DEATH ON THE FOURTH OF JULY

DEATH ON THE FOURTH OF JULY

*The Story of a Killing, a Trial,
and Hate Crime in America*

DAVID A. NEIWERT

palgrave
macmillan

First published 2004 by
PALGRAVE MACMILLAN™
175 Fifth Avenue, New York, N.Y. 10010 and
Houndmills, Basingstoke, Hampshire, England RG21 6XS.
Companies and representatives throughout the world.

PALGRAVE MACMILLAN is the global academic imprint of the Palgrave
Macmillan division of St. Martin's Press, LLC and of Palgrave Macmillan Ltd.
Macmillan® is a registered trademark in the United States, United Kingdom and
other countries. Palgrave is a registered trademark in the European Union and
other countries.

ISBN 1-4039-6501-3 hardcover

Library of Congress Cataloging-in-Publication Data
Neiwert, David A., 1956-
    Death on the Fourth of July : the story of a killing, a trial, and hate crime in
America / David Neiwert.
        p.   cm.
    Includes bibliographical references (p.)and index.
    ISBN 1-4039-6501-3
    1. Kinison, Christopher, d. 2000.   2. Murder—Washington (State)—Ocean
Shores.   3. Hate crimes—Washington (state)—Ocean Shores.   4. Trials
(Murder)—Washington (State).   I. Title.

HV6534.O27N45   2004
364.152'3'0979795—dc22

                                                                2003068939

A catalogue record for this book is available from the British Library.

Design by Letra Libre.

First edition: July 2004
10 9 8 7 6 5 4 3 2 1

Printed in the United States of America.

CONTENTS

ACKNOWLEDGEMENTS

LIKE MANY JOURNALISTS WHO DEVELOP SPECIALTIES, I've had occasion to be interviewed on television a number of times, identified as an "expert" on the subject of our conversation. But really, I'm not an expert (I just play one on TV). I'm a journalist, and as such have to rely on the *real* experts for both my data and ideas. Accordingly, there were a number of these real experts who contributed substantially to *Death on the Fourth of July* by sitting for interviews and engaging in e-mail conversations to explore the issues underlying the story. In the end, the book is a product of their thinking, synthesized, as it were, in attempt to give readers an overview of the problem.

In any event, I owe a deep debt of gratitude to them. They include: Frederick L. Lawrence, associate dean of the School of Law at Boston University; Donald P. Green of Yale University; Jack McDevitt of Northeastern University's Center for Criminal Justice Policy Research; Joan Weiss of the Justice Research and Statistics Association; sociologist Valerie Jenness of the University of California-Irvine; author Philip Dray; and Ken Toole of the Montana Human Rights Network.

I'm also extremely grateful to the many others who participated in the writing of this book, mostly because of their involvement in the Ocean Shores case, including Minh Duc Hong; Grays Harbor County Prosecutor H. Steward Menefee; Hong's attorneys, Monte Hester and Brett Purtzer; Dr. Gary E. Connor; Ocean Shores Police Chief Rich McEachin, and department spokesman David McManus; jury foreman Gene Schermer; Aberdeen *Daily World* editor John Hughes; Chamber of Commerce president Joan Payne; Ocean Shores Coalition president Carl Payne; Doug Chin of the Organization of Chinese Americans; and James Arima of the Japanese American Citizens League.

I owe a considerable debt to the many journalists who also covered the case, particularly in its first few weeks, since I relied heavily on their work for my initial information about the case before the trial. Leading this particular pack was the Aberdeen *Daily World* reporter, David Scheer, who also happened to be about the only other regular who covered each day of the trial. David is the model of the thoughtful young reporter who is both conscientious and thorough, and it was a pleasure working with him. I also want to acknowledge the contributions of Robert Jamieson and Hector Castro of the Seattle *Post-Intelligencer* and Alex Tizon and Joshua Robin of the *Seattle Times*, whose work covering the original incident I relied upon extensively.

My editor at Palgrave Macmillan, Brendan O'Malley, was extremely influential in shaping the final version of the manuscript, and his many suggestions played a major role in making the text more cohesive. I also owe a great debt of thanks for my agents, Frank Scatoni and Greg Dinkin of Venture Literary, who really made this project happen.

Finally, many thanks to the friends and family who helped make the book a reality: Shannon, Juston and Maiah Hubert; Ev Kara and Scott Fox; Deborah Leslie; Linda Hedenblad; Susan Clyde; and Debbie and John Anderson. Most of all, I owe the deepest debt to my wife, Lisa Dowling, who has kept us afloat and steady, both financially and emotionally, throughout; and to my daughter, Fiona Rose, who is both my muse and my inspiration.

—*Seattle, March 2004*

FOREWORD

by Mark Potok

AN AMERICAN TRAGEDY UNFOLDED ON THE FOURTH OF JULY several years ago in the aging tourist town of Ocean Shores, Washington. It involved a group of racist skinhead thugs, a police force that was reluctant to act, and an unfortunate young Asian American named Minh Hong. In the end, one man lay dead, a town's reputation was in tatters, and Hong was changed forever.

David Neiwert, a keen-eyed journalist, student of racial hatred and native of the Pacific Northwest, thought he smelled a story—a story that could throw light on the meaning of hate crimes and the need for the hate crimes laws that have sprung up across America since the late 1980s. And he was right. The encounter between Minh Hong and Chris Kinison, a brutal local white kid brandishing a Confederate battle flag, turns out to contain important lessons for the rest of us.

On the face of it, the collision was simple enough. Hong, his twin brother, and a friend who was also Asian-American pulled into a crowded Texaco mini mart in the predawn hours of July 4, 2000, looking for a snack. As they walked to the station, they were assailed by a group of young toughs led by the flag-waving Kinison, who screamed racial epithets at the trio. Frightened, Hong stole a pair of paring knives before he and his companions left the store. When Kinison attacked Hong's brother as the group tried to depart, Hong intervened, ultimately stabbing the unarmed Kinison twenty-three times. Kinison died in a pool of blood on the tarmac.

Was it simple murder? Had Hong "brought a pistol to a fistfight," in the Western vernacular of the region? Or was there something more to it?

Neiwert argues convincingly that there was. Kinison and his friends had been involved in an escalating series of serious racial confrontations with blacks and

Asians in the three days leading up to the killing. In each incident police, for reasons that in retrospect seem weak at best, declined to bring charges or even detain the whites, who were well known as local troublemakers. And, as Neiwert points out, the death threats and curses directed at the three Asian Americans before anyone was killed that July 4 almost certainly amounted to a felony hate crime—a critical and ignored fact that colors everything that happened in the minutes that followed.

But local prosecutors, police, and residents didn't see it that way. Minh Hong was charged with first-degree manslaughter—while none of the thugs who had threatened Hong and the others were even arrested. Town officials, police, and prosecutor Gerald Fuller all suggested that Kinison had acted inappropriately and perhaps even illegally, but that Hong was the real criminal. Townspeople reacted angrily to the attention the case brought to Ocean Shores, even as Kinison's high school friends built up a makeshift memorial of flowers and poems.

The essence of the Minh Hong case is not that unusual. Time and time again, local communities and their officials—particularly in rural towns like Ocean Shores that have precious little experience with major hate crimes—have tended to ignore and excuse local troublemakers as basically decent kids out for a rowdy good time. A part of the fault lies in an innate human tendency to make excuses for the people we went to school with and know well. But a bigger part of the responsibility is due to a lack of hate crime training that teaches police officers how to recognize and deal with the essential elements of a hate crime—a lack that is exacerbated by the failure of the federal and most local governments to pay for such training.

These shortcomings have resulted in uncounted instances of failed criminal investigations and prosecutions of hate crimes. They have buttressed the feeling of many minorities that much of rural America is a dangerous place, best left unvisited by the wise. And, in the case of Ocean Shores, they threatened to compound the tragedy of one young man's death with the martyrdom of another.

In this book, David Neiwert explores the killing of Chris Kinison, the trial that followed it, and the history and meaning of hate crimes legislation in America. At times, his writing is extraordinarily penetrating, using the details of a single death to flesh out and explore a history that began, as he shows, with early efforts to pass anti-lynching laws more than a century ago. It is a technique that, more effectively than any other, makes clear that the understanding and prosecution of hate crimes is not only justifiable. As Neiwert shows, it is essential to defending the democratic values that we, as Americans, should all feel bound to champion.

CHAPTER ONE

THE KNIVES

RAPPING, RAPPING.

The man with the Confederate flag was rapping his knuckles on the windows of the gas station, holding the flag up and then pointing at the three of them, beckoning them to come out. He began drawing his finger across his throat and grinning at them. Rapping, rapping.

He was big—about six feet tall and 200 pounds, much bigger than either Minh Duc Hong or his twin brother, Hung, or their friend Doug Chen, all of whom stood at about five-foot-six and weighed about 125 pounds each. And the looming figure had a bunch of friends.

The three young Vietnamese men had already encountered them on the way in, after they had pulled up and parked at the little Texaco station. There were about five or six of them, young white men, all with shaved heads or close-cropped hair, and the group of them had shouted racist epithets—"gooks" and "slant-eyes"—as the trio walked the fifty feet or so from their car to the door of the store. The one with the Confederate flag had walked alongside them, mocking their language, calling out "Ching-chong!"

The mini mart seemed to provide refuge. There were another four or five people inside, and neither they nor the clerk seemed to be paying any mind to the ya-hoos outside. Minh Hong looked around and found the cup of noodles he had been seeking for a late-night snack. Then Doug Chen came over and pointed out the man at the windows to him.

Rapping, rapping.

None of the three were prepared for this. Both of the twins were shy and studious young men, and neither they nor Doug Chen were the fighting kind. In fact, though the Hongs were twenty-six, this Fourth of July visit to the seaside resort town of Ocean Shores, Washington, had been the first trip they could recall taking away from their hometown of Seattle without their parents.

Minh Hong looked around the store, and now the seeming disinterest of everyone inside had a darker cast to it. The man outside was still going from window to window and rapping at them and waving his flag. And as before, when he could see Minh looking at him, he ran his finger across his throat and grinned.

Minh looked around the store. He could hear a woman with whom his brother had spoken tell the clerk to call 911; the clerk looked briefly outside, saw nothing within his view, and refused. It was clear that no one was going to help.

That's when he saw the two paring knives, packaged in shrink-wrap with cardboard backing, hanging from one of the racks. He sidled over and, seeing no one watching, stuffed them inside the pocket of his puffy yellow jacket.

❋

Small towns are vulnerable to hate crimes on two levels. It is not merely that certain conditions—such as racial and cultural homogeneity and an institutional disposition to paper over racial crimes—make rural areas prone to them. It is also that the ramifications from them are often so far-reaching that the communities themselves become chief among the victims.

Small towns are the kinds of places you're likely to find hate-crimes perpetrators, in no small part because of their racial homogeneousness. Contrary to popular conception, the typical hate criminal is not a skinhead inspired by hate groups, but is a fairly average person who otherwise fits in with his community—though of course, he also likely subscribes to an array of prejudices. The bigoted redneck and his violence-prone ethic is something of an overdrawn caricature, but he does exist—and in fact people with such attitudes are more likely to live in rural or suburban places precisely because they are predominantly white. Every town has them, and because they are known locally, their acts are often dismissed as mere rowdyism. And the winks and slapped wrists in turn are interpreted as permission.

When these people finally spiral out of control, only then does the town realize the consequences of its failures to act—which usually comes in the form of a severely damaged reputation. This is especially the case for a town like Ocean Shores, which relies on tourist dollars from nearby urban areas like Seattle and Portland, Oregon, for its economic health—not to mention its entire *raison d'etre*. A reputation for harboring racists can make all that dry up and blow away overnight.

Ocean Shores on a typical day is home to only about 3,000 people, but on busy weekends in the summers, crowds drawn by the five-mile expanse of bleached sand and pounding surf can make it grow to 50,000. The little police force of thirteen officers is typically undermanned and overworked anyway, and July Fourth can create an outright bunker mentality among beat cops.

More important, in a rural place like Ocean Shores—an hour's drive from Olympia, and three hours from Seattle or Portland—hate crimes are seen as alien things. Some of the myths about hate crimes, particularly those that represent them as the activities of organized hate groups like skinheads rather than the random acts they are typically, still hold sway with most law-enforcement officials, including prosecutors. When the cops know the perpetrators, perhaps as local troublemakers, they tend to deal with them on that level.

The natural reluctance of these towns to confront the problem because of fears for their reputations is reflected in national hate-crime statistics, compiled annually by the FBI. The bulk of the material contained in these annual reports is a series of long lists of law-enforcement agencies around the country reporting zero hate crimes—and the vast majority of these jurisdictions are in rural counties and small towns. In Washington state in 1999, for instance, nearly all of the 230 hate-crime incidents reported occurred in a handful of largely urban or suburban counties.

Since just the act of filing hate-crimes charges can bring intense scrutiny and headlines, small-town cops often treat such cases like the plague. That calculus played an important role in what happened on July 4, 2000 in Ocean Shores because the incident at the Texaco station was not the first hate crime in town that weekend.

✷

The first warning came the afternoon of Saturday, July 1, when a claque of local young men terrorized a group of Filipino tourists. Two families comprising six men, six women, and three children had stopped at the Ocean Shores Mall—a strip mall of mostly tourist and gift shops—to use the restrooms when a group of ten white men, many with shaven or close-cropped heads, confronted them in the parking lot in front of a kite shop. Some of them were in a pickup truck festooned with a Confederate flag.

Apparently their appearance drew some stares or fearful looks, because one of the men—later identified as twenty-year-old Gabriel Rodda, a local man who lived with his parents in town—demanded to know of one of the Filipino men, Jose Kalaw: "What are you looking at?" Kalaw and the rest of the two families fled to their cars and locked the doors. Rodda walked up and stood outside, screaming obscenities and slurs at them, so Kalaw, who had jumped into the front passenger's seat of his van, told the person in the driver's seat to roll up the window. This apparently infuriated Rodda, who according to the police report, ran to one of the vehicles and punched a window. The Filipinos later told reporters that the men began chanting, "White power!" and shouting racial slurs. "What are you doing in our town?" they screamed, and "Ocean Shores is my fucking town!"; all the while blocking the vehicles from leaving. They pounded on the windows and dared the Filipinos to come out. (The damage, police later said, was minor, mostly marks and scratches on the glass and paint.)

Jose Kalaw, however, had a gun for which he had a concealed-weapons permit, and reportedly he contemplated using it. Instead, he pulled it out and set it on the dashboard as a kind of warning. Rodda and his friends backed off, and the families in their three vehicles pulled out of the parking lot and fled down Chance a la Mer, the main boulevard in Ocean Shores.

They went only a brief distance before spotting Ocean Shores officer Donald Grossi, and Jose Kalaw pulled over and got out to flag him down. Someone else had phoned police that a fight was brewing, and so in short order another Ocean Shores cop, Chris Iversen, had arrived in the parking lot and confronted the group of young white men; he was soon backed up by officer J. W. Brouillard. The men claimed that the Filipinos had picked the fight, although Rodda did admit to punching the vehicle's window; his hand was bloodied.

What happened next remains in dispute. Jennifer Kalaw, one of the family members, later told Seattle reporters that she and others had insisted they wanted to press charges against Rodda and the others, but that Grossi had discouraged them. When it became clear that was the case, she said, they pleaded with him to escort them out of town to ensure they weren't pursued by Rodda and the others. For his part, Grossi reported that the family did not want to press charges, and he stands by that account today. Both sides agree that the Filipinos asked for an escort to the edge of town, which he provided.

"It's really sad," Jennifer Kalaw said later. "It's a nice place to go and visit, but now I'm too scared to go back."

A few weeks later—after accounts of the confrontation hit the papers—Ocean Shores city officials sent the Filipino families fruit baskets and letters of apology, along with an invitation to come back.

"We will never, ever go back there," said Jennifer Kalaw.

The officers who dealt with the young white men stayed with them long enough to ensure that the situation was defused. The men continued to rant about the Filipinos, referring to them as "fucking gooks."

"I called the local boys around and admonished them for their racial attitudes and actions, which they all denied," said Brouillard in the report he filed five days later, "and then told them that if they keep this kind of thing up that one of them will eventually get killed."[1]

✳

It may have seemed like only a summer fracas, but in reality, the Ocean Shores police had almost certainly arrived at the scene of a Class C felony. Washington state's malicious-harassment statute—its version of a hate-crime law—makes it a crime to "threaten . . . a specific person or groups of persons, or members of the specific group of persons, in reasonable fear of harm to person or property" if the act is committed "because of his or her perception of the victim's race, color, religion, ancestry, national origin, or mental, physical, or sensory handicap." In this case, though, the incident was merely put down to "boys being boys," and the perpetrators sent on their way.

Among those young men was a twenty-year-old named Christopher Kinison, the only child of a single mother who had lived in the North Beach area. He'd attended high school in Ocean Shores, gaining a reputation as a "troubled teen"; he had brushes with the law for, among other things, dangerous-weapon possession and malicious mischief.

Many of his friends, though, grow angry at suggestions that Kinison was a racist. One of his best friends is part Filipino, and an uncle with whom he had good relations is black. They all say he liked to fight, and some contend that he merely used racist language as a way to start a brawl.

However, the rhetoric he was known to use suggests that at some level he subscribed to racist and xenophobic ideologies. And he had a history of bigoted behavior dating back to 1997, when he was investigated for a racial-harassment incident in town involving a group of black teens; no charges were ever filed.

Eventually Kinison dropped out of school, left home, and drifted fifty miles east to Olympia. He picked up construction work and came to town occasionally to visit friends, which is what he was doing that Saturday when his friends harassed the Filipinos.

⚹

Three hours after police escorted the Filipino tourists to the town border, a similar fracas arose in the tourist town of Long Beach, about two hours' drive south of Ocean Shores on the Washington coast. A private gathering of people from Seattle was on the beach enjoying a party when a caravan of pickup trucks bearing Confederate flags crashed the festivities. A group of young white men got out and began harassing the one Asian and one black man at the party.

"They were talking smack and looking for trouble," Eric Li of Seattle told the *Seattle Times*. "They were calling me 'Kung Fu' and saying, 'We want to fight you.'"

The confrontation was broken up by Pacific County sheriff's deputies, who merely dispersed the crowd and sent the party-crashers on their way. No names were taken, so no one could verify whether it was Kinison's crowd. But the men reportedly favored the "skinhead" appearance that the young men were sporting in Ocean Shores that weekend.[2]

Two days later, on July 3, a black man from Seattle named Joe Scott was riding a moped along the drivable stretch of the beach near Ocean Shores when a
man in a pickup drove by and shouted racial slurs, again waving a Confederate
flag. Scott later said he thought it was Kinison, though he could not make a posi-
tive identification. He reported it to an Ocean Shores policeman, who did not
take a report but assured Scott that he was "going to handle it."[3]

Friends later said that Kinison had spent most of the day on the beach, hanging out for several hours drinking beer at a bonfire party at Point Brown, the
southernmost tip of the sandy peninsula on which Ocean Shores rests. As the
evening progressed, he and several friends—including Gabe Rodda and Brock
Goedecke, a Marine out on leave who was tight with Kinison—moved northward
a few miles to another beer party on the beach.

That same evening, Leo "Jay" Hayes, an Ocean Shores hotel employee who is
African American, says he encountered Kinison at one of those bonfires. Hayes,
who had arrived at the bonfire with a couple of white friends, said Kinison stepped
forward from a group of people who were directing racial insults at him and introduced himself as "Chris," then threw a can of beer at him, pulled out a knife and
threatened to stab him. "I turned and ran for my car," Hayes told an Aberdeen
Daily World reporter.

Hayes says the man did not chase him for long, and he and his friends fled the
scene in his car. Shortly afterward, a friend of Hayes's called him to say that he too
had been threatened at a bonfire by a man with a six- to eight-inch knife. Hayes,
waiting at the local Burger King, decided to call police. Two sheriff's deputies arrived and took down information. However, they took no further action, and had
Hayes—who'd decided he would rather be home watching wrestling on TV—sign
a waiver of prosecution.[4]

Later that night, Chris Kinison, Gabe Rodda, Brock Goedecke and several
other of their friends—all of whom had been drinking at the beach—made their
way into town, hanging out for awhile after midnight at the same Burger King from
which Hayes had called police earlier. Then, as the bars announced last call and a
nearby bowling alley closed up, everyone made their way across the intersection to
the Texaco station, loitering in the parking lot while friends grabbed a twelve-pack
to head home with. And then the gold Honda with the Asian guys inside pulled up.

❋

Minh Duc Hong and his twin brother, Hung, led remarkably protected lives for
26-year-olds. When they weren't working in their parents' little strip-mall diner,
they were attending school. They spent most of their free time with their family
or a small circle of friends in Seattle's Beacon Hill neighborhood or in Bellevue,
where they worked and attended school, and rarely strayed from that small world.

The family's teriyaki shop in Bellevue, as it happened, was not far from the offices of the newspaper where I worked from 1991 to 1996 as news editor, and I frequented the shop a great deal when I worked evening shifts (which was most nights). The teriyaki wasn't gourmet quality, but it was tasty, inexpensive, and ready quickly.

The shop's chief attraction, in fact, was the twin brothers, who were friendly and helpful and rather eager, both to please and to become acquainted. Both are slight, with thick glasses and scholarly mien, but they possessed great warmth and energy. Minh Duc Hong is slightly taller and somewhat shy but intelligent and well spoken, while Hung Duc Hong is more outgoing, with a sprightly sense of humor. They always engaged me in conversation, asking about the newspaper racket and that day's news, and after awhile it became clear they liked me not just as a regular customer but as a person. The feeling was mutual.

I only knew the twins by their first names, and when I moved to another job in 1996 I stopped going to their shop regularly, though if I had a good excuse I made a point of dropping in for a quick lunch. They always remembered me, but the connection grew thinner. And when the news came from Ocean Shores that summer, I did not connect their names with my two acquaintances, at least not until the first day of the trial.

But sometime in late June of 2000, the twins bought some fireworks and decided to go set them off in Ocean Shores for the Fourth of July. They made reservations at the Shilo Inn and convinced their parents to let them drive the gold family Honda on what would be their first excursion out of Seattle without their parents.

On Monday, July 3, Minh and Hung set out in the Honda, with a friend from high school, Doug Chen, riding in the back seat. Accompanying them were a couple of girlfriends, who drove in a separate car. They pulled into town midafternoon and checked in, then walked out on the beach for awhile. That evening, after dinner, they availed themselves of the hotel's swimming pool and spa, and hung out there for a couple of hours, until a little after midnight.

The swimming made them hungry. Someone suggested they go down to the convenience store and get some Ramen noodles that they could cook in their rooms. So the three young men piled in the car and headed out for what they thought would be a quick, uneventful trip to the store. And that was when they ran into Chris Kinison and his friends.

CHAPTER TWO

FIREWORKS IN RED

AS IT ALWAYS DID ON FOURTH OF JULY WEEKEND, Ocean Shores fairly bustled even late into the evening Saturday, with tourists tasting the warm breezes and savoring the arrival of summer. The Texaco was busy that night, which meant there were a number of people who witnessed what was about to transpire—in all, some twenty-five people were milling about. They ranged from a San Francisco tourist to former classmates of Chris Kinison's. And they were nearly all white.

All those witnesses, however, do not necessarily provide a clear picture of that night's tragedy. The multiplicity of viewpoints, to the contrary, means that the witnesses often contradict each other, leaving the truth to reveal itself in the lines between. Like a real-life *Rashomon*—the Akira Kurosawa tale of a murder from the perspectives of four witnesses, including the victim; all starkly different, all tainted and twisted by the teller's self-interest—the drama played out in bits and pieces on a broad stage. Most witnesses only saw small fragments of what happened, and their tales often conflict, as do (not surprisingly) the accounts of the surviving main participants. But there are broad areas of agreement, and from those some clear details gradually emerge.

No one is quite sure why Chris Kinison decided to attack the Hongs when they pulled up to the station at about 1:30 A.M. and got out of their car. Maybe the fancy gold Honda with gold-rimmed wheels got his attention. It was the kind of car that only city kids, and especially gang types, were believed to drive. Or maybe it was that they clearly were outsiders, tourists, and skinny, meek-looking ones to boot. One thing, though, unquestionably was on Kinison's mind: their race. They didn't look like "Americans" to Kinison, and they didn't even seem to speak the language. Considering that for much of that weekend's patriotic festivities, as it were, Kinison seems to have been involved in making threats against non-whites, what followed certainly was consistent with his day's theme.

All anyone really knows is that when the trio of Asians got out and walked the fifty feet or so from their car to the entrance of the convenience store, Kinison and his friends were on them, waving their Confederate flag and screaming at them. It's unclear who were among his cohorts in the verbal assaults; Brock Goedecke and Gabe Rodda were both identified by other witnesses as among the gang shouting racial epithets. But later on the witness stand, both men denied that they had even participated in the verbal assaults. In any case, everyone agrees that Chris Kinison was the ringleader.

"Gooks go home!" Kinison shouted. "White supremacy!" The Hongs tried to ignore him and kept walking to the store. Kinison walked alongside them, shouting more epithets and chanting, "Ching chong! Ching chong!"

Still, his three would-be victims made it safely to the door and darted quickly inside. For a few moments they could ignore the threats, and went about finding the midnight snack of Ramen noodles they had come for. However, when Kinison began rapping on the windows, waving his flag and pointing at the men inside, sliding his finger across his throat—and when it became clear that no one was going to help them—then, suddenly, the store seemed like a big glass trap. There was literally nowhere to turn.

Rhyana Von Kallenbach, a twenty-year-old visitor from Gig Harbor, had pulled up in a nearby parking spot with her sisters, and was entering the store at about the same time when she encountered the commotion. She was terrified. "There were four or five of them," she later testified. "They were white males and all of them had shaved heads. One had a cane." With the Confederate flag for added effect, she said, she thought they were "skinheads," and they clearly outnumbered and outsized the Asians. She left the Texaco quickly, fearing for her own safety and that of her sisters.[1]

She was not alone in feeling frightened. Matt Gonzales, a twenty-two-year-old from Olympia, was inside the store when the commotion broke out and watched as the three Asians made their way inside. Sensing trouble, he left, only to find himself confronted by Chris Kinison outside the door.

Other than a shock of jet-black hair, Gonzales does not appear to be Hispanic on first glance; he is tall and slender and fairly pale, and his facial features take after his Caucasian mother. Nonetheless, Kinison apparently sensed he was a minority and began shouting racial epithets at him. "White power, bitch!" he screamed, telling Gonzales, "Go back where you came from!"

Gonzales, who was nearly Kinison's match in size, took it coolly. "I told him to grow up," he later explained. "It seemed like he just wanted to fight. I wasn't interested. I told him if he kept it up, someone was going to get hurt." Gonzales turned away and walked across the street to the parking lot of the nearby McDonald's to talk to some friends, all the while keeping an eye on the unfolding drama at the service station.

Inside the Texaco, Amanda Algeo, the young woman who had chatted briefly with one of the twin brothers—whom she later (incorrectly) identified as Minh Hong—was disturbed by something else she said Hong told her at the end of their conversation. Looking at Kinison as he rapped on the window, she claimed that Hong muttered: "Well, he's going down." (Minh Hong would later deny on the stand that he said any such thing—or that he had even spoken with her.) Algeo had gone to high school with Kinison, and while they weren't close, she considered him a friend.

When it was her turn to pay, Algeo urged the clerk behind the counter to call police. The clerk, however, looked outside the station and said later that he didn't see any "misbehaving," so he declined. Algeo walked outside and bumped into Kinison; she asked him what he was making a scene about.

"It's called racism," he told her.

"It's called stupidity," was her response, adding that if he kept it up, "somebody was going to get hurt." She got in her car and drove home.

Randy Deibel was only at the Texaco by misfortune; his pickup's battery kept dying, and it had failed most recently at the Texaco that evening. He was trying to jump-start it when he saw Chris Kinison rapping on the windows and shouting racial threats at the Asian men inside.

Deibel, a twenty-seven-year-old who made a living in Ocean Shores as a carpenter, knew Kinison well even though they moved in different circles: "You pretty much know everybody because it's a small town," he testified later. He spotted a police cruiser making its way past the service station and warned Kinison to "cool it."

As the patrol car drove past slowly and circled in the grocery-store parking lot across the boulevard, Kinison quieted down and resumed chatting in the parking lot. But even as they waited for the policemen to leave—and they did eventually, after going once around the lot and heading out westward—he chatted up a young woman from Olympia named Alyson Green, asking her if she wanted to see a fight. He told another woman, a former classmate, that he was "going to kick some gooks' ass."

Meanwhile, no one had seen Minh Hong quietly steal the two packaged knives.

✳

The man with the Confederate flag stopped tapping on the window, and the seeming lull in the agitation outside persuaded Minh Hong and his companions that perhaps it was safe to return to their car, so they filed quietly out of the store. But no sooner had they come out the door than they found Chris Kinison and four or five companions between them and their car, lurking on the sidewalk, and the epithets resumed at full volume: "White power!" "Gooks go home!"

They tried walking around the men. Someone spat on them, and Hong said Kinison was in his ear, shouting: "You don't fucking belong here! Go back to your country!"

Terrified, they kept their heads down and walked in single file back to the car. A couple of witnesses later said the Asians returned the epithets with threatening gestures; one of them allegedly pulling up a pants leg to point at a knife, and someone shouted, "No knives!" However, other witnesses contradicted this, saying the trio went quietly and quickly. In any case, Minh Hong testified that they were relieved when they made it through the gauntlet and inside the relative safety of their car without being assaulted.

They waited a few moments and watched Kinison and his band seemingly lose interest and move back to the other side of the pumps. Hung Hong, in the driver's seat, backed out and then pulled forward around the pumps, evidently aiming for an exit onto the main boulevard, Chance a la Mer. It was not the closest exit—there was one behind their car that was closer, but it would have required extensive backing up and maneuvering. The Chance exit was more direct. But it also took their car directly past where Kinison and his friends were.

And Kinison wasn't done with them. Holding up his Confederate flag and waving it at them, several witnesses say he walked in front of their car and prevented them from leaving. Minh Hong says that something hit the back of their car, and the three of them suddenly realized that they were hemmed in.

Some witnesses say that they didn't see anyone surrounding the Hongs' Honda. Among them was William Keys, an excavator from San Francisco, who had pulled into the gas station in the slot next to the pumps that was adjacent to the Hongs' escape route. He had gassed up and returned to his Ford Explorer without realizing anything serious was afoot; he said he thought the commotion was just "roughhousing." It turned serious, he said, when the Hongs pulled up near him and stopped, but he said that he saw nothing preventing them from moving either way.[2]

Across the street, however, Matt Gonzales said he had a clear view as Kinison and his friends stopped the Honda, with Kinison waving his flag in front of the car. Two other witnesses corroborated this account.

Minh Hong pulled out his cell phone and dialed 911, but his service wouldn't connect. Convinced they were trapped, Hung Hong opened his driver's-side door and got out, apparently to flee. So did Doug Chen, from the car's back seat.

Instead, Hung Hong found himself suddenly face to face with Kinison. William Keys said he heard Kinison shout: "You fucking gooks! I'll take you all on!" Then Kinison swung just as Hung Hong, other witnesses say, put his hands up in a defensive position. Kinison aimed hard at his head, knocking off his glasses and staggering him. The white man came up and hit him a second time, knocking him to the ground. He seemed about to start kicking at Hung Hong on the ground when Minh Hong came flying out of the car from the passenger's side.

Minh Hong first attacked Kinison from the side. Someone—it might have been Kinison—hit him, and his glasses too went flying. Kinison grabbed him by the throat, and Minh Hong reached inside his pocket for the knives.

What happened at that point is difficult to determine, since the accounts are simultaneously vague and contradictory. Matt Gonzales came back across the street to see what was going on, and as he arrived, he saw Kinison flatten Hung Hong and Minh Hong rushing to his brother's aid. At that same moment, though, Doug Chen became embroiled in a fight with Brock Goedecke, who was standing nearby. Goedecke flattened Chen with a single punch. Gonzales, who was standing nearest to them, separated the two combatants, and that seemed to end the fight. This encounter took, Gonzales thought, only about twenty seconds.

Kinison and Minh Hong, however, were still going at it. No one saw any knives. They just saw Minh Hong flailing away at Kinison, six inches and seventy-five pounds his superior. Kinison swung and then draped an arm around Hong. They saw Hong's arms flying, swinging in low horizontal blows, striking Kinison repeatedly; William Keys described it as "like a sewing machine." Hung Hong got off the ground and groped at Kinison, briefly grabbing one of his arms. Keys testified that he saw Hung Hong pinning Kinison's arm behind his back, and Brock Goedecke also testified that Hong had done so. But forensics experts found that if Kinison's arm was held back, it had only happened very briefly—both of his arms showed wounds consistent with someone swinging and fighting.

Nonetheless, it was at about this point that Minh Hong struck Kinison three times in the chest with one of the paring knives. A few more blows may have landed afterward, but in those few seconds, the fight was over.

Kinison was still standing but he seemed to be dazed. Randy Deibel, seeing that Kinison was getting the worst of the fight, came running at the group of them. Doug Chen had already retreated back to the car, and the Hongs looked at each other and fled to the Honda as well. Another friend, seeing a pair of glasses on the ground, picked them up and handed them to Hung Hong through the driver's-side window, saying, "You better get the hell out of here."

Hong gunned the engine and peeled out of the parking lot. By then, Kinison had staggered back and was leaning against the pickup belonging to the man who had interceded. "It hurts," he told his friends, and sagged to the ground. They peeled off his now red-stained T-shirt and found blood pouring out of twenty-three stab wounds.

Gabe Rodda, one of Kinison's oldest friends, realized quickly how grievously his friend had been wounded and began screaming, "You stabbed my brother!" Though hobbled by an ankle injury that forced him to use a cane, he ran after the Hongs' car just as it was pulling out of the parking lot and flung his cane at them. It bounced off their back window as the Honda peeled away.

Brock Goedecke held his ailing friend and tried to close some of the worst wounds with his bare hands, but the blood flowed anyway, inexorably, and as he hugged the young man the life just ebbed out, like low tide on the big sandy beach.

✳

Finally summoned by a 911 call from the now-frantic Texaco clerk, Sgt. Paul Luck of the Ocean Shores Police Department got to the scene a few minutes later and found Kinison lying in a pool of blood. His eyes were half-open and he was no longer responding to queries. His friends, gathered in the parking lot, were in hysterics. Some of them were smeared with his blood.

A second Ocean Shores cop, Jeffrey Elmore, arrived shortly after Sgt. Luck, and found people still screaming and crying. "The scene was chaotic," he wrote in his report. An ambulance pulled up and work began trying to resuscitate Kinison even as they loaded him onto a gurney, then drove away with him. But they were far too late, and even if they had been there on the scene and had been able to stanch the flow of blood, it's unlikely they could have done anything to repair the three wide deep gashes to his chest; two of those, an autopsy would later reveal, had cut deep into the muscle tissue of his heart, and the third had ruptured the pericardial sac. Kinison was declared dead on arrival at the local hospital.

The two police officers tried to gather evidence and information from the many witnesses. Elmore wrote in his report that he first turned to Brock Goedecke, who admitted to them he had been involved in the fatal fight, and Gabe Rodda, whom they knew well as Kinison's close friend.

That, however, was a dry well. Both men, Elmore wrote, were "intoxicated and incoherent with emotion." Goedecke was nearly hyperventilating, screaming that they had stabbed his "brother." He also wanted revenge: "His fists were clenched, and he wanted to find the Asians."

Gabe Rodda was even more incoherent: "Rodda was weeping and posturing in a fist clenched muscle-man style stance," Elmore wrote.

Over the next couple of hours, Luck and Elmore would interview more of the witnesses, including Matt Gonzales—who told the officers that Kinison and his friends had "hemmed in" the Hongs' car, though the police did not include that detail in their written account—as well as Randy Deibel and a handful of others who had remained.[3]

They taped off the scene and tried to collect whatever evidence they could. There wasn't a lot—mostly just Chris Kinison's bloody and tattered T-shirt, and the red pools and drip patterns that spattered the asphalt and concrete. The large number of people who lingered at the scene meant much of the evidence had been compromised, but the police believed they had a pretty clear picture of what had transpired anyway.

What apparently never crossed the minds of any of the investigators was the possibility they might be looking at the scene of a hate crime. The police duly noted the racial taunts, but since there was no sign that hate groups had been involved, they proceeded as though they were dealing primarily with a homicide. There were few questions to the witnesses about the kind of threats that had been made, who had participated in them or how long they had been continuing. Brock Goedecke and Gabe Rodda were not questioned that night about their roles in the attacks on the Asians.

It wasn't as though the warning signs weren't there. Of the eight key indicators that law-enforcement specialists say are the earmarks of hate crimes, seven were present that night in Ocean Shores: (1) both the victims and witnesses perceived the assaults as being motivated by their race; (2) the perpetrator's comments and actions reflected that bias; (3) there were obvious racial and physical differences between the victims and the perpetrators; (4) there had been similar incidents throughout the weekend involving the same people, all attacking minorities; (5) the chief perpetrator was displaying a Confederate flag that signaled his sympathy with white supremacists; (6) there was a marked absence of common criminal motives, such as economic gain; and finally, (7) it all happened on the night of the Fourth of July, a holiday that always carries special significance for those "patriotic" types whose favorite color in the flag is white.[4]

Those signs failed to register on the radar screens of the Ocean Shores Police investigators, none of whom have ever received any special training related to bias crimes. So it is not surprising that none of the steps that those same experts recommend for investigating a hate crime—securing evidence related to the bias motivation, or stabilizing and reassuring the victims—were even considered. Potential witnesses walked away, and testimony about the assaults on the Asians was ignored.

What was different about this hate crime, of course, was that the primary perpetrator, and not his intended victims, lay dead. That made Chris Kinison—a young man the police all knew liked to pick fights—the only victim anywhere on the scene. In the eyes of Ocean Shores Police, then, this case was a murder investigation, and viewed through that lens, the fight at the gas station was treated as though it were an assault that spiraled into murder. In that context, of course, the three young Asians became their prime suspects.

Police did, however, find Chris Kinison's Confederate flag. It was lying in the right-hand turn lane of Chance a la Mer, next to the Texaco station.

※

Hung Hong was at the wheel as the trio of Asians drove in a blind panic out of the parking lot and fled into the darkness of Ocean Shores. The town is a short grid built around a couple of long avenues stretching six miles down the sandy beach peninsula, and at night you can drive straight into the darkness for a long time without ever turning. So without the least idea where they were going, they drove as fast as they could away from the scene, watching to make sure no one had followed them. (Minh Hong later reportedly told police that, somewhere along the way, he threw the knives out the window; however, later on the witness stand he denied saying this to police, insisting he left the knives back at the Texaco.)

After awhile the panic subsided and they realized they were lost, so they wound up driving around for a half hour before finally navigating their way back to the Shilo Inn, shaken and unsure what to do. Minh and Hung Hong had both suffered several cuts in the fight that needed tending. Minh Hong in particular was bleeding from deep cuts to his hands, which they wrapped with tape and tissue the best they could.

Back in their room, they caught up with the three young women who had come with them and told them of their ordeal. Their first impulse was simply to flee, so all six of them packed their bags and headed down to the lobby to check out, where one of the women dealt with the desk clerk. But outside in the parking lot, they conferred some more and gradually came to their senses, deciding they needed to call police and report the attack, still unaware that the fight had turned deadly. So they went to the hotel's front desk and asked the night clerk to call the police.

Hung Hong got on the phone with the dispatcher. "I went to try to get something to eat and we were getting harassed by some American kids," he said. "They were saying like racist stuff. Calling us gooks and stuff. One of them punched me."

The dispatcher asked how many were involved. "After they punched me, my glasses fell off and I couldn't see," answered Hung Hong. "He hit my car and stuff, too. I'm really afraid, because they are really racist and they have a whole group. I'm afraid to leave the hotel right now.

"They were waving like Dukes of Hazzard flags and stuff. They were yelling white power and [someone] punched me in the face."

At that point, Minh Hong says, he had no idea that anyone had been hurt. He knew he had used the knives, but did not know whether any of the blows had connected. But he believed that if he admitted to having stolen the knives, he'd likely be arrested for shoplifting. So when Sgt. David McManus of the Ocean Shores Police—an amiable middle-aged man with the friendly demeanor of someone who has put in twenty-plus years on the beat in small towns—arrived and began asking them questions, Minh Hong was less than forthcoming. At first he just talked about their attackers.

"They smelled like beer," he told McManus. "They came up to us and started yelling at us and calling us 'yellow.' It's not our fault that we're Asian."

"Absolutely," McManus said. "I totally agree. [It sounds like] you guys were defending yourselves. . . . But if you lie about something, it doesn't look good. . . . It doesn't look like you guys are innocent. . . . You've got to tell me the whole truth."

"It happened so quick," Minh Hong answered.

"Do you know where the knife came from?" McManus asked.

"No," Hong lied.

"Do you know where the knife went?"

"No."

McManus repeated the question a little while later, and Hong answered: "The only thing I saw was they were hitting my brother. These guys were like two to three times the size of me."

When McManus finished with the interrogation, another policeman took the Hongs to the hospital, and Doug Chen was released. In the meantime, a Seattle attorney called Ocean Shores police and said he had been asked by the Hongs' family to represent them. The police replied that the Hongs hadn't requested the services of an attorney yet.

McManus rejoined the Hongs a couple of hours later in their hospital room, and there he informed Minh Hong that Chris Kinison had died.

McManus also said that the Texaco clerk had reported the stolen knives. "I told him what we had found, and that I now understood why he was so afraid to tell us about the knife. I told him I still understood why he would want to arm himself before facing Kinison and his friends," McManus later wrote in his report.

The two brothers consulted with each other in Vietnamese, and then Minh Hong spoke. "He said he took the two knives from the Texaco, but his brother never knew he had them," McManus later testified. "He said he put one in his pocket and kept one in his hand. When Kinison attacked [Hung] Hong, [Minh Hong] began stabbing Kinison to get him to stop. He said he never intended to kill him, only to stop him."

McManus said he gave Minh Hong the number of the Seattle attorney who had called earlier, "and told him he should give him a call." Then he placed both brothers under arrest for suspicion of murder.

CHAPTER THREE

OPEN SORES

NEARLY ALL SMALL TOWNS HAVE DERISIVE NICKNAMES bestowed on them by the rebellious youngsters who bridle at their tight grasp, and in Ocean Shores it is "Open Sores"—an allusion, perhaps, to the somewhat shabby underbelly you can always gradually detect in tourism centers like this, little towns that try at all times to present their prettiest face. The locals, and the kids especially, know this underbelly all too well.

The death of Christopher Kinison was much more than a festering sore—overnight it opened up a gaping wound. The incident at the Texaco station was only the second homicide in the town's history, and it tore a hole through the placid community, in no small part because so many of the teens in town knew Kinison.

Although both Minh and Hung Hong were arrested the early morning of July 4 for suspicion of manslaughter, Hung was released the next day when it became clear that Minh had been the one wielding the knives. There was no evidence Hung had participated in Kinison's death—though there were scattered reports that one witness had seen Hung holding Kinison's arms behind his back while Minh stabbed him. These reports raised the anger level in Ocean Shores, among Kinison's friends especially, including many of his former classmates at North Beach High School.

A few days after the arrests, Grays Harbor County Deputy Prosecutor Gerald Fuller announced that Minh Hong was being charged with first-degree manslaughter, but that neither Hung Hong nor anyone else involved in the fighting that night would be charged. Trial was scheduled for late November or early December.

Minh's parents in Seattle promptly retained Monte Hester, one of the state's premier defense attorneys; Hester's partner, Brett Purtzer, became the chief workhorse on the case. "This is a self-defense case—no doubt about it," Purtzer told reporters. "Kinison was making racial slurs, saying they did not belong. He walked up to Hung and hit him in the face, knocking his glasses off. And Minh came to his brother's aid."

But prosecutors cited the large number of wounds that Kinison sustained: "You can talk about self-defense if you like," Fuller said, "but that [attack] was way over and above what was necessary under the circumstances."[1]

The pool of blood in the parking lot where Kinison had fallen was left untouched for several days, and the cyclone fence next to the spot became the site of a makeshift memorial. Friends and former classmates came by and left wreaths and bouquets of flowers, and attached to the fence poems, cards, and other mementos. Occasionally clusters of them could be seen gathering at the site, holding each other and crying.

"Nothing good has come out of this," a service station attendant told a reporter.

The Texaco station's managers originally had planned to remove the memorial a few days after the stabbing, but people kept coming by, weaving flowers into the chain-link fence and leaving cards. Someone also attached a white cross to the fence with a ribbon reading: "We love you, Chris."[2]

The mourners who gathered all knew Chris Kinison, mostly through school. He was "one of them." And perhaps because of that, they felt certain he had been wronged.

While everyone acknowledged that Kinison had picked the fight, most of them were angry that Kinison was killed by Minh Hong, and many questioned the charges that had been filed. "There was never anybody else after them," Randy Deibel told a reporter. "They could easily have beat him up, got in their car and left."

Zach Hoyt, a nineteen-year-old friend of Kinison's who had been with the group that night, told a reporter: "I thought everything was done with. Don't you think if they were scared for their lives, they would take off?"

"That's just murder," said Jesse Forvour, a close friend of Kinison's. "Those people had a chance to leave and they came back, with weapons."

Prosecutor Gerald Fuller answered the second-guessing: "I filed what I thought was the appropriate charge in view of the evidence I had."[3]

※

It isn't very easy to be a teenager in Ocean Shores. It's geographically isolated, located at the very end of the road—if you went any further, you'd be driving into the ocean. The nearest large town is Hoquiam, adjacent to Aberdeen, about twenty miles away, neither of which are exactly Excitement Central either. Most of Ocean Shores' adults are retirees, so the facilities and activities in town are geared to much gentler (or feebler, depending on your point of view) pursuits than those favored by teens.

Of course, teenagers everywhere rebel against local conditions, and their attitudes are shaped accordingly. In Ocean Shores, the tourists who are the town's lifeblood are also its bane—if anything makes life unpleasant in this town, it is the hordes of demanding and unappreciative visitors. Sometimes, like on the Fourth of July, as many as 50,000 of them can descend on the 3,800 souls who live there. These visitors are the focus of most of the teens' anti-establishment disgust. In the summer of 2000, you could hear the kids rename them *"terrorists."* That this was largely a joking reference became clear after September 11, 2001, when the nickname vanished from the local teen lexicon—but it suggests the extent to which they see the visitors as invaders.

Not all of this is the tourists' fault, of course. Some of it is the place.

There is the town itself. Nearly all tourist towns rely upon a façade of sorts, the face they present to the public that creates the kind of image visitors are seeking for their playgrounds. Some of these masks are shabbier and more transparent than others, depending on the town. In Ocean Shores, the façade is perhaps more obvious than elsewhere, partly because everything is so *new:* the city was only founded in 1960. Prior to then, it had seen a half-century of use as a cattle ranch owned by a homesteader, and before that, it had been a gathering spot for coastal Indian traders. Developers finally could not overlook the endless beaches on the massive, six-mile-long sandspit that forms the westernmost barrier between Grays Harbor and the open Pacific Ocean.

However, they also had grandiose visions of the kind of place Ocean Shores was destined to become. The boulevards in town were designed in huge swaths that would accommodate massive amounts of traffic, and the city center was built on large, spaced-apart blocks designed to accommodate lots of future growth. It never came. Larger and newer hotels have arrived in the intervening years, but the big land boom that many envisioned for years has never materialized. It's hard to say why: perhaps the town is just a little too remote, a little too isolated, a little too monochromatic.

Most of the hotels and motels are quite new. The older buildings in town, built in the 1960s and '70s, are not classic or charming in any way—largely, they're just shabby. Many of them sit on weedy lots with broken-out windows, waiting to be torn down and replaced with something new. Town fathers are hopeful: there's talk of a major aquarium project locating itself to Ocean Shores, which might give the town the added draw it needs. But for the time being, its pretty face has its share of dowdy wrinkles.

Still, its shabby edges notwithstanding, Ocean Shores is just what its residents say it is: a *nice* town, with nice people who live quietly and generally get along well as a community. Like most of small-town America, it feels safe, at least to people who live there.

Because it is built on a sandspit, nearly all of the infrastructure in Ocean Shores has a temporary feeling to it, as though a good tsunami could come along and rearrange everything overnight, if not wash it all away. Compacted sand is generally a decent building surface, but it is prone to shifting in an earthquake, of which western Washington gets its share. It also tends to settle, which means that doorframes can get out of whack. The paved roads—especially Ocean Shores Boulevard, which extends for most of the length of the peninsula—often buckle, and driving them can give you the sensation of being at sea.

Those wide boulevards now seem bizarre; the large, mile-long rectangle that frames the town is all four-lane road with a huge barrow pit in between the lanes, and it has a peculiar emptiness to it, like some of the strangely cheap roadways you find around Cancun, Mexico. There are no sidewalks along any of these four-lane thoroughfares (though a few exist on side streets), making the town even more inhospitable to pedestrians. Unlike most tourist towns, there is very little late-night wandering by visitors to Ocean Shores. Its streets at night are generally deserted. Except, of course, on the Fourth of July.

The town itself, situated at the northern end of the peninsula, comprises hotels and restaurants, gift and bike-rental and kite shops, a few gas stations, a few bars, a bowling alley and a grocery, all clustered together in a mile-long rectangular grid. While the main thoroughfares in town run north and south, its main drag—where the bulk of its retail businesses are located—is the main quarter-mile of Chance a la Mer, a four-lane east-west boulevard that begins near the Shilo Inn on the beach and largely ends at the intersection where the Texaco convenience store is located (the street actually continues for another half-mile as a narrow two-lane route out of town, but at that point is no longer a major thoroughfare). It is only one long block. Most of its businesses close at 9 P.M. during the tourist season; many of them are not even open in the off-season.

The beaches in Ocean Shores are breathtakingly beautiful—big, gray sandy expanses pounded by the steady roar of the surf. The sand turns peppery black when it is wet. The beaches themselves are huge and go on for miles, as does the wide swath of grassy dune building up behind them. Physically, Ocean Shores is growing steadily each year; the beach, because of wave action, does not erode, but actually expands a few feet westward annually.

This is also one of the only places on the Northwest's Pacific Coast where you can drive your car onto the beach. A few short stretches are off-limits to cars, but driving is allowed along most of the five-mile stretch of beach between the town and Point Brown, at the southern tip of the peninsula. So a lot of people cruise out to the shorelines to sate their appetite for fantasy by living their own car commercials, sometimes spinning into the water or goofing around, though most often just sitting and watching the sunset.

Sometimes such ventures do not end so well. Cars drive into soft spots in the sand and become stuck near the water just as the tide comes in, and the owners are forced to abandon them. At other incoming tides, couples parked on the beach will become otherwise preoccupied and may emerge from the arms of love to find themselves in deep water. No one has ever died in these circumstances, but they do help keep the police busy and amused.

At the height of the tourist season, the beach can become lined with cars for miles, which puts a bit of an edge on the free-spirited fantasy many are longing to live out. During the off-season, of course, the beaches become wide open, and this is when the local teens favor them. After awhile, the youths become somewhat proprietary about their haunts, which only makes them resent the tourists' inevitable invasion all the more.

Sometimes this feeling of ownership can play out in destructive ways. In 1994, a teenager from Ocean Shores went out driving on the beach and began targeting, just for kicks, the clusters of snowy plovers that roamed the shoreline. He drove his SUV at high speeds right into the rare and endangered birds, and wound up massacring several hundred of them, many of which were still attached to his front grill and undercarriage as he drove away nonchalantly. When Fish and Wildlife agents caught up with him, he told them he didn't think there was anything wrong with killing a few birds.

The beaches so dominate the landscape that they are almost all there is to the town. Even visitors can find themselves longing for something else to do after a few days on the endless sands. For a restless teenager who lives there day in and out, the monotony can be downright oppressive.

There isn't much to do. After hanging out at the beach (and probably drinking beer), kids can hang out at one or two locations along Chance a la Mer. Sometimes this just means sitting on a curb and shooting the shit, or skateboarding around the vacant parking lots. Sometimes it means getting into fights. After midnight, the town, as teens will tell you, is simply "dead."

Most of the kids who showed up to contribute to Chris Kinison's memorial had hung out with him on these street corners and on the beaches. He was the kind of guy a lot of people knew—very outgoing, very energetic, very gregarious. Some of his friends told reporters about his gentle side: buying long-stemmed roses for a friend's wife, or helping a friend haul furniture.

"His reward was just a smile and a thank you," Jenni Helm, a friend of Kinison's told a reporter. "He was content with that, never asking for money or saying, 'You owe me one.'"

Others were adamant that Kinison was not a racist at heart. His grandmother, Mary Lindau, told reporters: "My son-in-law is a Negro. The remarks [Kinison made during the fight] are remarks I've heard from other people, who should have known better. Orientals, I think, sometimes get judged pretty harshly. I don't know where he got that."[4]

Another old friend of Kinison's, Jesse Forvour, said the "white power" and racial remarks were only intended to spark a fight: "I'm like his brother, and I'm half-Filipino."[5]

Even Gabe Rodda talked to a reporter, saying: "It's all about whoever's . . . looking for a fight. We weren't searching for a certain race. Not at all."[6]

Kinison, it became clear, liked to fight. In all the testimonials offered by his friends, that theme kept appearing. It was also clear that they thought he might use any pretext to get into one. Randy Deibel, who was with him when he died and who told one reporter he was haunted by the death—"I can't get away from it"—likewise suggested that Kinison and his friends were just using the race talk and threats to start something: "They didn't believe what they said. They would say anything to start a fight."[7]

"Chris would have fought anyone," another friend, Ben Butler, told a reporter. "It didn't matter what color you were; it didn't matter how big you were."[8]

Indeed, Kinison was something of a legend: "I did not think he would ever go down," said James Bohrn, a 20-year-old friend who talked with reporters. "I've seen him take down 40-year-old guys."[9]

"He was a young man who had kind of an angry countenance," said George Vavrek, pastor of Ocean Shores Baptist Church. "But this town has not ever manifested any overt racist activities. There was a lot of alcohol talking there. The town views this as an aberration. We have blacks, Koreans and others living side-by-side here."

Local businessmen said the whole matter was overblown. "Some kid gets drunk and starts spouting off, that's it," said Carl Hansen, manager of an Ocean Shores resort. "If it doesn't get blown out of proportion, we're not worried. We're a tourist town, we welcome everybody."[10]

Not everybody, however, was so sure of that anymore.

✳

There were a lot of reporters in town that week, asking a lot of people a lot of questions. Indeed, the media horde raised its banner early on when the massive satellite trucks rumbled in and set up shop at various open lots around town. It was, as always, something like a signal for a black cloud to descend on the town, a certain sign that Something Bad had happened.

John Hughes, editor of the Aberdeen *Daily World*, observes that television news operations in particular love to "leap on any story that has any kind of a sex appeal and descends with the Panzer divisions of satellite dish trucks and does what I call the homage to Gore Vidal, the 'Visit to a Small Planet' school of journalism, where the local reports are always a stand-up routine in front of City Hall where they're saying, 'Back to you, Dave, where we're probing this act of racism that's divided all of Grays Harbor County.'" But of course, always accompanying the TV packs are the full phalanx of print reporters, some of them just as prone to facile, scripted story lines about how an incident has "divided" a community.

In reality, the community—at least in Ocean Shores—wasn't all that divided: Nearly everyone in town thought that what had happened to Chris Kinison was overkill, amounting to murder, and that both of the young Asian men should have been charged. Nor did anyone seem particularly concerned that not only Kinison, but many of his friends and cohorts, had committed a hate crime. This message came through pretty clearly, in fact, in most of the television interviews and many of the newspaper reports as well.

It probably did not help matters that a white-supremacist faction chimed in on the side of Kinison and his friends. An Olympia group calling itself the local chapter of David Duke's National Organization for European American Rights (NO FEAR) denounced the prosecution's decision not to pursue charges against Hung Hong. "This is an outrage," said David Jensen, the group's leader, in a press release. "This man is walking the streets today and being treated like a victim because he is an Asian American and Kinison—supposedly—used a racial slur. No one has asked the obvious question, 'is it now acceptable in Washington for minorities to kill European Americans for calling them names?' Why is the brother of this murderer, who aided him in his heinous act, not being charged with murder as well?"

Jensen spouted off to reporters as well: "I know what's right and what's wrong, and so far I have seen a violation of [Kinison's] rights," he told the Seattle *Post-Intelligencer*, hinting that David Duke himself might come to Washington State to observe the trial. "Kinison is taking the long dirt nap right now, and these two men are working at a restaurant, having a grand old time."

The combined effect of all these reports was to create a brief uproar around the Northwest, particularly in Seattle—the very place whence Ocean Shores derives the lion's share of its tourism dollars, as well as much of its residential base. (Seattle-based Boeing retirees are probably the largest single sub-community in the North Beach area.) The questions being asked by those TV reporters seemed perhaps not so silly: Was Ocean Shores, in fact, a hotbed for racism?

Op-ed commentary and letters to the editor questioning the response to the incident in Ocean Shores began appearing in the Seattle papers, with some writers accusing the town of harboring racism.

A letter to the editor of the *Seattle Times* from Bernadette Logue of Seattle cut to the quick:

> Interesting place, Ocean Shores.
>
> Chris Kinison, wearing a Confederate flag, screamed [racial slurs] at three Asian-Americans outside a Texaco there. He then led a mob of drunken white men in attacking the Asian-Americans. The three men fought back. Kinison was stabbed and killed.
>
> The word from Ocean Shores, according to all reports, including *The Times*, is that it is not a racist town; that Kinison was a troubled youth but basically a good guy—definitely not a racist. And Minh Duc Hong was not acting in self-defense when he stabbed Kinison.
>
> In Ocean Shores, apparently the custom on the July 4th weekend is to greet people of color by waving Confederate flags and yelling racist slurs. Maybe that's why, earlier, a police officer didn't take a report when Joe Scott, an African American, told him he'd been harassed. Maybe that's why no one aided a group of Filipinos, including children, threatened by 10 white men wavin' old Dixie in a parking lot. And maybe that's why no one working in the Texaco called the police while the shouting or the fighting was going on. Maybe that's why none of the other men involved with Kinison are in jail for hate crimes.
>
> Minh Duc Hong did what he had to do to save the lives of his brother, his friend and himself. They were outnumbered more than three to one, and they couldn't turn to anyone in Ocean Shores for help. Because in Ocean Shores they don't have a problem with racism.[11]

Another *Seattle Times* letter writer, Constance Daruthayan of Seattle, called on "the rest of the Asian community, other communities of color, and all who oppose bigotry to support Hong and demand that the city of Ocean Shores hold a meeting about the very real dangers posed by neo-fascist violence."[12]

And *Post-Intelligencer* columnist Chi-Dooh Li—a Chinese American whose politics are often right of center—offered a thoughtful response:

> To some, like Kinison, it might even seem that these immigrants are interlopers who have stolen their birthright. Could it be that the racial taunting is a bravado attempt to reclaim something they have lost by proclaiming superiority in the one area over which they have no control whatsoever—the color of their skin?

The news from Ocean Shores ought to trouble more than just the residents of that otherwise peaceful resort town. For some of us who may be regarded as outsiders because of our different skin color, it is a sobering thought that enjoying the fruits of the opportunities so freely offered to all in this great nation could incite resentment, and worse, in others.[13]

Even in Ocean Shores, voices were raised in question. *The Daily World* ran a story examining the Asian community's response. Most of them—especially business owners who seemed far more frightened of losing business over the incident than the prospect of its being repeated—thought that the community was largely free of racism's taint. But Ravi Agrawal, a thirty-seven-year-old Asian Indian beachfront homeowner, wondered if police and prosecutors had arrested the wrong people.

"They know that these people have been involved in a hate crime, but they have chosen to limit their focus to the killing," said Agrawal. "I'm not in favor of killing. Nobody is. But at the same time, being a minority, I can certainly say, when you are harassed purely on the basis of your race, your whole existence is completely questioned and denied." He urged the police to consider improving their understanding of hate crimes in order to better prevent them in the future.[14]

Such constructive criticism notwithstanding, the barrage on their town's public image from all sides left civic leaders in Ocean Shores bewildered and defensive. As a place that depended directly on urban tourists' dollars for its economic base, the last thing they needed was a reputation as a racist haven, and they bridled at the suggestions from civil-rights groups that they had provided one. At the same time, they feared that any effort to combat the image would just make it linger even longer, and worse yet, it might attract people like Jensen to the town. A sort of frozen denial became the official response.

"These types of things just don't happen here. This is the first crime of its kind in Ocean Shores. Lord, I hope it's the last," Mayor Peter Jordan told reporters. "We need to take a look at ourselves and ask how could this happen. Is there something we, as a community, missed?

"This has shocked the community," he added. "Shocked us silent."[15]

David McManus, the Ocean Shores police sergeant who had arrested the Hong brothers that morning and who doubled as the department's press spokesman, doubted that racism was systemic: "We are a small town. We'd see signs of something if it was building up. Everybody knows everybody."

Perhaps, as it turned out, too well.

※

After the shock of the media barrage settled in, so did the resentment. It arose from a well-established feature of the Grays Harbor landscape: the yawning rift between urban and rural cultures. The chasm is particularly pronounced here, in spotted owl country. The towns on the Olympic Peninsula are dotted with closed-down logging and sawmill operations, and the conventional wisdom is to blame environmentalists, who are identified with city dwellers. The resentment runs deep.

Perhaps this is no more so than in Aberdeen, the heart of the county. At one time, in the 1920s, it boasted the largest output of timber from anywhere on the Pacific Coast, since it was so ideally situated as a port for hauling out all that virgin old-growth Olympic timber. Since the 1960s, as the once-inexhaustible supply began to reach its limits, things have been in a gradual, long downturn. There was a brief uptick during the 1980s, when the Reagan Administration opened the doors to massive raw-log exports to Japan, but that all came crashing to a halt by the decade's end, when lawsuits and political pressure began shutting down the incursions into the final stands of the Peninsula's available old-growth timber. Aberdeen probably has even more boarded-up businesses, per capita, than Ocean Shores.

Indeed, if Ocean Shores has a slightly down-at-the-heels air, it is consonant with the depressed economic conditions that have pervaded life throughout Grays Harbor County for at least a decade, and in some places longer. Aberdeen is renowned globally, after all, as the hometown of the late grunge rock star Kurt Cobain, whose penchant for bleak and angry lyrics has often been traced to his years here as the child of a broken home. The town is not particularly eager to embrace his legacy, since he was a renowned drug user and a suicide, albeit one of the most influential songwriters in rock history. A well-graffitied bridge over the Wishkah River east of town, beneath which Cobain used to sleep when he was on his own and homeless, is the closest thing to a sort of memorial to his presence you can find in Aberdeen. But drive around the town awhile, and see for yourself the vacant businesses and broken lives, and you can see where a song like "Dumb" came from.

City dwellers, and environmentalists in particular, have borne the brunt of the blame for the poor economic situation, and there is little doubt that a certain callousness pervades most urban environmentalists' attitudes about the need for people to be able to make a living in the towns where they grew up and live. The reality, of course, is that the timber supply was never endless, but in fact had reached its economically justifiable limits. Moreover, many of the job losses were the product of market realities that had nothing to do with "green" sensibilities, such as the increasing mechanization of mill work that threw more than half of the existing mill labor pool out of work. Timber executives were themselves largely responsible for the recession caused by the bubble they had created in the 1980s when timber buyers delayed harvests in order to postpone the realization of losses on their federal contracts. Nonetheless, the urban elites—embodied by Seattle itself—were the popular scapegoats in timber country.[16]

There are cultural differences, too, the roots to which run deeper than the recent animosity over logging. Some are common to rural areas everywhere: a sense that rural life is simpler and purer, that old-fashioned values like decency and integrity matter more in the country, that hard work and fair play are what matters—in contrast to city life, which is viewed as shallow, fast-paced, thoughtless, and ultimately degrading. The decadence of city life is embodied in the minds of many rural dwellers in the rising prominence of urban gays and lesbians, who are typically viewed with a mix of horror and revulsion by the average person in a place like Grays Harbor County. People of other races are likely seen as outsiders too. What is most common in any event is a dismissive contempt for outsiders, and especially those from cities.

This simmering animosity welled to the surface in the weeks following the killing, especially as news accounts, some of them appearing in the nation's leading newspapers, began probing at the racial issues lying beneath the surface. Though stories about the case ran prominently in the Seattle papers and even the *New York Times*, it was the local paper in Aberdeen, the *Daily World*, that bore the brunt of the local ire at the media.

Reporter David Scheer, who handled most of the stories relating to the case, says that whenever the *Daily World* would run a piece, the paper's offices—and his desk particularly—would be flooded with phone calls complaining about the coverage. The paper was giving the whole county a black eye, in the view of many callers.

Letters to the paper's editor voiced similar views. One, by an Aberdeen resident named Vlad Ivanovich, contended the paper's coverage presupposed that "if you are white, then naturally you are the villain."

"I feel that in viewing the Hong twins as victims of a hate crime and taking away from the fact that at least one of them is a murderer, we as a community are taking a big risk with our youth," Ivanovich wrote. "The last time I checked, this was still a free country. That includes the freedom of speech.

"If this is approached as an epidemic of racism, and not approached for what it was—a murder—I am fearful that we will soon see racism become a true problem in this community."

Ivanovich, like many in the community, felt that the charges against Minh Hong weren't enough: "As for our prosecuting attorney, I feel he should have been a kindergarten teacher instead of a prosecutor, seeing that he has chosen to handle not one but two cases of murder in this county with kid gloves in not seeking the death penalty. To me, this shows the lack of concern for the people of Grays Harbor by Mr. Prosecutor."[17]

Another letter writer, T. Evenrout of Ocean Shores, attacked Minh Hong's defense: "I think the self-defense notion is ridiculous! Two men ganging up on an intoxicated person and stabbing him twenty-two times is murder in MY eyes—no matter how you look at it. How nauseating! This was an act of pure cowardice on behalf of the two men from Seattle.

"As far as the media coverage about racism goes, I do not believe this was a factor. It sounds to me as if Kinison would have picked a fight with ANY stranger who came to the Texaco station, regardless of his race. The media always blows things out of proportion just to make for an interesting story."[18]

However, these voices were not the only ones being raised locally. David Scheer says he kept a tally of the phone calls that came in to him, and they wound up about equally divided between those criticizing the paper's coverage as too sympathetic to the concerns about race, and those who either praised the paper's work or felt that it was too quick to dismiss charges of bigotry within the community.

Sean Izzarone of Aberdeen wrote *The Daily World* a letter that castigated its coverage for papering over the racial tensions in Grays Harbor, arguing that racism ran deep in the community: "If anyone is guilty, we, the citizens who allowed this event to transpire and continue to justify and defend the racist diatribe of Christopher Kinison in our efforts to shift the blame to 'the other,' are the guilty ones.

"We should all be on trial for our complicity in allowing racism to thrive in our communities, not Minh Duc Hong. We are ALL racists. We are all GUILTY."[19]

The same kind of division manifested itself among civic leaders in Ocean Shores. A number of local businesses, led by the Chamber of Commerce, understood the depth of the problem it faced and began organizing a local civil-rights group called the Ocean Shores Coalition to take a prominent stand against racism in the community.

But if Mayor Jordan had been contemplative about the crime when it first occurred, the weeks of negative coverage had indeed shocked him silent. He refused any further comment on the case, citing the pending trial and "potential litigation." Likewise, City Council members decided to stay mum.

Neither was there any indication that Ocean Shores Police intended to pursue any hate-crime charges against any of the other participants in the incident.

✵

An array of Seattle-based civil-rights groups had been monitoring the case but had largely been silent publicly; at the Japanese American Citizens League (JACL), for instance, chapter president James Arima counseled caution, since he considered it entirely possible that the young men were guilty. But as details of events that weekend began to emerge—especially the previous attack on the Filipino family and suspected attacks on other minorities by Kinison and his friends—it became increasingly clear to these organizations that something was wrong in Ocean Shores.

Finally, frustrated by the inaction of local law enforcement to take concrete steps against the local whites, the Asian American groups raised the stakes to another level. On October 2, they released to the press a letter they had jointly sent to the Seattle FBI seeking help from the agency in the case. The letter made front-page news in both the *Seattle Times* and the *Post-Intelligencer* and was a top story on several of the city's TV newscasts that night.

Leading the charge were the JACL and the Asian Bar Association, both of which questioned not only the inaction of Ocean Shores law enforcement before the incident, but the town's seeming willingness to rally in sympathy of someone who had been involved in what clearly appeared to be a hate crime.

"The police see these cases as just boys will be boys," observed Karen Yoshitomi of the JACL. "That's just hooey. This group of whites was clearly targeting people of color. The police response was to do nothing. And that's why we have to go to the FBI.

"There's a feeling that nothing has been done to recognize a hate crime when it happens."

The JACL, the Asian Bar Association, and the Organization of Chinese Americans (OCA) together sent a letter to the FBI arguing that police inaction before the incident could have prevented the crime and concluded: "Our community remains frustrated over what is perceived as the failure of law enforcement to pursue hate crimes against Asian-Americans and the ability of law enforcement to protect us."[20]

Yvonne Kinoshita Ward, president of the Asian Bar group, said local police had plenty of warning that trouble was brewing when Kinison and his friends assaulted the Filipino family: "Had they intervened, perhaps the tragedy would not have happened."[21]

Maxine Chan, president of the OCA's Seattle chapter, urged "Asian Americans and other people of color to think three times before taking a trip to the Ocean Shores area."[22]

The FBI ultimately declined to investigate, however, since federal hate-crime statutes require a federal crime to have been committed—which is to say, one that occurred on federal property or in the commission of a federal activity—and there was no evidence that was the case here. When the bureau made its announcement on October 14, JACL officials agreed with their assessment.

But the effort—combined with the specter of an orchestrated boycott of Ocean Shores by the Seattle groups—finally spurred Ocean Shores officials to action. On October 23, the city council passed a proclamation denouncing racial intolerance and hatred as "not representative of the character of our community." The proclamation emphasized that Ocean Shores "values the racial and cultural diversity of all its citizens and visitors."

However, the council managed to muffle the effect, passing the measure in the dead of night at the end of a closed-door session. Local reporters didn't pick it up until the next day. Both city councilmen and Mayor Peter Jordan sheepishly declined to talk about it in the context of the Hong case, citing "potential litigation."

"We felt (the proclamation) was something that needed to be said," said Councilman David Creighton. "Other than that, there wasn't anything more to it than that really. . . .

"I never thought we had a problem to begin with. The whole thing was an absolute shock. I hope we don't have any more problems like that in any way, manner or form. Someone dying is a horrible thing."[23]

But if the city's officials were slow to react, its Chamber of Commerce—recognizing a looming disaster—took the lead in organizing a concerted community response to the incident. Led by board president Mike Pence (who doubled as the city manager), an ad hoc committee of eighteen community leaders met two days after the city issued its back-door proclamation and agreed to begin putting together a long-range organization designed to address racial tensions and to promote understanding and diversity in the community. Eventually they would name themselves the Ocean Shores Coalition.

At that first meeting on October 25, the group was treated to some remarkably sound advice from Bob Hughes, a retired mediator for the U.S. Justice Department whose specialty had been helping communities set up task forces to resolve just this kind of racial conflict. He'd had previous experience dealing with the disruption wrought upon communities by white-supremacist groups in the inland Northwest, and stressed that pretending the problem doesn't exist won't make it go away.

However, Hughes correctly noted, the majority of hate crimes are not committed by people with organizational ties but rather by "thrill seekers" who act on their own and may not even identify themselves as racist. Regardless of the motive, any hate crime, Hughes stressed, should be treated as "a wake-up call."

In communities where hate groups have taken hold, the problem "has been lack of acceptance that there is a problem," he said. "First it was isolated: 'We've never had anything before and we've never had it again.' . . . But it's good to have a wake-up call—to accept what we have seen (in hindsight) was most likely a precipitating incident.

"One of the things I recommend to any community is to start documenting any racial activity. (After a while) a pattern might start to emerge.

"If the data is changing, we should all welcome this. It makes a community look bad to have high numbers, but it means a community is being honest. I think it's to our advantage in the long run that we risk looking bad compared to another community that is not reporting hate crimes."

All this sensible talk impressed the JACL's Karen Yoshitomi. "I am extremely pleased by the steps that they have taken," she told *Daily World* reporter David Scheer the next day. "I think it takes a tremendous amount of courage to take a hard look at what has been happening in their city and to take some steps."

At meeting's end, Mike Pence was satisfied that things were off to a good start: "It's never too late to do the right thing."[24]

✳

Perhaps the good common sense was too good to last. A few days later, things began to turn downright absurd.

At the *Daily World,* editor John Hughes penned an editorial chiding Peter Jordan and the Ocean Shores council for hiding behind the cloak of "pending litigation" instead of confronting the community's problems head-on: "He should have said, 'It's a silly city policy, and I am duty bound to come to the defense of my city by telling you the plain truth.'" Hughes then proceeded to outline what the mayor should have said.[25]

A week and a half later, Jordan responded with a long and testy letter that proceeded to march off into fantasy:

> One other aspect of the recent media blitz which nobody has yet mentioned, is that this pattern of behavior by the special interest groups involved may well be intended to influence potential Grays Harbor County jurors in an effort to obtain a change of venue or a jury nullification verdict in the manslaughter trial currently pending in Grays Harbor County Superior Court. Could it be that these special interest groups have arbitrarily decided that the citizens of Grays Harbor County cannot provide a fair and impartial forum in which to try the criminal case, and are in fact acting on that unilateral decision?
>
> During the several days it has taken me to draft this letter, *The Daily World* has continued to print sensational "news" in high-visibility space. It is interesting to note that much of this space is dedicated to the point of view espoused by special interest groups who have no firsthand knowledge of life in Ocean Shores. Perhaps, in a perceived need to validate their existence as political advocacy groups, problems must be acknowledged to exist in order to justify the groups' demands for simplistic solutions. Failing that, perhaps problems must be invented. I am reminded of a paraphrased simile from G. B. Shaw, "If there were not a devil, it would be necessary to create one."[26]

Fortunately, Jordan's bizarre accusation of "jury nullification"—which John Hughes considered "outrageous" and said so in a follow-up editorial—did not travel very far, and failed to derail the nascent efforts to build bridges with the Asian American community and repair Ocean Shores' damaged image.

That effort came to fruition at a gathering organized in mid-November by the Chamber-sponsored Ocean Shores Coalition. It brought together officials from racial-diversity organizations—namely, the OCA and Asian Bar Association, as well as the Seattle-based Northwest Coalition for Human Dignity, which had a long history of organizing local communities to combat hate groups and the crimes they inspired—with state officials and members of the Ocean Shores community.

One of the Coalition leaders, a retired mechanical engineer named Richard Mayo, said he hoped the organizations would "educate the town and perhaps prevent a future tragedy. That's not an easy thing to do. We need education here. We need a method to move the information along."

"I applaud you," said Tony Orange, from the state's Commission on African American Affairs. "You have a lot of people of good will here and you have a lot of resources here."

Even Maxine Chan, who had harshly criticized the community only a few weeks before, was laudatory: "These folks have lots of work ahead of them. . . . All of these things you talked about tonight [at this gathering] were wonderful.

"The first step is to say, 'no,'" she said. "A community has to come together to say no to a bias crime—to say it will not be tolerated here. That's a powerful message you send to folks."[27]

For all the warm feelings, though, there was also a paternalistic tone to the exchanges—wise city folk counseling the wide-eyed country dwellers. Perhaps that was reflected in the attendance. Only twenty-five people were in the audience.

Earnest hopes notwithstanding, the real and very raw question that lingered was whether the effort would ever move beyond mere words. The first real test of the newfound collaborative spirit in the community lay just ahead: at Minh Hong's trial.

CHAPTER FOUR

WHITE FACES

IF MINH HONG FELT ALONE AND HELPLESS THAT NIGHT at the Texaco station, those feelings must have been magnified a hundred times when he finally went on trial in early December.

Although Hong's mother and father took turns attending the trial and his girlfriend was there throughout, he was confronted daily in the courtroom with a sea of white faces, many of them decidedly unfriendly. There were a couple of Asian men from Grays Harbor County who dropped in from time to time, and an observer from the Department of Justice's Community Relations Service, an African American woman, was there every day. James Arima and Karen Yoshitomi of the Japanese American Citizens League put in regular appearances. And scattered among Chris Kinison's friends in the audiences were a few colored faces—notably, Kinison's uncle, an African American who made it clear to reporters he doubted the claims that Kinison was a racist, and Jesse Forvour, Kinison's half-Filipino friend. However, everyone else at the trial—the judge, the prosecutors, the jury pool, even Hong's own lawyers—was white.

This became an issue in selecting a jury, which was when the larger problem of racial diversity in Grays Harbor County reared its head. Naturally enough, defense attorneys Monte Hester and Brett Purtzer were concerned about the panel's makeup, since much of their planned defense drew on racially sensitive issues, and public confidence in the verdict might hinge on having a racially representative jury. But since 92 percent of the county's population is Caucasian, they didn't have much to work with. And both prosecutors and defense attorneys were concerned about the intense media coverage the case had engendered. Nearly everyone in the county knew about the case, and the lawyers were unsure whether the news stories would prejudice potential jurors, in either direction.

David Foscue, the Superior Court judge overseeing the trial, was also concerned about jurors' ability to serve if the trial turned into a long one, with the Christmas holidays rapidly approaching. So he ordered an unusually large pool: some 145 people. From that random draw, only one—an elderly black woman—was obviously a minority.

The setting for the trial itself was unusual. Montesano, a smallish town ten miles east of Aberdeen, is the county seat. An earthquake a year before had badly damaged the stately ninety-year-old sandstone Grays Harbor County Courthouse and forced major renovations that happened to be in full swing when the trial was scheduled. So court officials moved the proceedings across the street to the adobe-roofed Montesano City Hall, in an upstairs meeting hall with wooden floors, high ceilings and lousy acoustics.

On the first day of jury selection, the open room was in more or less a state of chaos. The size of the pool didn't help matters; jurors were being questioned one at a time, which meant the room was full of people sitting around card tables on folding chairs with a lot of nothing to do. Some played board games like Trivial Pursuit or card games. Others knitted or read books. The constant conversation created a loud murmur in the room throughout the day. When Foscue went to address the crowd or to call out the next juror's name, he usually had to shout.

The jurors were examined in a small kitchen across the hall from the meeting room, where the judge and the attorneys had gathered. Minh Hong and his attorneys sat next to a three-basin sink, while the prosecutors had placed chairs next to the oven. Judge Foscue sat near the dishwasher. When a juror came in the room, he or she was offered a seat next to the refrigerator.

Most of the questioning focused on the jurors' awareness of the case from news reports. Chief deputy prosecutor Gerald Fuller, who was in charge of the county's case, repeatedly asked interviewees whether they were able to set aside anything they had read or heard about the case beforehand. Fuller stressed that sometimes media accounts could be incomplete or incorrect.

Nearly every one of the potential jurors responded that they could. Most of them said they had in fact read newspaper accounts of the incident, but not very many of them could recall details of the case. Pressed further, none of them mentioned one of the more prominently reported facets of the Fourth of July fight—that Chris Kinison had been waving a Confederate flag.

A handful, however, said they had in fact formed opinions about the case and probably couldn't hear the trial even-handedly. One man was insistent that Hong should have simply driven away. Others cited religious beliefs for refusing to participate; one man said his background as a Jehovah's Witness meant he could not sit in judgment of another person.

Monte Hester, Minh Hong's attorney, was more interested in the potential jurors' racial views. At the end of each session, he simply asked each interviewee to look at his client and answer a single question: "Can you say to Minh, as you look at him, 'I presume you to be innocent?'"

Most of them replied that they could. But a few candidly answered, "No."

✳

Only seventy-five people out of the 145 in the jury pool were interviewed the first day, and the African American woman who constituted the sole non-white face among them did not make the initial cut. So when proceedings started out the next day, Brett Purtzer raised a red flag, entering a motion to restart the jury-selection process with a fresh pool of potential jurors, in hopes of obtaining a more representative sample of the county's population.

Gerald Fuller immediately objected. The jury pool, he argued, was chosen at random from among the county's licensed drivers: "To do it any other way would be other than random, and that is what the law requires us to do."

Judge Foscue surveyed the fifty-six remaining would-be jurors. Only three identified themselves as minorities, and two more raised their hands when asked if they were one-fourth minority. Those numbers, however, roughly reflected the 92 percent/8 percent white/nonwhite split in Grays Harbor County's census. Satisfied that they were working with a racially representative pool, Foscue denied the motion, and the jury selection proceeded.

Once the remainder of the initial jury pool had been interviewed, the winnowing process began in earnest. Hester took the first day's line of questioning a notch further, asking the jurors whether they would try to defend themselves or their loved ones if some assailant were to threaten them—and how far they would go to do it.

"When do you quit?" Hester asked. "When you are dead?"

Then he pointed out to jurors that quitting too early had its consequences as well—namely, it would risk their lives and their loved ones. "Have you ever heard the phrase, 'dead wrong'?" he asked. It was clear he was setting the stage for arguments he would present in trial.

Prosecutors likewise sharpened their questions. Fuller's deputy, Andrea Vingo, asked the panelists if they had ever been involved in a fight or had seen one. "Do you think there are sort of unspoken rules about fair fighting?" she asked.

The question brought mixed responses. One answered that "you don't kick the person, especially in the crotch." Another emphasized: "And no weapons."

By the day's end, they had managed to whittle the list down to a jury of twelve people, with two alternates in reserve. The final list was a reasonable cross section of the community: an oyster-dredge operator, a retired funeral-home owner, a couple of homemakers, local businessmen. A genial, white-haired former Aberdeen High chemistry teacher, Gene Schermer, was chosen as the jury foreman.

One of the five jurors to raise her hand indicating she was a minority was among them, as was one of the two alternates. In the end, Purtzer and Hester were satisfied.

"There is nothing about these particular jurors that concerns me," Purtzer told reporters as he left. "Overall, they seem to be objective people who have no prejudice."

Still, the predominantly white makeup of the jury left lingering doubts. Purtzer observed that it was likely to leave members of minority communities "nervous" about Minh Hong's chances for a fair trial.

✹

It was already clear that a personality clash was brewing in the courtroom—namely, between defense attorney Monte Hester and prosecutor Gerald Fuller. But then, it was unlikely you could find two lawyers who were less alike.

Monte Hester is a tall man from Oklahoma with a basketball player's large frame, fit and white-haired with large glasses that fit his square face. He is an imposing figure, and his rumbling tenor resonates well in a courtroom. He also is a refined man with highly attuned sensitivities, and he plainly is practiced at manipulating an audience's emotions with well-crafted rhetoric. His bearing is not exactly aristocratic or cold—he has a nice common touch, and he can be passionate at times—but rather is carefully dignified.

Fuller, on the other hand, is a working-class kind of everyman—balding, a little plump, a bit ruddy when the blood is flowing—who looks like he comes from Grays Harbor. He laughs easily and is good at bantering with reporters and witnesses. "Jerry," as he is known outside of court documents and news stories, is a regular guy who is well liked, and he parlays that persona well in the courtroom. Most of the time, no one on a jury will mistake him for an overzealous prosecutor—he seems too reasonable, too regular, too much like them.

It was apparent that the men rubbed each other the wrong way, and it went well beyond a mere difference in styles. Monte Hester clearly had grave reservations about the prosecutors' conduct thus far in the case—charging a victim who acted in self-defense and then ignoring the likelihood that some of their witnesses had been participants in a hate crime suggested a certain lack of racial enlightenment, if not outright bigotry. Jerry Fuller obviously chafed at this, and resented deeply the implications of racism behind Hester's attitude.

Keeping the two egos from erupting was a chore that befell David Foscue, the Superior Court judge from Montesano. Foscue is a smallish man—quick to smile, with a shock of white hair and an easygoing but learned demeanor—but he never seemed intimidated by either of the two attorneys who sometimes loomed before him. Despite the tensions bubbling beneath the surface, he managed to keep the trial on an even keel throughout.

Hester's right-hand man, Brett Purtzer, was more in Jerry Fuller's mold, physically speaking—average height and a stocky but fit build, thinning hair and a square jaw with a friendly disposition. He complemented Hester nicely, particularly on cross-examination, displaying a knack for calm, efficient dissection of a witness' testimony. It was clear, however, that he shared much of his boss's animus toward Fuller and the prosecution team over the direction in which they had taken the case.

Fuller's deputy, Andrea Vingo, a brunette of medium height and build, complemented her boss in much the same way. She was neat and efficient where he tended to the rough and unkempt, and her cross-examinations were deliberate and unthreatening. It was clear she kept the gears turning smoothly in presenting the prosecution team's case.

Fuller also had his hands full for much of the trial with Molly Kinison. Chris was her only child, and her grief was like an open wound that flooded the courtroom every day. Tall, taut and dark-haired, she usually sat in the first or second rows of chairs with a group of friends who accompanied her most days. She made a striking visage, crying frequently and making occasional verbal outbursts. It was clear that at least a couple of jurors were emotionally caught up by her presence.

But Fuller handled her nicely. He had an employee from his office's grief-counseling services, Michaelan McDougal, at her side at all times during the trial, and either Fuller or Andrea Vingo spoke to her regularly during breaks and before and after the daily sessions. Throughout the two weeks the ordeal lasted, Molly Kinison's grief was treated with care and compassion. Fuller may have gained some sympathy from the jurors for the treatment, but it was clear the concern was genuine.

Minh Hong, in contrast, sat with his lawyers at a table facing the jurors, consistently impassive, his head bowed. He looked frail, as though the prospect of prison was perched heavily on his shoulders. His gaze was straight ahead and he made no eye contact with anyone. People who knew Minh beforehand knew this was not an act—he was always shy and likely to look down.

His parents also attended the trial each day, sitting usually in the second or third row nearest the defense's table. They more or less traded turns so that someone could mind the teriyaki shop, but on most days, Minh's mother was the one who drove down. She was not demonstrative, and in fact stared straight ahead through most of the proceedings, her eyes locked onto her son. Nonetheless, throughout the trial anyone observing her was likely to see those eyes welled with tears.

I was somewhat stunned when I first saw Minh Hong's mother—by the recognition. She passed by me just as I first entered the courtroom the first day, before I had seen Minh, her eyes fixed straight ahead. And I knew who she was, of course, from all those teriyaki dinners she and her sons had served me over the years. I looked over and saw Minh Hong and was again hit with the shock of recognition.

I had become interested in the case because of my previous work involving white supremacists, hate groups, and hate crimes. I thought the case had the potential to reveal a lot about the nature of all of these, as well as giving me a chance to explore small-town life. So I had pitched the story to the editors at *Salon* and set about to cover the trial.

I'd read the names in the paper, of course, but had never connected them with my young friends at the teriyaki shop. And now the connection, frankly, left me somewhat stunned.

Of course, I was concerned that my foreknowledge of the suspects would taint my ability to cover the trial fairly. But this was not the first time this had happened; most small-town reporters indeed know many of the characters they wind up writing about in court trials, and I had been no exception. On the other hand, what I already knew about the Hong brothers did not jibe with the portrait that the prosecutors had been painting in the papers: big-city Asian gangsta wannabes who got into a fight with local kids and stabbed one to death.

The flip side of all that courtroom experience, though, is the ingrained knowledge that even someone you think you know may have a hidden side you're completely unaware of. I had seen such revelations emerge in court before. It was possible that Minh Hong indeed was, away from his parents' shop, a thuggish, vengeful killer. I would be surprised, but not shocked. So I dutifully opened my notebook and my mind, waiting to see if Jerry Fuller could demonstrate that it was so.

✳

Montesano became the county seat of Grays Harbor almost by default, though not without a fight. It was one of the first towns in the county, and won the 1886 vote to place the first courthouse there after a brief tussle with the harbor town of Cosmopolis. But by 1909, Aberdeen had blossomed into the largest town in the county, and there was a two-year legislative battle over its city leaders' efforts to split the county in two and establish a new seat there. But it lost, and in 1910 the large sandstone courthouse was built in Montesano, cementing the town's hold on the seat.[1]

In the intervening years, Aberdeen and adjacent Hoquiam continued to grow and prosper, and for awhile both were economic powerhouses, though in recent years much of that glory has faded. Montesano, meanwhile, has changed relatively little. It is still a small town, and in many respects, the county is its main industry, the courthouse still the epicenter of its economic life. It closer resembles quaint, quiet little Elma (home of the Annual Slug Festival) just a little ways down the road to the east than it does its larger neighbors.

There's one good-sized supermarket, a handful of gas stations, and a downtown business district mostly clustered around the town's main intersection (and only traffic light), at the junction of a couple of backroads highways labeled 107 and 108, respectively, roughly two blocks away from the main freeway to Grays Harbor, State Route 8 (which parallels much of 108). There's a family restaurant called the Busy Bee and a coffee shop and an Italian restaurant, a few clothing shops, a Subway sandwich store (the only chain business in town), a couple of banks. Not a lot, but enough to live comfortably, especially with Aberdeen a fifteen-minute hop down the highway.

And Montesano is a comfortable place. The people who live there are generally genial and open, and they like where they live. It's quiet, it's safe, it's close to the outdoors. In the spring it is a gorgeous green, and in the fall the trees along the boulevards create the traditional autumnal spray of fading color. It has all those small-town virtues people like to retire to—and there are indeed a number of senior citizens who live there.

Most of the businesses, the restaurants especially, were a little eager to see the trial begin, since media people are renowned for racking up the dining and lodging expenses. But there was a general uneasiness, because people were well aware that the cloud hovering over Ocean Shores was one that hung over the whole county, of which they obviously were part. The arrival of satellite-TV trucks was as ill a harbinger for Montesano as for their neighbors to the west.

Everyone seemed to understand that the harsh spotlight had been turned on their larger community, demanding to know: Was Grays Harbor a haven for racists? The question hung in the air like the harbor fog on cold December mornings, though many chose to ignore it, as they would the mist.

Clerks in the stores and waitresses at the restaurants were mostly tight-lipped about the trial. On the other hand, a few people acknowledged what was at stake, and whether it was true. The owner of the little coffee shop, who had only taken over the business the summer before, declined to give her name, but wondered aloud about whether a reputation as a racist community was deserved.

"You know, people have been real nice to me, and I'd never really seen any sign of racial prejudice," she said. "Gays—that's another thing. But I was really surprised the other day. I was at the [restaurant a couple of doors away] one morning and I heard someone at a table in the back room launch into this big long rant about Hispanics—'Spic this,' and 'fucking Spic that,' you know, 'they're all a bunch of lazy criminals.' I was surprised.

"But I guess that there is some racism here. You just don't usually see it."

A middle-aged Latino woman leaving the Italian restaurant seemed a little nervous about talking to a reporter, but smiled and said, "No, no," she hadn't ever really experienced any racism. "People have always been nice to me. It's a nice place."

But, she admitted, she had heard of "others who didn't really have such a good time."

✳

The businessmen's hopes for a free-spending media horde vanished, alas, the morning of the first day of the trial, December 6, a Wednesday. All they had for a horde was David Scheer, the reporter for the Aberdeen *Daily World*, Jamie D'Antoni, a reporter for *The North Coast News*, the Ocean Shores weekly, and me. I was staying with friends in Aberdeen, and am notoriously cheap anyway.

For some reason, the Seattle media chose not to cover the trial for the most part. The city's two newspapers were in the midst of a long and difficult strike and were so short-staffed they did not assign reporters to the story, relying instead on the Associated Press wire stories that were re-edited versions of Scheer's pieces. The *Post-Intelligencer* (which did not even bother to run an AP story until December 12) did finally assign someone to the trial its second week, sending Bill Miller, normally a metro editor but now pressed into service as a reporter. No reporter from the *Seattle Times* ever appeared. The city's four network television stations—evidently following the newspapers' leads, though they were not striking—did not send anyone to Montesano until the final day, when the verdict was announced (and even then, only two stations were present).

So the town was almost preternaturally quiet that morning—except, of course, for the steady trickle of patrol cars cruising up and down the streets, on the lookout, apparently, for David Duke and his minions.

The Duke rumors had evidently been flying for months. David Jensen, the Olympia man who ran the local chapter of Duke's National Organization for European American Rights (NO FEAR) had been spending the ensuing months since the stabbing touting Chris Kinison as a martyr for the white cause. The campaign, however, seemed to be gaining little traction, especially since Kinison's family and friends had publicly repudiated the effort. But Jensen reportedly had told people that Duke himself was going to attend the trial, and was threatening to bring a large contingent to watch the proceedings.

It was all bluster, of course, but local police (probably wisely) decided that prudence was the better part of valor. No one would officially admit to an "emphasis patrol," but there was an unusually high number of cruisers on the streets of Montesano that morning.

Inside the city hall and upstairs in the converted meeting room, it was quiet. There was a small audience of about fifty people gathered in the rows of chairs, with Kinison's family and friends forming a large cluster seated near the gallery that had been built for the jury. The chaos of the jury-selection process had largely vanished, and a reasonable semblance of a courtroom had been created in the big ballroom.

Instead of having benches and banisters, the room was arranged with folding tables serving as dividers and chairs arranged in rows for jurors and the audience. Because there were no microphones and the room was so large, everyone— witnesses especially—had to project loudly, as if they were on a stage. On the sunny days when the courtroom grew warm and windows were opened, the sound of a truck driving by on the street below would rumble through the courtroom and drown out anyone speaking.

That morning, however, there was little activity outside, except of course for the occasional police cruiser drifting by. Conversation was kept to a low murmur of general anticipation.

Then the lawyers, with Minh Hong in tow, filed in and took their seats, followed by the jury, who found their places in the little gallery. Shortly after, everyone rose as Judge Foscue entered the room, and the trial began.

CHAPTER FIVE

GROWING UP AMERICAN

MOLLY KINISON HAS A SCRAPBOOK FULL OF PICTURES of her only child, Christopher, that she likes to show to people. The pictures in it show a blond, smart, happy boy: a child with the charm and verve that will carry someone a long way in life. Someone with a bright future.

He spent many of his boyhood years in Hawaii, where his parents lived while still together. His father was a career officer in the Navy, and they were stationed there for five years. And so many of the class pictures of young Chris Kinison are taken in Hawaii, where, being white, he was in the distinct minority. In a couple of class photos, he is one of only two white faces in the crowd. Most of them are Asian.

There are pictures of Chris playing on soccer teams and middle-school foot-ball teams in Maryland, where the family later moved, and again, he is surrounded by mostly black teammates. And there's a picture of young Christopher with his arm around a childhood pal who is black.

Chris, Molly Kinison insists, was raised to be racially tolerant. He had many minority friends growing up, and never showed any signs of having a racist bone in his body.

"My son is not a racist," she told David Scheer when she granted him an in-terview, a week after the trial. "He was not a skinhead. . . . I wouldn't stand for it. I wouldn't stand for anybody to be treated badly."[1]

Many of his friends, of course, were also outspoken in denying that Kinison was a racist. They all cited his Filipino friend and black uncle, and all claimed that, though it was true he liked to fight, he merely used racist language as a way to start a brawl. That same violent streak, however, hints at another side of the young man.

However multiracial and tolerant Chris Kinison's background may have been, something appears to have changed about the time he got into high school, after his parents divorced and Molly moved to Ocean Shores in 1994. Certainly that was when he developed a taste for fighting. Chris began getting into trouble with the law for, among other things, possessing pot and dangerous weapons and engaging in malicious mischief.

Kinison dropped out of school in October 1997, early in his senior year at North Beach High. People in town say Kinison and his crowd were people who lived on the fringe, many of them dropouts. Minh Hong's lawyer, Brett Purtzer, called them "punks and drunks," a description even his friends were unlikely to dispute. It was, if anything, a description they were rather proud of.

A little while after he dropped out, Chris began drifting. Dave McManus, the Ocean Shores Police sergeant who later interviewed the Hong brothers, said that Kinison lived "on the Beach"—staying in friends' spare rooms and basements or couches, spending his days and evenings either hanging out on the beach or wandering the town or hanging out with friends, drinking beer around bonfires. His contact with his mother grew infrequent.

At about the same time, Kinison was at the center of a feud between his crowd of friends (which included Gabe Rodda and Brock Goedecke) and a gang of Indian teens from the Quinault Reservation, some thirty miles north of town. The violence came to a head in late October, when an injured Kinison was delivered to the front doors of the Ocean Shores police station on Point Brown Avenue.

According to Kinison, a "carload of Indians" had attacked him as he walked down a nearby street. The injuries—mostly massive bruises on his legs—rendered him unable to walk, and he was transported by ambulance to the local hospital, where he was treated and released after determining no bones had been broken.

Things turned a little uglier a few weeks later, when Kinison's predilection for harassing minorities first emerged. Kinison, according to a group of black teenagers, had pulled up alongside them as they walked through Ocean Shores, called them "niggers," and threatened them with harm unless they got out of town. Police investigated but eventually the black teens, who were on vacation, declined to file charges.[2]

"Chris was a scrapper," said Gail Canady, who got to know Kinison when she hired him for a few weeks in 1999 at the Subway sandwich shop she manages on Chance a la Mer. She said she nearly fired him one day for fighting with a fifteen-year-old boy, whose father later came into the shop and threatened Kinison. She did fire him the next day when he was late to work.[3]

Sometime in 1999, Chris drifted fifty miles east to Olympia. He picked up odd construction jobs and came back to Ocean Shores occasionally to visit friends. Apparently too broke to afford a car, he caught a bus to Aberdeen on June 30, 2000 and friends picked him up at the downtown depot.

According to people who knew them, Kinison and his crowd liked to talk about how Ocean Shores had been "taken over" by foreigners. And indeed there was an increased minority presence in town, though in reality the percentage of the town's minority population remained roughly the same. There was, notably, a certain higher ethnic profile: Korean Americans owned one of the largest resorts in town, and two of its three gas stations, and East Indian families operated three large new hotels.

For the most part, this kind of diversification of the town's population was considered a welcome sign of its growing maturity, especially to officials at the local chamber of commerce: "We have always been a welcoming community, and the new faces we've been seeing recent years are real proof of that," boasts Joan Payne, the chamber's executive director.

Not everyone feels that way, she admits. And indeed, there was a tiny segment of the community, including some of Kinison's gang, who felt they had been "invaded." They wondered why those businesses weren't owned by "Americans" and why they didn't hire "American" kids like themselves.

What better time to stand up for all things "American" than the Fourth of July?

✳

It is hard to say where Christopher Kinison obtained that Confederate flag. No one among his friends seemed to know. At least, if any of them do know, they aren't talking. But it appears he brought it with him on that bus from Olympia.

There is no evidence that Kinison had ever been involved in any kind of hate group or even a right-wing militia. The only signs of racist or extremist beliefs came in the threats against the black kids he made in 1997—that, and his apparent involvement in the series of incidents that culminated in his death on the Fourth of July.

The claims of his mother and friends—that he simply liked to use racism as an excuse for getting into fights and harassing tourists—has a certain credibility. After all, what few minorities live in town are usually well known, which means any other racial minority who shows up is quickly pegged as an urban tourist. And that Kinison loved to get into fights of any kind is beyond dispute. So, it must be said, is the racially inclusive environment in which Kinison was raised.

Unfortunately, even the most skilled, disciplined, and successful parents can find their children caught up in white-supremacist beliefs, and Kinison may have been no exception. It is important to remember that he was in economic straits and had been for some time; he clearly harbored some reservoir of resentment for his low social position. He also had become unmoored from his family—Molly had lost control of him years before—and young people's values often drift in such vacuums. These traits fit the psychological mold of a typical recruit for white supremacists. And when people begin to develop such beliefs, they often become adept at hiding it from their friends, outside of a select few. Even their oldest friends can be shocked to discover what new ideas they have cultivated.

Chris Kinison is plainly a much more complicated case than his friends will admit. There was, first and foremost, the Confederate flag—even outside the South, widely considered a symbol of white supremacists and racist rednecks. And in the Northwest, it was also associated with the Aryan Nations' neo-Nazis, who were known to decorate their pickups with the flags.

And then there were his actions, even before meeting Minh Hong: participating, albeit perhaps from a distance, in the harassment of the Filipinos. Allegedly threatening two different black men, one of them with a knife. Harassing Matt Gonzales as he emerged from the store. All of them clear cases of harassment in which the racial hatred was a prominent feature of the threats.

He went beyond the usual well-known epithets of skinhead stereotype ("White power!") to ideologically based abuse of the Nativist variety ("This is my country! Gooks go back to where you came from!"), indicating some strong beliefs behind the assaults. It is also clear he knew exactly what he was doing; his retort to Amanda Algeo—"It's called racism!"—was unmistakable.

These were the images that confronted Minh Hong and his brother and friend that night at the Texaco: the close-cropped, muscular young man shouting racial slurs at them; the Confederate flag, the fingers run across the throat; the cluster of other young white men, some with shaved heads. That image is almost the classic Hollywood portrait of a hate crime: the blood-crazed skinhead who lusts for the chance to stomp the defenseless "gook," while his gang of leering pals look on. If Chris Kinison was only imitating a hate crime, he was damned good at it.

The reality, however, is that this kind of assault is *not* the typical hate crime, nor is a skinhead the typical hate criminal. Only a small handful of all hate crimes are committed by people with any kind of organizational ties to "hate" groups or who practice "hate" ideologies. Most hate crimes in fact are committed by "thrill seekers" who think committing the acts is a clever way to have fun. And in that respect, Chris Kinison probably did resemble the classic hate criminal. As did his friends.

✳

One of the pitfalls of the popular stereotype of a hate criminal as a tattooed, leather-clad skinhead with a spike collar is that police often succumb to it, too.

Unless they've been trained to know otherwise, the possibility that a crime scene they've happened upon might be a bias crime doesn't cross the radar of many officers, because there are no skinheads in sight. This is particularly the case when, as at Ocean Shores, they're just "local kids."

The reality is that those "local kids" are in fact the most common perpetrators of bias crimes. Numerous studies have demonstrated that only a small percentage of hate crimes are committed by people with any connection to or background involving organized "hate" groups. One of these (conducted by Dr. Edward Dunbar, a clinical psychologist at the University of California at Los Angeles) found that fewer than 5 percent of the perpetrators of the 1,459 hate crimes committed in the Los Angeles area in the period 1994 to 1995 belonged to any kind of racist organization.

What these studies have found instead is that the majority of bias crimes are committed by seemingly normal, mostly law-abiding young people who often see nothing wrong with their behavior. Bias-crime offenders are predominantly young white males, typically from working-class or middle-class backgrounds.[4] And though ties to hate groups are rare, the perpetrators often are clearly inspired by these groups' rhetoric, shouting their well-known slogans, parroting their political rhetoric, and displaying such symbols of white supremacism as the swastika or the Confederate flag.[5]

Of course, alcohol and drugs also often play a role in these crimes, but the predominating impulse is bigotry—a personal animus toward a group that the victim represents. These prejudices so deeply color the perpetrators' judgment that they fail to see the criminality of their actions.

There are, according to experts, three major types of hate-crime perpetrators:

- Thrill-seeking offenders
- Reactive offenders
- Mission offenders

Thrill-seeking offenders represent far and away the most common kind of perpetrator; they commit roughly 60 percent of all hate crimes. They typically act in groups of five to ten teenagers or young people, and they rarely are ever associated with any kind of hate group. Their primary motivation is the psychological or social thrill that comes with committing the crime; sometimes, the acts are perpetrated as a way of gaining acceptance from one's peers, or to win "bragging" rights of some kind or other.

The thrill-seekers' victims are almost any member of a vulnerable group. Typically, people belonging to these groups are believed by the offenders to be inferior. Yet their hatred of the victim is almost superficial and often is a pose to seem "different" or "tough." Offenders of this kind, studies have found, in fact are read-ily deterred from repeating the crime if there is a strong response from the com-munity or society at large condemning the act.

Indeed, this is a significant aspect of the research about hate-crime perpetra-tors: The evidence is overwhelming that a community or, for that matter, society at large, can effectively intervene through education and effective law enforce-ment, as well as efforts to eliminate the conditions that give rise to many forms of violence, particularly those among young people. It is clear that hate crimes are not necessarily random, uncontrollable, or inevitable occurrences. Strong signals of disapproval from the community, and especially law enforcement, are very ef-fective deterrents.

Conversely, because of the seeming ordinariness of the criminals, police are less likely to attach significance to the bias aspects of the crime, which enhances the likelihood the offenders will not face punishment. And because of the num-bers of people involved in most of these crimes, each group member's participa-tion is often limited to a specific aspect of the larger crime. This enables each of the perpetrators to avoid either acknowledging the seriousness of the crime or fac-ing its consequences.

Reactive offenders are the second-most common type, representing about 30 percent of all hate crimes. These are people who have a strong sense of entitle-ment regarding their rights or their way of life, and this sense extends neither to the victim or his identity. What sets off a reactive offender is some kind of per-ceived threat to these things; and they often react violently or threateningly, em-phatically exceeding the force they might apply to someone who does not pose this "threat." In all of these cases, the perpetrator is motivated not only to protect or defend against the perceived menace, but also to send a "message" that will repel the "outsiders." (Most hate-groups members who commit crimes in fact are reactive.)

The victims of reactive hate crimes are always individuals from the group that the perpetrator believes constitutes the threat; most of the time, these are people of color, Jews, or homosexuals. The crimes most often happen in the of-fender's own neighborhood or community. And the offenders rarely feel guilt be-cause they usually believe they are fully justified in whatever violence was required to "get the job done."

Mission offenders are the rarest kind of bias criminal, constituting less than 5 percent of all the crimes. These people are often psychotic or have some impaired ability to reason; they are unstable and violent and will erupt entirely at random. Often, they believe they have been instructed by a higher order to rid the world of evil; they also believe they must avenge misfortunes they have suffered. A com-mon trait is that mission offenders see conspiracies being perpetrated by the groups targeted. Their victims are any member of the group perceived responsible for their miseries. These crimes are always of a violent nature, and often end with the perpetrator's suicide.[6]

There is some crossover among these three categories; there are always a certain number of criminals who will at least partially fit two of the categories at once, though rarely all three. Chris Kinison could probably be described as both a thrill seeker and a reactive criminal.

Organized hate groups, associated in the popular view with bias crimes, in fact can inspire offenders in all three categories. Moreover, the tiny percentage of actual hate-group involvement in such crimes—combined with the common appearance of hate-group rhetoric when they are committed—suggests, perhaps, the breadth of the reach of these groups' ideologies well beyond their actual membership.

It is important, especially for law-enforcement officers investigating the scene, to understand that not everyone involved in a hate crime is equally culpable. Most hate crimes are group events, like the events of the Fourth of July. Most of the time there are multiple offenders. And it's important for officers to recognize that different participants play varying roles in these crimes:

- **The leader:** The person whose idea it is to commit the crime, and who often plays the primary role in fomenting the violence. This is the person primarily culpable for the crime, but is rarely solely so.
- **The fellow traveler:** These persons form the immediate circle around the leader and are most likely to follow through on his directives and urgings, or imitate him. They are unlikely to have committed the crime in the leader's absence, but can be nearly as culpable, depending on the level of participation.
- **The unwilling participant:** These persons neither condone the crimes nor participate in the violence in any fashion other than their presence. These people usually have minimal culpability.[7]

Psychologists have found that the prejudice that motivates most hate-crime offenders, particularly the "leaders," is usually rooted in an environment that disdains people who are "different," and that frames this difference as a threat to the original environment. The Other—an indefinable abstract force that represents essentially any person or entity, particularly a religion, ethnicity or sexual orientation, outside of the subject's sphere of knowledge or accepted range of behavior—is a powerful motivator for bias criminals. And the change that the Other represents is a source of anxiety and fear. As such, hate criminals in the United States often display fetishes with "being American," and their crimes are often a way of affirming their own Americanness by denying and quashing that of another.

As sociologist Barbara Perry explains it in *In the Name of Hate: Understanding Hate Crimes:*

> Paradoxically, perpetrators of hate crimes, who are motivated by fears of cultural changes, construct themselves as victims of these transformations. They are the "new minority," vulnerable to the threat presumed to be represented by people of color. From the perpetrators' perspective, their violence is legitimate, since they are protecting themselves and "their" country from the threat of outsiders—from the invasion by the "darkened hordes." The offenders become the champions of the race as they reassert the relative belongingness of whites in contrast to the outsider status of others.
>
> Equally important as the reestablishment of whiteness as Americanness is the role hate crime plays in punishing those Others who have attempted to overstep their boundaries by assuming they, too, are worthy of first-class citizenship. Again, this is evident in anti-immigrant sentiment and its corresponding violence. But it is also apparent at more localized points of contact where whites feel their identity—or safety—threatened by unwelcome intrusions of people of color. [A 1997 study] uncovered such a sense of community loss in their interviews with white working-class men. These subjects expressed a "felt assault," a sense of "no longer belonging" in their own neighborhoods—sentiments they attributed to the influx of minorities "who they clearly position as the other."[8]

The self-righteousness that often accompanies these kinds of sentiments also acts as a barrier to any kind of self-awareness on the part of the criminal about the moral depravity that their crime actually represents. Indeed, in many cases, bias criminals perceive that society actually sanctions (sometimes at a level "beyond the law") the attacks they have perpetrated. In some settings—particularly on their home turf—offenders perceive that they have societal permission to engage in violence against the target group; this is especially common with bias crimes against homosexuals.

From a psychologist's point of view, all of these traits suggest one thing primarily: that the typical perpetrators of bias crimes suffer from a syndrome known as Antisocial Personality Disorder. Dr. Gary E. Connor, a Seattle psychologist who examined the Ocean Shores case, says that people with these traits are noted for their aggressiveness and displays of anger and hate as well as their utter lack of empathy for others, along with a flagrant disregard for the well-being of others and a lack of remorse for any pain they cause.[9] People who exhibit this syndrome, he says, are "capable of an enormous amount of damage" and, moreover, are frequently untreatable.

"The law hasn't really caught up with what the average hate-crime perpetrator is about," says Connor, who notes that law enforcement tends to focus on the status of the victims while often failing to accurately assess the perpetrator's motives. "The problem the law has is that these people appear competent," he says. "And yet these disorders are intractable as far as treatment goes, so they are likely to escalate their behavior if it goes unchecked by a strong response from society, and especially law enforcement."

Connor says that scapegoating is an essential feature of the psychological makeup of people with Antisocial Personality Disorder. "These people always blame out, never in," he says. "It's always someone else's fault. Especially when their lives fall apart, as they always do."[10] Likewise, most "hate" ideologies espoused by skinheads and neo-Nazis, and often used (as it was by Chris Kinison) by non-affiliated "thrill" offenders, prominently focus on ethnic or religious scapegoats; and in the case of "reactive" offenders, bias crimes are often specifically an act against the targets of their ideological venom.

A 1996 study conducted by Donald P. Green of Yale University revealed a great deal about the nature of hate-crime perpetrators, who it found were quite distinct from members of hate groups. "It was a very odd paper, because we took seven years' worth of newspaper clippings and culled from them the names of people who were arrested in connection with hate crimes, or whose names appeared in connection with hate group demonstrations,"[11] says Green. The survey interviewed these people by telephone as part of an ordinary poll of people's political and racial attitudes; this gave researchers a "normal" base to compare attitudes with their selected subjects. It also avoided many of the pitfalls of the usual academic surveys of white-supremacist attitudes, because the subjects were not made to feel conscious they were being questioned because of who they were.[12]

"What was interesting about it is we found that the Confederate flag is one of the critical symbols that differentiate hate-crime perpetrators from white supremacists. A typical white supremacist has a much more highly developed ideology than a typical hate-crime perpetrator. Even though those samples are very small, the idea was to see whether you could predict who was who based on their survey attitudes. And one of the key predictors of who was a hate-crime perpetrator was they have a kind of visceral reaction to intermingling of people. Their attitudes toward interracial marriage were the best predictors of which group are they in." White supremacists, on the other hand, were colder and more calculating, and driven by ideology rather than emotion. They were more likely to refer to symbols such as swastikas or the Dixie Battle Flag:

> Members of supremacist groups are much more likely to see a need for white activism and to condone the use of force to protect tradition. The distinctive

orientation toward collective action extends also to symbols of white solidarity. The issue of banning the Confederate flag elicits a distinctive response from the supremacist, but not from the hate-crime perpetrator. In sum, the supremacist harbors a more elaborately structured set of ideological views.[13]

"That's perhaps part of what was going on that night," says Green. "Whether [Chris Kinison] was a white supremacist or a typical hate-crime perpetrator, we'll never know. It may be that this is one of those rare and interesting instances where he was both."

✺

While data and studies have given us a pretty clear picture of the typical hate-crime offender, no one has ever compiled a psychological profile of the typical hate-crime *victim*. This is partly because these victims are notoriously difficult to study; most of them are so traumatized by the crimes that they often refuse to participate in such work.

Mostly, however, it's because hate crimes can happen to literally anyone and can occur at any time, in no small part because of the random elements in the perpetrators' victim-selection process—that is, most victims are complete strangers to the offender, chosen only because of their perceived membership in the target group. Nearly any race, religion or sexual orientation can inspire bias-motivated violence, and indeed one need not even actually belong to the target group to fall victim to a hate crime; witness the not-insubstantial number of heterosexual victims of gay-bashing.

That said, it is clear that in twenty-first-century America, minorities are far more likely to be victims of hate crimes than anyone else. In 2001, for example, 10,898 of the 12,020 victims of hate crimes reported to the FBI were various kinds of minorities. A pattern of victimization risk also emerges from the data: race is the most common motivator, with African Americans the most vulnerable targets; Jews and gay men are the second- and third-most likely targets, respectively.[14]

Perhaps just as significant, the data reveals that these are more likely to be violent crimes. Criminal-justice expert Barbara Perry points to FBI statistics that reveal wide disparities in the levels of violence between bias crimes and "normal" street crimes. "It is apparent that hate crime . . . is much more likely to involve physical threat and harm to individuals, rather than property," she writes:

> Consequently, such victims are also more likely to be at the receiving end of excessively brutal violence. To the extent that hate crime perpetrators are motivated by fear, hatred, mistrust, or resentment of victims, for example, they

are more likely to engage in extreme violence—violence which is beyond that necessary to subdue the victim.[15]

Uniformly, studies have found that the experience of being the victim of a hate crime induces extraordinary levels of fear of extreme physical harm while the crime is being committed. Dr. Gary Connor, the Seattle psychologist who examined the case (and who in fact was scheduled to testify in Minh Hong's defense but was never called), describes a phenomenon that occurs in incidents like these called "hyper-vigilant decision-making": "It's what happens when someone encounters a situation that appears either lethal or likely that great bodily harm will happen." The result is a classic "fight or flight reaction": Connor says the condition is characterized by tunnel vision and limited hearing; there is a faster heartbeat and breathing, and hand-eye coordination worsens. Thinking "tends to deteriorate rapidly. It's not even what you would call 'thinking.' They will try anything that shows promise, which helps them escape from the terrifying experience—never mind the consequences."[16]

The presence of a symbol like the Confederate flag—a symbol of white supremacists and hate groups—along with racial slurs can heighten that fear and apprehension, according to Robert Crutchfield, chair of the sociology department at the University of Washington. "I don't think it's unusual for a person of color, when confronted with that flag, to fear bodily harm," he says. "It's not surprising they [the Hongs] had a strong reaction."[17]

The sense of a person facing such a threat, Connor says, is "terror, chaos, loss of control. It's like what happens in a war." Different people will respond to threats in different ways, however: "If you're trained, and are prepared to deal with these kinds of threats, you have a different reaction," he says. "You tend to think your way out. It's entirely different for someone faced with a lethal threat when they've never been subjected to anything like this in their lives."

Nonetheless, Connor points out, hyper-vigilant decision-making in fact often results in relatively high-quality decisions that tremendously improve the victim's ability to avoid harm. And sometimes, he says, fighting back—especially given no other option—is the best thing to do (though he stresses that an escape plan is always the first and best course of action for people caught in such situations).

What we also know about the victims of bias crime is that they are substantially harmed well over and above what befalls victims of the simpler versions of the same crimes, perpetrated with ordinary motives (what is known as the underlying or "parallel" crime behind these acts, such as simple assault, vandalism, or threatening); for instance, some studies have found that bias-crime victims often experience post-trauma psychological stress syndromes similar to those experienced by rape victims, because the sense of violation can be so profound. The result is a commingling of shame, fear and rage.

"Short-term, the impact is the acute, intense paranoia of 'Do I go out of my house? Do I have deliveries brought in, or can I trust that person, either?'" says Susan Xenarios, director of St. Luke's-Roosevelt Hospital Center Rape Intervention Program/Crime Victims Assessment Project in Long Island, New York. "The other extreme is pure rage. Or sometimes you get rage and fear together, and that's hard to stabilize." And over time, she adds, "if you don't deal with the crisis reactions, they become worse."[18]

"There's something different about being attacked simply for who you are—for your basic identity as a person, as opposed to being selected for what you have or what you are doing," says Joan Weiss, executive director of the Justice Research and Statistics Association and former executive director of the National Institute Against Prejudice and Violence, who studied bias crimes and their victims extensively between 1981 and 1992. "This is not to minimize the harm that befalls people in any kind of violent crime. But when your identity is assaulted as well, it creates another level of trauma. And we see this manifest itself with bias-crime victims in all kinds of ways: severe depression, a heightened level of persistent anxiety, extreme withdrawal, a profound sense of isolation."[19]

Indeed, one of Weiss' studies—a survey of violence in the workplace—found that bias-crime victims were significantly more likely to experience psychophysiological symptoms, some of them debilitating, than people who had experienced non–bias-related crimes. And although white victims of bias crimes were just as likely as non-whites to experience increased trauma, non-whites were more likely to adopt certain defensive behavioral postures as a result, including watching their children more closely, making themselves "less visible" and moving out of their old neighborhoods.[20]

There is also a secondary level of victimization that can occur with hate crimes: they create a fear of exposure, particularly if the kind of minority group to which the victim belongs experiences real discrimination or social difficulties in the community anyway. Lesbians and gay males are the most vivid example of this; most of them fear, not unreasonably, that merely admitting to being the target of a hate crime implicates them as homosexuals, essentially forcing them "out of the closet" when in many cases they have personal and professional reasons to keep their status private. More to the point, gays and lesbians can in many states lose their jobs, face evictions from their housing, or be denied access to public services and accommodations, and legally so—all if their sexual orientation is disclosed as the result of a gay-bashing assault.[21]

This is true of other minorities as well, particularly immigrants, many of whom may fear deportation if they report a crime perpetrated against them, and may themselves mistrust authorities if they come from a culture with a corrupt or oppressive police force. In communities with a history of conflict between minority groups and police, this distrust is often amplified. "So even if you promise them that this is not going to be an issue if they press charges, they don't believe you," says Joan Weiss. "Why should they believe you? It can feel too risky."

In addition, other obstacles arise in such situations: language barriers can create misunderstandings; many minorities may not even be aware that what has befallen them is a serious crime; and cultural differences and private fears can prevent the victims from being completely forthcoming. A person from a traditional and deeply law-abiding background who has stolen a kitchen knife in the process of defending himself during a bias crime may well lie about the theft to police out of simple fear of being in trouble with the law for committing even the minor crime that the theft represents.

All of these factors combine to make hate-crime victims, and minorities especially, deeply reluctant to even participate in an investigation, and ultimately less likely to report the crimes as well—something that the studies of bias-crime victims have repeatedly observed. This in turn raises the critical role played by police and other law-enforcement officials, particularly prosecutors, in their handling of both the victims and the crime scene itself.

"One of the biggest problems with untrained police departments is, even if they're well-intentioned—even if they believe, 'OK, we should do something about this, we should treat it as a hate crime,'—they don't understand that they may miss the hate crimes for not knowing what to look for—not knowing the questions to ask," says Weiss.

Moreover, these kinds of failures are endemic to small departments facing demographic changes, and where training in these matters is often minimal at best. "So many times there is a real lack of understanding on the part of law enforcement of the profound implications for immigrant communities and other minorities of dealing with police, of the problems that exist in understanding the law and the justice system and how they work," says Weiss.

She notes, pointedly, that while many of these problems arise out of ignorance or misunderstanding, in some cases they have a basis in actual bigotry, too: "It isn't always a case of simply saying one didn't understand."

✳

Minh Duc Hong and his twin brother, Hung, were very much in the mold of the traditional immigrant children: kept at close reach by the parents, who depend deeply on them, and more or less socially cloistered. When they weren't working in their parents' teriyaki shop, they were attending school.

Their beginnings were far less secure. Born in 1974 near Saigon, their father fought on the American side as a sailor in the South Vietnamese Navy until the war's end in 1975. He was then forced to serve three years in a Communist "reeducation" camp. When he was reunited with his family in 1978, he promptly smuggled them all out to Hong Kong. While they remained there, he came to Seattle in 1979, found a job and moved his wife and two young sons to America later that year.

Though they lived in Seattle, the twins chose to attend Interlake High School in Bellevue. This meshed with the family project the Hongs launched in 1988, when they opened a little teriyaki restaurant in Bellevue. The twins became its primary workforce, putting in twelve-hour days—preparing food in the mornings, then manning the place in the afternoons and evenings when they got out of school.

Their parents were in charge of the kitchen, while the boys—who were far more fluent in English—dealt with the customers, served cheap lunches and dinners, cleaned tables and dishes, and kept the cash register ringing. After graduating from Interlake in 1992, the twins became students at Bellevue Community College, keeping more or less the same routine intact.

The Hongs' restaurant is a fairly nondescript place, and its food's chief virtue is that it is simple, tasty and inexpensive. It has about eight tables with utilitarian furniture, and the food is ordered and delivered at the front counter. The twins, in fact, were among its main draws, because they gave it a lively personality. Though they are physically indistinguishable when you first meet them, it does not take much time around them to begin telling them apart. Hung Hong is faster and funnier, always joking and asking questions. Minh is much more serious, quieter, but he always has something to say—reserved, but not painfully shy, either.

For both brothers, being American was something special, in no small part because of where they came from. Minh Hong says he can remember being smuggled out of Vietnam as a small child, and he remembers how happy they were at last to be in America. He took citizenship courses as a boy and took the oath in his early teen years.

"I remember saying the Pledge of Allegiance every day at school, and I remember how important that was to us," he says now. "It was really important to my parents, but I remembered where we came from too. Being American—we were just really proud to be American."

Hong says he encountered racial bigotry every now and then from classmates and others, but he mostly ignored it. "We were too busy working and going to school to give it much thought, actually," he says. "To be honest, I was pretty naïve."

Everyone who knows them describes them one way: "They're *good* kids." Both are good sons in the best traditional sense, devoting the bulk of their lives to making their family business successful and never, ever, bringing shame on the family. They never before had a single brush with the law in their lives, not even a speeding ticket.

Ironically, it was their compunction about the law that brought them to grief. The twins had bought some fireworks at an Indian reservation in late June 2000, but setting them off anywhere in Seattle or Bellevue is illegal. They determined that the best legal place to use them was in Ocean Shores, a three-hour drive from the city. So they cajoled their parents into acquiescence and proceeded to make the necessary plans for their big excursion out of town.

On the morning of July 3, they set out in their family's new gold Honda with Doug Chen riding in the back seat. They had reservations at the Shilo Inn, and dreams of a glorious Fourth on the beach, lit by the glow of their fireworks, all red, white, and blue . . . and little inkling that a few hours later, one of them would be stealing knives from a convenience-store shelf.

CHAPTER SIX

THE TRIAL, DAY ONE: RASHOMON

AT THE MOMENT HE LOOKED DOWN AND SAW THOSE KNIVES on the shelf and shoved them in his coat pocket, what was going through Minh Hong's mind?

When he saw Chris Kinison rapping, rapping on that window and waving that Confederate flag and running his finger across his throat, was he angry? Did he want revenge? Or was he frightened out of his wits?

In the end, Minh Hong's trial turned on this question. Even at the outset, during opening arguments, it was the hinge on which the two different versions of reality presented by each side turned.[1]

All criminal trials ultimately are a matter of competing narratives: one side presents its version of events, the competing side another. The success or failure of the respective cases depends in the end on how well one side or the other succeeds in persuading the jury or the judge that its version represents the true reality. Sometimes evidence and testimony is enough to win the day, but it always helps to be a convincing narrator at the start.

And Monte Hester, Hong's defense attorney, is nothing if not convincing. Using his imposing size and his deeply resonant tenor to dominate the stage, he stalked about the room, changing his tempo and inflection to reflect the story he was telling, his answer to the question of what was in Minh Hong's mind that night. And it was a compelling one.

Put yourself in Minh Hong's shoes, he told the jury. You're in Ocean Shores for a weekend away from home to enjoy yourself and shoot off some fireworks. You go down to the local convenience store for a late-night snack. And when you get out of the car, you suddenly find yourself confronted by a gang of angry white men.

"They have all of that look," Hester said. "You know it: Shaven heads. Big, athletic. Screaming at them: 'Gook go home!' 'Fucking chinks!' 'This is OUR country!' Mr. Kinison wasn't alone. There were several people who were making these statements. He and his confederates made it look like a mob was after them."

And so they fled into the Texaco, Hester said, and indeed it provided a temporary refuge. They mingled about inside, bought some items, hoping it would quiet down. "Minh Hong looked around and he noticed that everyone else was white, and the clerk was white. He heard someone request a 911 call, but the clerk ignored that. And then he looked outside and saw Chris Kinison: Waving that Confederate flag, knocking on the glass and pointing, and doing this"—and Hester ran his finger across his throat. Minh knew he was defenseless, he said, and the knives seemed like his only chance to survive the night.

That, in a nutshell, was the defense's version of what was in Minh Hong's mind that night: He was frightened out of his mind, fearful he was about to suffer who knows how severe an assault, how horrific a death. Hester laid out the rest of the scenario: The departure from the convenience store, the continuing assaults ("They now are spit on, called vulgar names"), and the attempt to leave, only to be blocked by Chris Kinison in the front and others from behind: "This convinced them they were at terrible risk," Hester said. He described in detail how Hung Hong got out of the car and was promptly assaulted by Kinison, and how when Minh Hong went to his aid, Kinison hit him too and knocked off his glasses, leaving him almost blind.

"And so he fought for his life," Hester said. "The stabbings took only seconds. And when it was over, he did not know he had even stabbed him."

Jerry Fuller's narrative was quite different. The picture the prosecution painted of Minh Hong that night at the Texaco was not of a terrified tourist but of an angry and vengeful city-bred tough who had decided he was going to get the best of "this rube" from the country. Fuller contended that the Hongs could have fled had they wanted to, but instead drove to where they could attack Kinison, separate from his friends. A woman inside the Texaco, he said, had heard Minh Hong remark that Kinison was "going down." He charged that the Hongs were not blocked at all but stopped entirely on their own.

And, perhaps most damningly, he charged that Hung Hong had grabbed Kinison's arms and held them behind his back while Minh had flailed away with the knife (though this claim, of course, begged the question: Why not charge Hung Hong as an accessory then, too?). He remarked on the number of wounds, and invoked a basic law of combat: "You don't bring a knife to a fistfight."

"Chris Kinison did something that was really stupid, really offensive, and racist," Fuller said. "But he didn't deserve to die."[2]

It was an argument tailored to the nearly all-white jury from Grays Harbor, where the population is about 92 percent white and about 99 percent resentful of all things Seattle (except, of course, its tourist dollars). The urban-rural split runs deep here, and the macho ethic endemic to logging and fishing towns runs even deeper. Being the wrong race was less likely to hurt Minh Hong with this jury than being from the inner city. And regardless of how frightened he may have been, Fuller raised doubts about the proportionality of his response. As long as he could persuade the jury that what Minh Hong faced was comparable to a bar fight—and that he responded out of malice and not terror—his version of events was likely to win out.

That narrative, however, began to spring leaks within the morning. And by the end of the afternoon, it was taking on water over the bow.

✳

In *Rashomon*, Akira Kurosawa's 1952 cinema classic, the audience is invited to examine a crime: a Japanese noble is escorting his wife through a forest when they are attacked by a notorious bandit, who kills the husband and then sexually assaults the wife. We see four different versions from four people: the captured bandit, who laughingly describes how he terrorized the pair and ravished the flighty wife—who then, he says, demanded he kill her husband so she did not have to live with the shame; the woman, who describes her husband's contempt for her "shame" after being raped, and implicates herself in his death by suggesting she went insane with grief; the husband, who speaks through a medium, and describes his wife's betrayal of him because she wants to be rid of him; and finally, a woodcutter who happened to witness the whole thing in secret, and who describes instead the folly and cowardice of all three participants, culminating in senseless tragedy. Yet, in the end, we discover that even his testimony is tainted with self-interest.

The "Rashomon effect" in ensuing years has entered the lexicon to describe the way that multiple perspectives will lead to multiple interpretations of the same "facts." The truth, in essence, is more likely to be found in sorting through a totality of different perspectives, which in the end may even then be incomplete, but nearer to the heart of things than a single viewpoint.

Criminal courts, of course, have confronted the Rashomon effect over the years; it is a common factor in nearly every trial, particularly those in which there are numerous witnesses, and this was especially the case in Minh Hong's trial. For every bit of testimony, it sometimes seemed, there arose a view of events that conflicted with the description provided by previous witnesses, creating a web of questions about competing self-interests, and the extent to which they colored different witnesses' testimony. The way jurors viewed the credibility of these witnesses often depended upon their seeming objectivity.

For the first four witnesses, credibility was not an issue. They were all evidentiary witnesses, brought to the stand to try to establish the basic facts of the case. Paul Luck, the Ocean Shores Police sergeant who had been first on the scene that night, described what he found. Luck drew a diagram of the Texaco station's layout on a large sheet of paper that was displayed in the courtroom for much of the rest of the day—it became a sort of guide for much of the ensuing testimony—and explained where he found Kinison when he arrived and what the general scene was like. Jeffrey Elmore, the second Ocean Shores officer at the scene, described the scene in similar terms, and explained that he set about interviewing people at the gas station. And then David Raines, a night clerk for the Shilo Inn, described his contact with the Hongs and Doug Chen and how he helped summon police to the hotel.

With the fourth witness, however, a few leaks began to appear in the hull of Jerry Fuller's narrative. This was Dr. David Selove, a self-employed forensic pathologist who had examined Chris Kinison shortly after his death. Selove provided a horrifyingly dispassionate inventory of Chris Kinison's injuries: Three wounds on the neck. Nine stab wounds on the back, some penetrating up to three inches. Four wounds that penetrated the ribs; one of these punctured a lung. There was also a minor wound on the left forearm, and two wounds on his fingers. But none of these wounds were fatal. What killed Chris Kinison were three stab wounds to the chest; the two uppermost penetrated the heart, and one penetrated the pericardial sac.

These are the kinds of deeply disturbing details that are always part of murder trials, and they are always difficult for family and friends of the dead person to sit through. Molly Kinison was no exception; she began sobbing, mostly quietly but visibly. Kinison and her supporters had seated themselves closely to the jury, and it clearly began to affect some of them.

Her sobs became more audible as Brett Purtzer began cross-examining Selove. Was the multitude of wounds that Kinison sustained exceptional in any way? No, answered the pathologist; the "number of wounds was average or typical of what you see in this kind of case."

Was there any sign his arms had been held back? "There was no evidence that his arms had been pinned behind his back," said Selove. In fact, he said, the evidence (particularly the wounds on his arm and fingers) suggested he had full use of his arms.

This was all too much for Molly Kinison, who cried out: "He's DEAD!" Shaking, she quieted down, and the brief interruption subsided. The eyes of one of the women jurors watching her filled with tears.

Already, Jerry Fuller's claim that Chris Kinison's twenty-three wounds were beyond the pale was looking shaky—this was, after all, the prosecution's own witness—and Selove's testimony now threatened to undermine his claim that Hung Hong had pinned back Kinison's arms while Minh Hong stabbed him. When it was his turn again, he vigorously questioned Selove about the issue. The pathologist insisted there was no proof either way—there was no evidence his arms were held back, but that did not rule out the possibility.

Fuller also pressed him about whether the wounds indicated if Kinison was defending himself or attacking. Again, Selove demurred: "I'm not saying that he was assaulting or defending himself," he answered. "This is consistent with either scenario. I can't say with reasonable medical certainty that it's one, exclusive of the other."[3]

If Fuller's case looked shaky that morning, it seemed to get a big shot in the arm that afternoon with the first eyewitness: William Keys, a San Francisco project manager and excavator on vacation that weekend in Ocean Shores, described how he had a front-row view of the unfolding drama from the driver's seat of his SUV, which he was filling with gas at the front pump near where the action occurred.

There were "four or five guys goofing around" near the pumps, he said, but he looked up when he heard Kinison yell out, "You fucking gooks, I'll take you all on!" He said that when Hung Hong got out of the car, Kinison hit him, and he then saw the "person in the yellow jacket" attack him from behind with a "broken bottle." Hung Hong, he said, grabbed Kinison's arms and held them behind his back while his brother flailed away.

"It seemed like ten times to me at that point, but he was moving so fast I couldn't tell," Keys testified. "It was like a sewing machine."

But there were problems with Keys's testimony, as Monte Hester found on cross-examination. First he pointed out, with the help of the diagram clipped to the board, that Keys would have had difficulty seeing as much of the fight as he claimed, because the pumps would have obscured much of his view. Keys essentially agreed with this. And then there was the problem with the initial statement Keys gave to police, portions of which Hester read aloud: Keys had said then that he "didn't know of any contact between the Asian kids and Kinison," and that he had only seen the three people getting into their car afterward.

Keys's testimony was damaged, but not fatally; it was always possible that he had simply been reluctant to get involved initially, but it was also possible he had simply embellished his story—though if so, it was for reasons no one could discern. However, only one other person was to testify that he saw one of Kinison's arms being held, but he said they were not pinned back, and said it occurred only briefly. Others with better views said no one had held him at all. And Minh Hong was to later specifically repudiate the accusation. In a court of law, such accusations usually need some kind of corroboration in order to hold up, and none ever arrived for Keys's version of events.

The next two witnesses, John Hohstad and Christina Fleming, were both friends and former classmates of Kinison. They described the events leading up to the fight, but did so in a way that depicted Kinison as the only participant in the verbal assaults. But both had made initial statements to police indicating otherwise, as Purtzer demonstrated on cross-examination; Fleming, for instance, had told police that "Chris and some other people started calling them names."

Both of them, though, offered a tantalizing tidbit that was to remain something of a mystery in the case: While they knew nearly everyone in the parking lot, they also described a stranger with a shaven head who was there among the crowd and was reportedly egging Kinison on. "I had never seen the guy before in my life," Hohstad testified.

However, when the day's last witness, Gabe Rodda, took the stand, the prosecution's narrative took on a positively surreal cast. Rodda, an athletic, dark-haired twenty-year-old with what was then an extremely close-cropped head, explained to the court that he had known Kinison for six years and had been close with him since school days—he considered him "my brother." He described what he saw of the fight—claiming he hadn't been involved in the verbal assaults—simply: "I saw the two Asian men; they rushed Chris," and both of them, he said, stabbed Kinison. He also described how he was hobbled by an ankle injury that forced him to use a cane, and how he had thrown the cane after the gold Honda as it departed.

No one brought up Rodda's leading role in the attack on the Filipino family two days before the stabbing—for good reason, since Judge Foscue had, during pretrial hearings, barred any evidence or testimony about Kinison's prior behavior from the trial. But Rodda began to crumble under Hester's cross-examination. He admitted he had consumed eight or nine beers that night, but: "I was doing pretty well—I was not inebriated at all." He admitted he hadn't seen the beginning of the fight. Pressed for details about simple facts in his accounts that seemed to keep changing—was his friend trying to fix a flat tire or get a jump start?—he grew flustered and covered his brow with a hand.

"I'm having major memory problems right now," he sniffled.

"Do you agree your memory is such that we shouldn't rely on it entirely?" Hester asked?

"That's not true!" Rodda protested. "I'm sure about what I saw."

By that point, no one else in the courtroom was.

CHAPTER SEVEN

HATE, AMERICAN STYLE

ONE WEEK LATER, WHILE THE JURY WAS DELIBERATING HIS FATE, Minh Hong and I talked outside the courthouse. Minh, as always, spoke quietly. The conversation came around to what was going through his mind that night. About why he took the knives. About why he fought so hard. He talked about how frightened he was, and why. It all crystallized into one thought.

"I just knew I didn't want to end up like that guy in Texas," he said.

✳

"That guy" was James Byrd, a forty-nine-year-old unemployed black man who led a life of alcohol-damaged anonymity in Jasper, Texas, until the night of June 7, 1998. That was when he caught a ride in the back of a pickup with a trio of white men who wound up beating him severely, then chaining him to the back of the truck and dragging him three miles down the backcountry roads until his body literally came apart. Byrd's head was found near one of his arms nearly a mile away from where his torso came to rest.

In an earlier era, Byrd's gruesome death might have been relegated to a back-page news item, if not outright ignored. But in 1998, its sheer brutality created a nationwide sensation. However, the interest ran deeper, perhaps because the ghosts of one of the ugliest legacies of our culture—the lynching of black Americans, once a commonplace event—had apparently reawakened in the Texas backwoods. The major networks, newspapers, and news services all carried the story prominently. It seemed as if everyone in the nation had become riveted by each day's developments in Jasper.

In short order, authorities arrested three men in the murder, two of them locals: Shawn Berry, the twenty-four-year-old manager of a local moviehouse; Bill
King, also twenty-four and an ex-convict; and his thirty-two-year-old ex-jailmate,
Russell Brewer. Among the evidence at the murder scene, one of them had left
behind a lighter with the symbol of the Ku Klux Klan engraved in it. Then it
emerged that, while in prison, King and Brewer had belonged to a Klan offshoot
called the Confederate Knights of America. King reportedly had told his companions they were "starting *The Turner Diaries* early."

A race war, in other words, had been the men's intent. *The Turner Diaries* was
a title that already had made its mark on the American landscape: posing as a
novel, it in fact is a neo-Nazi blueprint for fomenting a second American civil war
divided along racial lines, and it has inspired a whole generation of haters to commit various acts of violence, including the murderous neo-Nazi gang called The
Order, and Oklahoma City bomber Timothy McVeigh.

But if Byrd's killers had hoped to set off a fresh cycle of retribution and bloodshed between whites and blacks in Jasper, it did not happen. Some members of the
black community reportedly threatened to fight back, especially if it appeared that
local authorities were going to whitewash Byrd's death, as had happened with so
many other Texas lynchings over the years. And there were fears, too, that Byrd
was just the start of a bloodletting aimed at Jasper's blacks. But the talk dissipated
as it became clear that this time, the dynamic had dramatically changed: this
time, the nation's media had descended on the little town, and whole world was
watching. There was no chance that this could be swept under the rug.

Moreover, had there been any doubts in the popular mind that Byrd's murder
was a case of racial violence, they were by now thoroughly erased. The media coverage, already massive, intensified twofold, and reporters began describing the
killing with a term that they rarely explained: hate crime.[1]

What, exactly, is a "hate crime"? The term does not appear in the law, except
as the generic title of various statutes, either state or federal. These laws, in fact,
are intended to cover "bias-motivated" crimes, and typically they increase the
punishment for violent acts committed with a bias against the victim's race, ethnicity, or religion. "Hate crime" is mostly a descriptive term, since the bias motivation of these crimes is typically the product of old hatreds. But inside the
courtroom, the word carries little weight; what matters there is evidence both of
the perpetrator's bias and that he was acting on that bias.

Thus, while "hate crime" neatly describes our intuitive understanding of
these kinds of acts, and thereby gives journalists and advocates a useful shorthand,
it also creates widespread misunderstanding about the laws and how they work.
Many believe mistakenly that the laws are aimed primarily against activities by
so-called hate groups. Others argue against them by suggesting that "all crimes are

hate crimes." Still others believe that the mere expression of racial hatred is criminalized by the laws, or that any kind of interracial violence is a hate crime.

When reporters on the scene in Jasper, or network anchors in New York, described the Byrd case as a "horrendous hate crime," they rarely ever observed that the three suspects were not actually being charged with a hate crime, under either Texas or federal law. The federal hate-crimes statute, for instance, limits Department of Justice prosecutions to crimes committed on federal property, such as a courthouse or post office, or in the process of a federal activity, such as voting in a national election. As such, the Byrd case wasn't eligible for federal prosecution, though the law did allow Justice officials to provide Texas officials with federal grants (eventually totaling some $300,000) to support their handling of the case.

And then there was Texas' hate-crimes law, which was widely considered constitutionally unsound. It enhanced punishment for crimes committed "because of the defendant's bias or prejudice against a person or group," a vague formulation that had not been tested in the higher courts (only two prosecutions ever fell under its auspices), but which legal scholars believe failed the standards set by U.S. Supreme Court rulings. Moreover, its penalty enhancements were insignificant in this instance, since prosecutors already intended, using the state's capital murder laws, to seek the stiffest punishment possible for Byrd's killers: the death sentence.

Bill King, Russell Brewer and Shawn Berry were indicted by a grand jury for capital murder in early July 1998. Prosecutors, who announced they intended to seek the death penalty for all three, decided to try the men separately. King's case, covered daily by the networks, began on February 15, 1999, and lasted only seven days. The jury deliberated a mere two-and-a-half hours before delivering a guilty verdict; two days later, it sentenced him to die by lethal injection. Russell Brewer's September trial lasted slightly longer, and the jury deliberated four hours before finding him guilty. He too was given the death sentence. Only Shawn Berry, whose November trial focused on his claims that he had been a passive participant in the violence and was unaware that Byrd had been chained to the pickup, was spared the executioner; his jury found him guilty as well, but sentenced him instead to life in prison.

During the long ordeal, Jasper had become a crucible for the state of race relations in America. On the day of James Byrd's funeral, members of the Black Panthers appeared on the streets of Jasper, while across town near the courthouse, a small contingent of Klansmen gathered. Two weeks later, national Ku Klux Klan leaders organized a rally in Jasper that drew only eighteen members, and their demonstration was cut short by police when a much larger crowd of Panthers and their supporters, with whom the Klan followers exchanged racial epithets, threatened to turn the event into a melee. Police had to form a cordon to keep back the crowds as the men in white sheets, prevented from fleeing in a pickup that refused to start, made their final getaway by crowding six Klansmen into a Yugo.[2]

The townspeople of Jasper, black and white alike, tried their best to keep their heads amid the madness that had descended upon them. After the initial conflagrations, life settled into a more normal routine as the town awaited the trials and endured the constant presence of media figures. "Community outreach" meetings were called in the hopes of spurring an open discussion of race relations in Jasper, and a forty-member task force was formed to confront the problem. Despite their best efforts, though, Jasperites were dismayed to find that their little town had become a national byword for racial violence. In response, community leaders closed ranks and held firm to the claim made by Jasper's black mayor, R. C. Horn, that "this is not a racist community."

Many of the town's blacks, however, were far from reassured that such a change had occurred virtually overnight. After all, East Texas had been a hotbed of Klan activity beginning at the turn of the century and continuing through the 1960s, and those old sympathies could be found readily in the countryside. While the lynchings that once had been common in the South were rare events now, racial violence aimed at blacks never went away completely either. In particular, black skeptics pointed to a Klan hate campaign to drive out blacks from the nearby community of Vidor in 1994, as well as a number of black prisoners who had died in the custody of white lawmen. In one of these cases, the police chief of the town of Hemphill and two of his deputies were eventually convicted of murder.[3]

While the Jasper public-relations campaign—which included a press event in which the fence that had divided the white and black cemeteries in Jasper was torn down—won plaudits from the national press, many local blacks concluded that it did little more than merely paper over a history they knew all too intimately.

"A lot of white people would tell you there's no racism," local resident Gloria Glenn told an Associated Press reporter. "That's because they're not living it."[4]

✵

Nearly eighty years before James Byrd was lynched by three white men, something similar took place under very different circumstances in the little East Texas town of Center, about sixty miles due north of Jasper.

This time, the victim was a black teenager named Lige Daniels, who was accused of killing an elderly white woman who lived in Center. When word reached the governor that mob violence was imminent, he wired the captain of the Seventh Cavalry stationed nearby to protect the prisoner. The cavalry, however, never showed. The captain later explained that he had been unable to "find any members of his company in time for mobilization."

So at about noon on August 3, 1920, a mob of about one thousand men stormed the Center jail, knocked down the steel doors, and dragged Daniels outside, where they proceeded to beat him severely. A rope was thrown over a nearby oak tree, and Daniels was then hung.

A photo postcard that was available for many years afterward, mostly in the backwaters of trinket shops, recorded the event. It is a remarkable photo, and not only for the warm glow of the sun peering through the oak tree and bathing Lige Daniels' corpse, hanging from the bough, in an almost angelic light. What makes the portrait unforgettable instead is the crowd gathered below—stern-faced fathers and laborers, all looking quite proud of themselves; and a handful of children. One young boy (he appears to be about ten), dressed in his Sunday shirt and tie, is beaming beatifically. He probably remembered that day till he died.[5]

There were many such postcards. Perhaps the most notorious were those from the lynching of another black teenager, Jessie Washington, by a mob of several thousand residents of Waco, Texas, on May 16, 1916. Washington, who was retarded, had confessed to the murder of an elderly Waco resident. At the moment his conviction (with four minutes' deliberation by a white jury) was announced, the mob surged forward into the courtroom and dragged Washington outside, where he was stripped, beaten, stabbed, and wrapped with a chain, which was draped over a tree limb, just above a pyre of wooden crates. Washington was then jerked twice into the air, and his body lowered onto the pyre, where he was sprinkled with coal oil and set alight. Afterward, mob members proudly strung the charred corpse back up for a brief public display, after which Washington's body was lassoed by a horseman and dragged around the town until the skull bounced loose. Some motorists then tossed his remains into a black bag, tied it to the back bumper of their car, and tooled around the countryside with it in tow. A constable finally retrieved the bag from a nearby town, where it was left hanging.[6]

The lynchings of Daniels and Washington were mere drops in a bucket of bloodshed. Between 1882 and 1942, there were 468 lynchings in Texas, of which 339 were perpetrated against black victims. (All but fifteen of those occurred in the eastern half of the state.) Moreover, Texas was only part of a nationwide trend that was especially pronounced in the South: during those same years, according to statistics compiled by the Tuskegee Institute, there were 4,713 lynchings in the United States, of which 3,420 involved black victims. Mississippi topped the list, with 520 blacks lynched during that time period, while Georgia was a close second with 480; Texas' 339 ranked third.[7] And most scholars acknowledge that these numbers probably are well short of the actual total, since many lynchings (particularly in the early years of the phenomenon) were often backwoods affairs that went utterly unrecorded. In that era, it was not at all uncommon for a black man to simply disappear; sometimes his body might wash up in one of the local rivers, and sometimes not.

Lynching may not have been the original American hate crime; many would argue, with some validity, that the litany of atrocities committed against Native Americans during the centuries leading up to their eventual near-eradication in the so-called Indian Wars of the 1800s—and certainly many of the acts of butchery committed during those wars—better fit the description. Such carnage as the 1864 Sand Creek massacre and the 1890 Wounded Knee massacre were clearly of the same vein: acts of extraordinary and dehumanizing violence whose main purpose was to terrorize and oppress an entire racial population. Slavery, the predecessor to the lynching phenomenon, was likewise rife with murder and unimaginable violence, and its entire existence was predicated on racial subjugation.

One respected authority on lynching with whom I have corresponded suggests that acts of this nature have been with us throughout human history, and the impulses behind them probably are "rooted in some very fundamental sociobiological concepts of group or tribal identity, fears of miscegenation, loss of sexual dominance, and 'The Other'"—though he is quick to note that such subjects are probably beyond his sphere, as they are mine. Regardless of their progress, in American history, it was in the lynching phenomenon that the terrorism at the heart of these acts crystallized into an almost ritual form that stamped itself permanently on the character of American race relations.

The word "lynch" comes from the name of a Virginia justice of the peace named Charles Lynch, who during the Revolutionary War oversaw a makeshift court at his home in Chesnutt Hill that enabled locals to deal with such miscreants as horse thieves and Tories, who were often summarily horsewhipped in the judge's yard. Moreover, "Lynch's Law" eventually was given the imprimatur of the Virginia legislature, which agreed that it had been an appropriate response to the stresses brought on by the war. The term soon was applied to the many acts of vigilantism that became part of the American frontier experience, where the distances from any kind of lawful authority meant that crimes went unpunished without the intervention of the victims' fellow citizens.[8]

During the years leading up to the Civil War, blacks in the South were rarely the victims of lynchings—since they were viewed as property, it was considered an act of theft to kill someone else's slave. There was an exception to this: putting down slave revolts. The fear of black insurrection (and there were a handful of real slave revolts, notably Nat Turner's 1831 Virginia rebellion, in which some sixty whites were killed) was so pervasive among Southerners that any rumor that one might occur could bring swift death to the alleged conspirators, even if, as was often the case, it later turned out there were no such plans. In any event, when lynching did occur in the years before the Civil War, the victims predominantly were whites. Many of these were in the antebellum South, where lynch-mob treatment was often administered to abolitionists and other "meddlers."[9]

If blacks' slave status largely protected them from racial violence before the Civil War, then its abolition also left them remarkably vulnerable to such assaults upon the South's defeat. This became immediately manifest, during Reconstruction, when black freedmen were subjected to a litany of attacks at the hands of their former owners that went unpunished. As documented by Philip Dray in his definitive study, *At the Hands of Persons Unknown: The Lynching of Black America*, these crimes turned up in hospital records and field reports from the federal Freedmen's Bureau, all of which described a variety of clubbings, scalpings, mutilations, hangings and even immolations of former slaves, all within the first year after Appomattox.[10]

In 1866, the violence became discernibly more organized with the emergence of the Ku Klux Klan, which originated with a claque of Confederate veterans in Pulaski, Tennessee, and spread like wildfire throughout the South. Initially much of the Klan night riders' activities were relegated to whippings, a punishment intended to remind the ex-slaves of their former status. But as the assaults on blacks increased, so did the intensity of the violence visited on them, culminating in a steady stream of Klan lynchings between 1868 and 1871 (when the Klan was officially outlawed by the Grant Administration); at least one study puts the number at twenty thousand blacks killed by the Klan in that period. In the ensuing years, the violence did little to decline, and in fact worsened, despite the Klan's official banishment.[11]

Moreover, in addition to the night-riding type of attacks, mass spectacle lynchings soon appeared. These were ritualistic mob scenes in which prisoners or even men merely suspected of crimes were often torn from the hands of authorities (if not captured beforehand) by large crowds and treated to beatings and torture before being put to death, frequently in the most horrifying fashion possible: people were flayed alive, had their eyes gouged out with corkscrews, and had their bodies mutilated before being doused in oil and burned at the stake. Black men were sometimes forced to eat their own hacked-off genitals. No atrocity was considered too horrible to visit on a black person, and no pain too unimaginable to inflict in the killing. (When whites, by contrast, were lynched, the act almost always was restricted to simple hanging.)

The violence reached a fever pitch in the years 1890 to 1902, when 1,322 lynchings of blacks (out of 1,785 total lynchings) were recorded at Tuskegee, which translates into an average of over 110 lynchings a year. The trend began to decline afterward, but continued well into the 1930s, leading some historians to refer to the years 1880–1930 as the "lynching period" of American culture.

There is considerable photographic documentation of these lynchings, many of which became postcards, because the participants were rather proud of their involvement. This is clear from the postcards themselves, which frequently showed not merely the corpse of the victim but many of the mob members, whose visages ranged from grim to grinning. Sometimes, as in the Lige Daniels case, children were intentionally given front-row views. A lynching postcard from Florida in 1935, of a migrant worker named Rubin Stacy who had allegedly "threatened and frightened a white woman," shows a cluster of young girls gathered round the tree trunk, the oldest of them about twelve, beaming as she gazes on his distorted features and limp body a few feet away.[12]

Indeed, lynchings seemed to be cause for outright celebration in the community—even more so than most public executions, which had long enjoyed such status in rural communities. Residents would dress up to come watch the proceedings, and the crowds of spectators frequently grew into the thousands. Unlike public hangings, the crowds were openly encouraged to participate in the violence. Afterwards, memento-seekers would take home parts of the corpse or the rope with which the victim was hung. Sometimes body parts—knuckles, or genitals, or the like—would be preserved and put on public display as a warning to would-be black criminals.

That was the purported moral purpose of these demonstrations: not only to utterly eradicate any black person merely accused of a crime against whites, but to do it in a fashion intended to discourage future perpetrators, to "send a message"—the unstated portion of which was a warning to blacks not to attempt to rise above their station. This was reflected in contemporary press accounts, which described the lynchings in almost uniformly laudatory terms, with the victim's guilt unquestioned and the mob identified only as "determined men." Not surprisingly, local officials (especially local police forces) not only were complicit in many cases but acted in concert to keep the mob leaders anonymous; thousands of coroners' reports from lynchings merely described the victims' deaths occurring "at the hands of persons unknown." Lynchings were broadly viewed as simply a crude, but understandable and even necessary, expression of community will. This was particularly true in the South, where blacks were viewed as symbolic of the region's continuing economic and cultural oppression by the North. As an 1899 editorial in the Newnan, Georgia, *Herald and Advertiser* explained it: "It would be as easy to check the rise and fall of the ocean's tide as to stem the wrath of Southern men when the sacredness of our firesides and the virtue of our women are ruthlessly trodden under foot."[13]

Such sexual paranoia was central to the psychology of the lynching phenomenon. In the years following black emancipation—during which time a previously tiny class of black criminals became swelled by the ranks of impoverished former slaves—a vast mythology arose surrounding black men's supposed voracious lust for white women, a legend for which in truth there was scant evidence, and one that stands in stark contrast to (and perhaps has its psychological roots in) the reality of white men's longtime sexual domination of black women, particularly during the slavery era but afterwards as well. In any event, the omnipresence of the threat of rape of white women by black men came to be almost universally believed by American whites.[14] Likewise, conventional wisdom held that lynchings were a natural response to this threat: "The mob stands today as the most potential bulwark between the women of the South and such a carnival of crime as would infuriate the world and precipitate the annihilation of the Negro race," warned John Temple Graves, editor of the *Atlanta Georgian*.[15] Such views were common not merely in the South, but among Northerners as well. The *New York Herald*, for instance, lectured its readers: "[T]he difference between bad citizens who believe in lynch law, and good citizens who abhor lynch law, is largely in the fact that the good citizens live where their wives and daughters are perfectly safe."[16]

The cries of rape, for many whites in both South and North, raised fears not merely of sexual violence but of racial mixing, known commonly as "miscegenation," which was specifically outlawed in some thirty states. White supremacy was not only commonplace, it was in fact the dominant worldview of Americans in the nineteenth and early twentieth centuries; most Caucasians believed they represented Nature's premier creation (having been informed of this by a broad range of social scientists of the period, whose views eventually coalesced into the pseudo-science known as eugenics), and that any "dilution" of those strains represented a gross violation of the natural order. Thus it was not surprising that a number of lynching incidents actually resulted from the discovery of consensual relations between a black man and a white woman.

Underlying the stated fear of black rape, moreover, was a broad fear of economic and cultural domination of white Americans by blacks and various other "outsiders," including Jews. These fears were acute in the South, where blacks became a convenient scapegoat for the poverty that lingered in the decades following the Civil War. Lynching in fact was frequently inspired not by criminality, but by any signs of economic and social advancement by blacks who, in the view of whites, had become too "uppity."

There were, of course, other components of black suppression: segregation in the schools, disenfranchisement of the black vote, and the attendant Jim Crow laws that were common throughout the South. But lynching was the linchpin in the system, because it was in effect state-supported terrorism whose stated intent was to suppress blacks and other minorities, in no small part by eliminating nonwhites as competitors for economic gain. These combined to give lynching a symbolic value as a manifestation of white supremacy. The lynch mob was not merely condoned but in fact celebrated as an expression of the white community's will to keep African Americans in their thrall. As a phrase voiced commonly in the South expressed it, lynching was a highly effective means of "keeping the niggers down."[17]

✳

Lynchings unquestionably had the short-term desired effect of suppressing blacks' civil rights; the majority of African Americans in the South during that era led lives of quiet submission in the hope of escaping that horrific fate, and relatively few aspired beyond their established station in life. Those who did often migrated northward, where lynchings were hardly unknown (some of the most notorious occurred in places like Indiana and Minnesota, and they in fact were recorded in nearly every state in the Union), but were not as endemic. However, the awfulness of the mobs' brutality, often reported and photographed in gruesome detail, ultimately also inspired a reaction that gave birth to the Civil Rights movement and eventually the demise of the racial caste system lynching was intended to enforce.

The first voices raised against lynching were heard in the 1890s, even as the bloodbath was cresting. Civil rights pioneer Ida B. Wells, a well-educated black woman who had risen to the editorship of a leading black newspaper in Memphis, began questioning the myths underlying the popular rationale for condoning the killings. As she gathered statistics about lynching, she noted, for instance, that even though the threat of black rape was the foremost excuse for the phenomenon, in fewer than one-third of the lynchings was rape even alleged. (Later, more complete statistics particularly bore this out; congressional testimony in 1922 indicated that only 28.4 percent of the blacks lynched between 1889 and 1918 had been accused of raping or attempting to assault a white woman. This remained the case over time as well; the Tuskegee Institute's lynching data for 1882 to 1951 indicate that lynching victims were accused 41 percent of the time of felonious assault, 19.2 percent of rape, 6.1 percent of attempted rape, 4.9 percent of robbery and theft, 1.8 percent of insulting white people, and 27 percent for miscellaneous offenses. Moreover, among the lynching victims between 1882 and 1927 were 76 black women.) Often the accusations of rape were completely spurious.

Indeed, in two-thirds of the cases, Wells found, lynchings were for incredibly petty crimes such as stealing hogs and quarreling with neighbors. A black person could easily face an agonizing death at the hands of a mob merely for trying to vote, or for testifying against a white man or getting into a fight with him, or asking a white woman to marry—and sometimes for no offense at all.

Wells also attacked the myth of black men's sexual voraciousness. She adroitly observed that during the Civil War, many slave owners willingly left their wives and daughters in the care of their black manservants, who were frequently entrusted with the defense of the home during those years. And if black men were prone to sexual assault, there was little evidence of it before the war as well; contemporary historian Ulrich B. Phillips, for instance, examined Virginia's court and criminal records from 1783 to 1863, and found only 105 blacks convicted of sexual assault over the eighty-year span.

Wells (who became Ida Wells-Barnett in 1895 after her marriage to Chicago attorney Ferdinand Barnett) ultimately published her findings in a widely distributed 1901 book titled *Lynching and the Excuse*. She was soon joined in her crusade by other leading African Americans, including W. E. B. DuBois, Frederick Douglass and William Monroe Trotter. It was their view that the systematic oppression of black Americans needed to be confronted directly, and lynching was the system's most egregious component. In 1905, DuBois, Wells-Barnett, and other black leaders organized the Niagara Movement to demand full citizenship rights for African Americans: freedom of speech, an "unfettered and unsubsidized" press, full voting rights, full civil liberties, and recognition of the principle of human brotherhood. The Niagara Movement's manifesto, written mostly by DuBois, did not address lynching directly, but observed: "The Negro race in America—stolen, ravished, and degraded, struggling up through difficulties and oppression—needs sympathy and receives criticism, needs help and is given hindrance, needs protection and is given mob-violence, needs justice and is given charity, needs leadership and is given cowardice and apology, needs bread and is given a stone. This nation will never stand justified before God until these things are changed."[18]

However, the leading black figure of the time in the minds of most Americans was Booker T. Washington of Alabama's Tuskegee Institute, acclaimed for its pioneering work in education young black people. His famed 1895 speech (which came to be known as the "Atlanta Compromise") before a mostly white audience at the Atlanta Exposition had counseled black Americans to give up agitation for political rights and social equality in exchange for the opportunity to work and prove themselves, suggesting that racial segregation was an acceptable and perhaps even desirable state. Washington urged blacks to steer away from dreams of returning to Africa: "Cast down your bucket where you are," he counseled. He admonished them instead to focus their efforts on their own resourcefulness and hard work, and to emphasize the honor of common labor. For these sentiments, Washington was widely praised by white politicians across the American spectrum, but other black leaders were unconvinced. The Niagara Movement, with its emphasis on open agitation for blacks' civil rights, represented a direct challenge to Washington's compromise.

Though this nascent organization mostly foundered, its underlying principles came fully to life in 1909, when DuBois, Wells-Barnett, and other Niagara leaders joined forces with white civil-rights reformers to create the National Association for the Advancement of Colored People. The NAACP's principles were broad-ranging, but within the first year of its existence it became clear that the primary challenge it faced was in organizing a national campaign to combat the practice of lynching—and for the ensuing three decades, leading the fight against lynching and mob violence was the organization's major preoccupation.[19]

It was clear to the NAACP's leadership that Booker T. Washington's "compromise" was not only counterproductive, but his prescription for black Americans—steady forward progress by embracing the all-American values of hard work, integrity and individual enterprise—was in fact a recipe almost certain to invite vicious repercussions in the form of a lynch mob. As the NAACP began systematically compiling information about lynchings, it became clear that blacks who succeeded economically and socially (particularly those who became landowners) were the frequent targets of lynching, and any indications of civic advancement by blacks often met violent opposition. Among the many victims of lynchings were black postal clerks, grocery owners, farmers, and white-collar professionals, such as doctors. Black veterans returning from action in World War I were sometimes lynched merely for wearing their uniforms in public.

Likewise, it was becoming increasingly clear, even to the public, that the rationales proffered for decades to justify the lynch mobs' actions—particularly the threat of black rape—were not merely flimsy but entirely hollow, a cover for the real motivation for lynching, which was to terrorize and subjugate the black community. A 1918 lynching case, nearly as notorious in its time as James Byrd's some eighty years later, drove this point home in horrific fashion.

It began on May 16 when a white landowner in rural Valdosta, Georgia, was shot to death at his home. His wife accused a black man named Sidney Johnson, and a lynch mob soon formed with the purpose of carrying out summary justice for the farmer's murder. However, when it was unable to locate Johnson, the mob turned its wrath on five black men who'd had the misfortune of being in the vicinity at the time and lynched them instead. Among the five was Haynes Turner, a former employee of the murdered farmer.

Turner's wife, Mary, was eight months pregnant, and when she heard of the murder, she vowed publicly to find the men responsible, swear out warrants against them, and ensure they were punished in the courts. Not surprisingly, her vow to seek justice doomed her; as an Associated Press report of the affair put it, Mary Turner had made "unwise remarks" about the execution of her husband, "and the people, in their indignant mood, took exceptions to her remarks, as well as her attitude." The local sheriff placed her under arrest, reportedly for her protection, but then surrendered her to a mob of several hundred white men and women—as well as a number of children—determined to "teach her a lesson." At a place outside town called Folsom's Bridge, they stripped her, tied her ankles together, and hung her upside down from a tree. Dousing her with gasoline, they slowly roasted her to death. While she was still alive, a man using a knife ordinarily reserved for splitting hogs walked up and cut open the woman's abdomen. "Out tumbled the prematurely born child," wrote a news reporter covering the event. "Two feeble cries it gave—and received for the answer the heel of a stalwart man, as life was ground out of the tiny form." Hundreds of bullets were then fired into Mary Turner's body. Sated, the mob left her body by the roadside. She and her child were buried in a shallow grave near the bridge.[20]

✴

Mary Turner's murder—which made clear irrevocably that lynching more often than not had nothing to do with black rape—made national headlines. On its heels came the "Red Summer" of 1919; there were seventy-six blacks lynched that year, but even more horrifying were the "race riots" that broke out in twenty-six cities, including Chicago; Washington, D.C.; Omaha, Nebraska; Charleston, North Carolina; and Knoxville, Tennessee. These insurrections in fact were massive assaults by whites upon local black populations, often sparked by an imagined offense. Two years later in Tulsa, Oklahoma, where a prosperous black population was literally bombed out of existence over two days of complete lawlessness, the rioting was set off by a black youth's alleged assault on a local white girl that later turned out to be harmless consensual contact. Nonetheless, a Tulsa newspaper had publicly called for the young man's lynching, and when a group of local blacks attempted to ward off a lynch mob, the fighting broke out. By the time the violence had subsided, as many as three hundred black people were believed killed, many of them buried in a mass grave, and thirty-five city blocks lay charred.[21]

Such horrors, and many others of similar brutality, lent real credence to the NAACP's anti-lynching campaign. Its black-white coalition made steady gains in attaining widespread respect for its cause, both with public officials and the public at large, in the decade after its founding. A 1915 nationwide boycott of D. W. Griffith's film *The Birth of a Nation* (an overtly racist paean to the Ku Klux Klan and the virtues of the lynch mob), was reasonably successful and helped attract a broad range of supporters. Moreover, the fledgling organization worked tirelessly to lobby local and state officials about the pernicious nature of lynching and to act to correct the injustices.

Central to the NAACP's strategy was building public outrage over the horrifying litany of lynchings. At its headquarters in downtown New York City, the NAACP hung a large banner that flew over Fifth Avenue announcing, each time a mob killing occurred: "A Man Was Lynched Yesterday." Throughout most of the northern states, sympathy for the NAACP's cause gained considerable traction, especially among middle- and upper-class whites.

In 1921 the NAACP took its campaign to the national level, when Rep. Leonidas Dyer—a Missouri Republican who represented a largely black St. Louis district—introduced "An Act to assure to persons within the jurisdiction of every State the equal protection of the laws and to punish the crime of lynching," a piece of legislation that would come to be known simply as "the Dyer Bill." Many states had anti-lynching laws on their books, but they were inconsistently enforced at best, and overtly ignored in most Southern states. Dyer's legislation was the first attempt to make lynching a crime that could be enforced by federal authorities if the states failed to act.

At its May 1919 National Conference on Lynching at New York's Carnegie Hall, the NAACP had called for congressional investigations of the lynching phenomenon. But later that year it wisely withdrew the proposal, perceiving (probably correctly) that such hearings could be extended interminably as a way to forestall concrete action. Instead, the NAACP leadership—primarily James Weldon Johnson and Walter White—decided to focus on securing federal legislation that would punish both lynchers and the lawmen who abetted the murderers, particularly in cases where states were reluctant to act. Dyer's bill, which had the NAACP's full backing, proposed to do just that.

Its chances of passage appeared strong. Republicans, who were generally sympathetic to blacks' civil rights, controlled both houses of Congress, and President Warren Harding had already indicated he would support anti-lynching legislation. Moreover, public opinion polls found overwhelming support for the measure, particularly in the northern states, though predictably enough, it was widely viewed in the South as another attack on its culture and states' sovereign rights.

These concerns, as well as traditional arguments in support of lynching, were voiced loudly in the searing debate that followed when the bill came up for passage in the House in December 1921. Even as the NAACP presented evidence that less than 30 percent of black lynching victims had even been accused of sexually assaulting white women, defenders of lynching continued to claim that the practice was necessary to prevent rape.[22]

"As long as rape continues lynching will continue," contended Rep. Thomas Upton Sisson, a Mississippi Democrat. "For this crime, and this crime alone, the South has not hesitated to administer swift and certain punishment. . . . We are going to protect our girls and womenfolk from these black brutes. When these black fiends keep their hands off the throats of the women of the South then lynching will stop."[23]

However, the bill's opposition also raised serious constitutional issues about its attempt to federalize crimes previously under the jurisdiction of the states, an

argument that eventually formed the core challenge to later federal efforts in dealing with crimes of this nature. Rep. Clarence F. Lea, a California Democrat, observed: "The question before us is not whether there shall be a law to punish
lynching. Such a law is on the statute books of every State in the Union. Under
the theory and practice of our Government for more than 130 years such offenses
have been within the sole jurisdiction of the State. The question is whether or
not we shall duplicate the State function by conferring the same power upon the
Federal Government as to this class of crimes."[24]

But even this argument became couched in emotional terms. The specter of a
young girl supposedly raped and slain by a black man was raised by Rep. Benjamin
Tillman, a South Carolina Democrat, even as he claimed that the Dyer Bill would
eliminate the states and "substitute for the starry banner of the Republic, a black
flag of tyrannical centralized government . . . black as the face and heart of the
rapist . . . who [recently] deflowered and killed Margaret Lear."[25]

Another, less emotional, argument against the Dyer Bill would continue to be
raised against similar measures in succeeding decades—namely, that there was no
real distinction between lynching and simple murder (an argument nowadays for-
mulated as "all crimes are hate crimes"), and that the anti-lynching legislation as
such was an unwarranted intrusion on the law. "Lynching is but murder; and if, as
Mr. Gogg says, we can by Federal statue punish the crime of lynching perpetrated
by individuals composing a mob, there is no escape from the conclusion that by
Federal statute we can extend the jurisdiction of the Federal Government into all
the States and against all crimes affecting life, liberty, or property of citizens of the
various states," argued Rep. James Pleasant Woods, a Virginia Democrat.[26]

The fight over the Dyer Bill grew so contentious that at one point the doors
of the House were locked with members inside, and warrants issued for truant
members, since Southern representatives' planned absences had denied the House
a quorum. Eventually, though, Republican leaders shepherded the measure before
the full body on January 26, 1922, and it passed with ease, 231 to 119.

However, the Dyer Bill faced a much tougher road in the Senate, where the
Southern states held more power (due largely to the less representational nature
of the body, since every state possesses two votes), and where rules made a filibuster more likely to succeed. Through most of 1922, Southern senators success-
fully delayed the legislation through various tactics. As the bill slowly progressed,
though, it became increasingly clear that the Southern bloc fully intended to filibuster the bill, and it was far from clear that Republicans possessed enough votes
to overcome it; moreover, many Republicans were privately hesitant to support
the measure because of the federalism issues it raised.

In response, the NAACP mounted a major publicity campaign, placing full-
page advertisements in the nation's largest newspapers denouncing the practice of

lynching and calling it the "Shame of America," and inquiring of readers: "Did you know that the United States is the Only Land on Earth where human beings are BURNED AT THE STAKE?" The ads had their intended effect, and public pressure in support of the Dyer Bill mounted steadily. However, it soon became clear that the Republican leadership was unwilling to go to the mat for the measure; when Southern senators seized the floor on November 27, 1922, and began their filibuster, Republicans made some half-hearted attempts to end it. But on December 2 they folded their tent, withdrawing the measure and thus effectively killing it. They defended the move as necessary in order to enable the Senate to conduct the rest of its regular business.[27]

✵

There were subsequent attempts to pass anti-lynching legislation. The Dyer Bill was resurrected in 1926, but again did not survive the Senate. In 1934, a pair of Democratic senators—Colorado's Edward Costigan and New York's Robert Wagner—offered a measure that would have punished law-enforcement officials who by neglect allowed their charges to be taken by a mob. Again the legislation had the NAACP's full-fledged backing, and again the public support was overwhelmingly in its favor (indeed, one poll found even that 65 percent of Southerners supported a federal law outlawing lynching). Ultimately, however, it met the same fate as the Dyer Bill; it passed handily in the House, only to succumb to a fatal filibuster by Southerners in the Senate. Two later efforts in the 1940s to pass anti-lynching legislation met similar fates.

These failures, however, were anything but. What no one expected was that even though the effort to enact federal anti-lynching laws did not succeed, the broad national debate it had inspired achieved nearly spectacular results in undermining the lynching phenomenon. By the 1930s lynching was no longer celebrated in the public view, but widely condemned as barbarous and unjust by nearly every responsible segment of society. Even in the South, the views of such Caucasian organizations as the Association of Southern Women for the Prevention of Lynching had come to hold sway.

Over the course of the succeeding decade, from 1922 to 1932, lynching deaths—which had somewhat steadily declined in frequency after 1904 anyway—dropped dramatically, from fifty-nine black lynchings in 1922 to only six in 1932. The trend continued during the 1930s; only ninety-three black lynchings were recorded during the entire decade.

The nature of lynchings changed dramatically during this period—driven, almost certainly, by the stigma that had become attached to mob justice, and the clear withdrawal of public sanction for such murders. The mass spectacle lynchings, which had seemingly reached their apex in the bloody "Red Summer" of

1919, virtually disappeared over the course of the 1920s. By the 1930s, lynchings had largely reverted back to the form in which they first manifested themselves during the early Reconstruction period: furtive affairs involving midnight riders, arsonists and shooters, usually involving only a handful of perpetrators. By 1952, when there were no black lynchings recorded at Tuskegee (though it must be noted that, even then, this did not necessarily mean that none had occurred), the era of the lynch mob seemed to have become a thing of the past.

This watershed change in the American cultural landscape occurred with virtually no official or legal support from Washington, D.C. Congress, of course, never enacted an anti-lynching law. And the Supreme Court, for most of the lynching era, had declined to involve itself in lynching cases, preferring to leave them to the jurisdiction of state courts. A handful of decisions, however, gradually turned the tide in the courts, and simultaneously left a permanent impression on the larger body of criminal law: *Moore v. Dempsey* in 1923, which overruled the death sentences of six black men convicted (in a lynch-mob atmosphere) of insurrection following a rural Arkansas "race riot," for the first time stipulated that in light of the requirements of the Fourteenth Amendment, any denial of due process was the concern of the federal government; *Powell v. Alabama* in 1932, which overturned the verdict in the infamous case of the "Scottsboro Boys," nine itinerant black workers who were convicted on flimsy evidence of raping two white women, and which further stipulated that the right to an attorney was an indispensable part of due process; *Norris v. Alabama* in 1935, which overturned the third conviction delivered against the Scottsboro boys, on grounds that the exclusion of blacks from the jury violated the equal-protection clause of the Fourteenth Amendment; and finally *Brown v. Mississippi* in 1936, which found that a Southern sheriff's extraction of a murder confession from a black suspect by torturing him was likewise a violation of a defendant's constitutional rights. However, most of these rulings came well after the lynching era had begun its decline, and only *Moore v. Dempsey*—delivered at a crucial juncture in the national debate—could be said to have had any appreciable role in the sea change of public attitudes about mob justice.[28]

Where the legal system failed, though, it is clear in retrospect that the moral suasion that was imbued in the campaign to combat lynching succeeded. While the NAACP's campaign to pass a federal anti-lynching law fell short, its broader campaign to debunk the myths that had been used to defend lynching, and to permanently stigmatize the practice as inimical to basic American values of justice and fair play, were remarkably effective. It could be argued that this tends to support the position of Caucasian anti-lynching organizations like the Association of Southern Women for the Prevention of Lynching, which had opposed federal anti-lynching laws as an unnecessary intrusion on a natural process of incremental change in cultural attitudes wrought by moral persuasion and not the law. But the historical record is also clear that when anti-lynching statutes were properly enforced—as they were, for example, in Illinois after 1911—the laws were remarkably effective tools for changing social mores regarding lynching.[29] This suggests that a federal anti-lynching law in 1922 could have been an effective tool for changing the way society treated lynching, and may have helped precipitate the decline of lynching even sooner; certainly, if nothing else, it would have given law enforcement officers around the nation both the mandate and the motivation, as well as the means, to stop mob justice in its tracks. As such, the failure of Congress to pass an anti-lynching law stands not as accidental wisdom on the part of the nation's chief legislative body but one of many instances of its abject failure to adequately address one of the nation's great miscarriages of justice.

Although lynchings declined, they did not disappear altogether, by any means. Certainly, the deep racial animus that had always inspired them was still alive and well, particularly in the South. They continued to occur periodically, but instead of being treated as commonplace, they became the subject of intensive international news coverage. The 1955 lynching of a Chicago teenager named Emmett Till, on vacation in Mississippi, for being "fresh" with a white woman, became a national cause célèbre, playing a prominent role in the claims of civil-rights advocates that justice for black people did not exist in the South.

For those Southerners still dedicated to the tenets of white supremacy, and who permanently opposed the substantial gains made during the 1950s and '60s for African Americans' civil rights—in particular the desegregation of schools and other facilities that began with the Supreme Court's landmark *Brown v Board of Education* ruling in 1950—lynching continued to hold its longtime value as a tool for terrorizing the black community. But without the cover of public sanction, lynching and racial violence became a surreptitious crime that was strategically deployed in a vain attempt to stem the tide of the Civil Rights movement. As such, lynchers frequently targeted the persons they saw as the source of the agitation. The 1964 slayings of three civil-rights workers in Mississippi, which became a landmark in rising national attitudes supporting the movement, was in most respects a classic lynching. But now the lynchers also turned to other kinds of violence: burning and bombing African American churches, attacking civil-rights marchers, and assassinating the leaders in the movement.

These crimes, too, declined over time, particularly as the Civil Rights movement's successes mounted through the 1960s and '70s, and the broader society came to embrace the changes. But the desire by some Americans to impose a racial caste system, and their willingness to resort to violent crimes as a means to terrorize minorities, never completely went away. Instead, the targets expanded, coming to include Asians, Hispanics, Indians, Jews, and eventually homosexuals:

anyone deemed The Other by white supremacists and nationalists. The crimes became atomized, as it were—events involving only one or two perpetrators, and usually only one or two victims, though in fact the communities they represented were often the real targets (much like the early Reconstruction-era Klan violence). As such, they often were simply woven into the general fabric of violence in America, and at times seemed indistinguishable from ordinary assaults and murders.

Yet, even though lynching largely faded from the public scene, it has remained a raw living memory for most American minorities—not merely blacks, but other ethnic and religious groups who know all too well how deeply racial and religious bigotry remain imbedded in the nation's cultural makeup. While most American whites tend to shun that chapter of their history, the litany of horrifying murders produced during the lynching era lingers, generations later, as a wellspring of deep distrust and fear among minorities, and blacks particularly. Moreover, the drumbeat of crimes inspired by racial and religious hatred that has continued well into the 1970s, '80s and beyond, less frequent and more random though they are, seems to have been clearly drawn from the same sources. When a man with a Confederate flag begins brutally assaulting a minority person in a small rural town, even a relatively sheltered Asian like Minh Hong knows that what he is seeing is a part of the American psyche that every person of color dreads deeply—and for good reason.

Many times still, these crimes so resemble a classic lynching that the ghosts of the first half of the century are almost reflexively resurrected. James Byrd's murder in 1998 was just such a case. But by then, hardly anyone referred to it as a lynching. It had a new name: hate crime.

✳

Though it is part of the lexicon now, the term "hate crime" was unknown even as recently as the early 1980s. But for those who were dealing with the remnants of white-supremacist ideology and its attendant violence, no one needed such a term. Like pornography, they knew what they were looking at when they saw it.

The first sign in northern Idaho was the fliers. No one knew who was handing them out, but several came across my editor's desk at the *Sandpoint Daily Bee* in the rural Panhandle in the spring of 1979, brought in by a reporter on his rounds or an ad salesman who had picked it up around town. They were crude mimeographs, and even cruder humor: An "Official Running Nigger Target," it was labeled. It showed a cartoon silhouette of a black man with a large Afro and monstrous lips, sprinting, arms akimbo, in apparent full flight. Numbers designated different scores for different parts of the anatomy, with a relatively low score for a head shot, and the highest score for hitting his feet.

There was never a shortage of crackpots in the Idaho backwoods, and normally a sheet like that would have disappeared into the round file. But the sentiments behind it were so nakedly hateful, and the violence it condoned so disturbing, I tucked it into a special file I was keeping.

No one knew for sure who was behind the fliers, but we had a pretty good idea of the general direction from which they were coming. Just down the road from Sandpoint, about forty minutes' drive south, a group of fringe dwellers from Southern California who called themselves the Church of Jesus Christ-Christian had purchased a wooded parcel near Hayden Lake, set up a compound, and began calling it the "Aryan Nations." The church's leader, Richard Butler, promised to be a good neighbor, but there were reports of cross burnings at the compound; and then Butler began advertising his call for other like-minded supremacists to move to northern Idaho and create what he envisioned as a "white homeland."

This was the shabby state into which the ideology of white supremacy, once the dominant worldview of white Americans, had declined: forced into exile in a backwoods lot, shouting its defiance at the rest of the world, and vowing impotently to wreak vengeance. Where once Butler's claims that African Americans were a subhuman species bent on the destruction of whites might have been roundly applauded, now they only confirmed his status as a social pariah.

At the time, Butler's pronouncements were generally dismissed as lunacy by those of us in the mainstream press, including his call for a "white homeland"—after all, northern Idaho couldn't have become much more white than it already was. But what none of us anticipated was that even though the numbers that Butler recruited were generally small, their impact on the community was dramatic. Many of the people who moved to settle in the new "white homeland" were ex-cons, recruited into white supremacy while in prison. Others were radical ideologues who were fully inclined to take to heart Butler's urgings to engage in a "race war"—guys like Robert Mathews, who moved to nearby Metaline Falls in northeastern Washington to be near to Butler's church, and found work in the local zinc mines. Mathews would later gain national notoriety as the leader of the murderous gang of neo-Nazi bank robbers known as The Order.

And they were changing the face of the northern Idaho community. The region was historically considered among the more liberal precincts in the state, particularly compared to the Mormon-dominated southern half; mining- and timber-rich northern Idaho had a long history of labor activism dating back to the previous century, and in fact had played a key role in the development of radical labor organizations like the International Workers of the World. Now, an undercurrent of reactionary sentiment latent in the landscape (the region had also been home to a number of Confederate Army veterans who settled there after the Civil War), brought to life by the Aryan Nations, began to manifest itself in ugly ways. The file I was keeping at the *Daily Bee* was an attempt to keep track.

At first, it cropped up in nasty but relatively harmless ways, like the "running nigger" fliers—hateful, but not criminal. Then it began crossing the line:

- A Jewish restaurateur in Hayden found his business vandalized with anti-Semitic graffiti and swastikas, as well as a sticker with the message, "Do Not Patronize This Place."
- A Hispanic family in Coeur d'Alene, some fifteen miles south of Hayden, was terrorized by someone calling late at night and making death threats; when they refused to leave, someone tried to set fire to their trailer, then killed their dog by slashing its throat. The family packed up and left.
- A cluster of young thugs associated with the Aryan Nations assaulted a pair of teenagers (a minority boy and a white girl) outside a bowling alley.
- Crosses were left burning on the lawns of two area families. One of these was an all-white family who, police believe, were targeted mistakenly.
- A Baptist church and a printing business in Coeur d'Alene were both defaced with swastikas.

The threats and intimidation came to a head in September 1982, thanks largely to one of the more troublesome hooligans attracted to northern Idaho by Butler's church: an ex-convict named Keith Gilbert. He had moved to the region after doing time at California's San Quentin prison for having 1,500 pounds of dynamite at his Glendale home, which he later claimed was intended to assassinate Martin Luther King at a 1965 appearance in Los Angeles. Gilbert had been a follower of Butler's in California, but shortly after moving to Idaho he had a falling-out with Butler, so Gilbert struck out on his own with a white-supremacist organization based in nearby Post Falls. Gilbert, who later admitted responsibility for distributing the "running nigger" targets, then began his own campaign of threats and intimidation.

His chief target was a Coeur d'Alene family headed by a white woman named Connie Fort who had been married for several years to a black man and had three children with him. Gilbert began by walking up to the eldest boy and spitting on him, saying: "Your life is condemned. You shall be served in front of the devil." Having discovered where Fort's family lived, Gilbert began driving by the home and shouting threats and obscenities at the children. He mailed an envelope containing a death threat for "race traitors" who engaged in "miscegenation." Another mailing contained a news clipping about the corpse of a black man found floating in Spirit Lake, shot through the head.

Police were initially hesitant to charge Gilbert, partly because Idaho law made racial slander only a misdemeanor. But as the threats escalated, he eventually was charged and convicted of misdemeanor assault, and fined $300 with a forty-five-day jail sentence. Gilbert merely laughed it off.

The rest of the community, however, did not. Local churches circulated petitions in support of Connie Fort's family and managed to gather hundreds of signatures. And Fort herself decided that something had to be done about the failure of Idaho law to adequately address this kind of hateful harassment. The previous year, a coalition of church leaders, city and law-enforcement officials, and businessmen from throughout the county had already formed, calling itself the Kootenai County Human Relations Task Force. As Fort's story gained publicity in the local press, the KCHRTF took up the task of gaining public support for changing the law. It organized town-hall meetings to discuss the issue, and found that its support was deep and broad; at a panel discussion set up by the Idaho Human Rights Commission in 1982, other participants included the Justice Department, the American Civil Liberties Union, and law-enforcement officers.

Out of those discussions, the Human Rights Commission composed legislation—similar to a law recently passed in Washington state, also largely in response to the activities emanating from the Aryan Nations—that would make it a felony to intimidate or harass another person because of their race or religion, either with physical assault or with threatening words. The bill was introduced in the Idaho Legislature's 1983 session with considerable fanfare, and its advocates claimed the support of over a hundred voluntary organizations in the state that supported its passage.

However, the bill encountered considerable opposition among legislators from the state's notoriously conservative southern half. Many voiced concern that the law would trample on constitutional rights to religious freedom and free speech. Others accused the sponsors of secretly supporting the United Nations genocide convention—which, in the John Birch Society–heavy politics of southern Idaho, was akin to a kiss of death. Richard Butler testified against it: "This bill would take away sovereign, inalienable rights of white Christians," he told legislators.

The tide slowly turned in the bill's favor, however, as the breadth of support for it became apparent. Kootenai County Prosecutor Glen Walker—a conservative Republican—traveled to Boise and patiently explained to lawmakers why the law was needed, particularly as a tool for dealing with a kind of crime they all recognized had deeply corrosive consequences for their community. Walker also shepherded several compromises to the legislation, including a clause that would specify it was not intended to imply support for the United Nations, thereby mollifying the Bircher contingent.

The *coup de grace*, however, was delivered by Keith Gilbert himself. He created a phony "Anti Defamation League" lobby, concocted a letterhead and a nonexistent leader named "Rabbi Schechter," and sent letters to all member of the Legislature under "Schechter's" signature voicing full support for the bill. Gilbert assumed that such "Jewish" support would inspire legislators to oppose the measure—but his ruse was discovered and publicized instead. Angered by his brazenness, legislators rushed to support the bill, and it wound up passing handily.

✳

Idaho thus became the ninth state in the nation to pass what would become known as a hate-crime law. California was the first to do so, in 1978; Washington and Oregon followed suit in 1981, while Alaska, New York, Rhode Island, and Pennsylvania passed similar laws in 1982. By 1998, forty-five states and the District of Columbia had passed such laws.

As in Idaho, many of these states had found that even though white supremacy, culturally speaking, had been relegated to the fringes of society, its remaining adherents were every bit as willing to resort to violence to achieve their ends as they were in the days of the lynch mob. And it was also clear that the violent crimes that resulted were not ordinary assaults and murders and threats, but had several special qualities to them. For one, they were inherently more violent, and much more likely to result in severe harm. More significantly, they clearly victimized not just the immediate sufferer, but the larger racial, ethnic or religious community to which that person belonged—and that in many cases, that was exactly what the perpetrators intended, as a way of "putting them in their place." This not only extended the reach of these crimes, but it made clear that they were perniciously anti-democratic, and clearly destructive in a society supposedly dedicated to racial justice and equality.

While in Idaho the passage of a hate-crimes law was in most respects a grassroots effort, this frequently was not the case elsewhere. As the laws gained momentum, a variety of different interest groups became involved in their passage—particularly civil-rights groups like the NAACP, for whom support for the hate-crimes laws clearly descended from their earlier campaigns to pass anti-lynching laws. But there were others as well: victims' rights advocates, the women's rights movement, and ultimately gay and lesbian rights activists. The Anti-Defamation League of B'nai B'rith became a leading advocate of the laws, and continues to offer model legislation for states seeking either to pass or improve their statutes. All of these groups played prominent roles in organizing and passing legislation in a variety of states.[30]

This was particularly the case with efforts to pass a federal hate-crimes bill. The first such attempt, in 1985, is credited with originating the term "hate crime," and although it did not pass, some of its core provisions would eventually make their way into law in 1994, with the passage of the Hate Crimes Sentencing Enhancement Act (HCSEA). (Two previous federal hate-crimes laws—the Hate Crimes Statistics Act, which gathered data from various states, and the Violence

Against Women Act—had passed in 1990 and 1994, respectively.)[31] The HCSEA represented in many ways the fruition of the NAACP's long years of effort to pass an anti-lynching bill, even though by 1994 lynching had come to be viewed as only one of many kinds of crimes that could be used to intimidate and threaten minorities. However, it was a limited victory, since the HCSEA was notable as well for the shortness of its scope; the law only considered violent crimes committed on federal property or in the pursuit of a federal activity (such as voting in an election) as potential hate crimes. As such, it continues to be only rarely prosecuted.

The laws came in many different forms. Many of the earlier versions were like the "malicious harassment" laws passed in Washington and Idaho—freestanding statutes aimed specifically at a selected species of behavior, and moreover distinguishing bias-motivated violence from other criminal acts. Others, like California's 1987 statute (which largely superseded its 1978 law), outlaw bias-motivated crime as a violation of civil-rights protections. Still others are sentence enhancements that expand the sentence for an assault, say, if it is committed with a racial or religious bias as its motive. Some modify pre-existing statutes by reclassifying a crime for a bias motivation; and some "coattail" bias-motivated crimes by embedding them into standing criminal codes.

The categories of bias motivation that were targeted for punishment also tended to vary widely. Race, religion and national origin were the three arenas on which nearly everyone could agree—though a handful of states, including Texas, chose to pass laws that named no categories of bias whatsoever, thereby effectively rendering them useless. Some states included bias against gender, or against persons with disabilities, while others included age and political affiliation as criminal bias categories. A number of states also chose to make bias against a person's sexual orientation—that is, if they were gay or lesbian—one of the designated hate-crime categories.[32]

Opposition to the passage of these laws was often fairly tepid, particularly in states with sizeable urban populations, where the support of civil-rights groups was at times overwhelming. However, in a handful of mostly conservative rural states—Wyoming, Indiana, New Mexico, South Carolina and Arkansas—local opposition killed the passage of hate-crime legislation, making them the only states without such laws on the books. The majority of this opposition was similar to that raised in Idaho—namely, a concern that the laws might somehow abridge free-speech rights.

This same concern was the focus of the court cases that arose from the inevitable legal challenges to the state laws. Most of these challenges remained within the sphere of state courts, where the majority of the laws were upheld as constitutional. However, two cases—both arising in the Midwest—made their way to the U. S. Supreme Court, and the resulting decisions wound up defining and ultimately endorsing hate-crimes laws.

The first came in 1992: *R.A.V. v. St. Paul,* which dealt with a case in which a white teenager (known only by his initials) was arrested for burning a makeshift cross on the lawn of a black family, a violation of St. Paul's ordinance banning cross-burnings. Overturning a Minnesota Supreme Court ruling upholding the law, the justices unanimously ruled the statute unconstitutional, though for differing reasons. Justice Antonin Scalia's majority opinion found that the government could not outlaw so-called "fighting words" on the basis of their content, or viewpoint, while the remaining justices mostly found the law to be unconstitutionally overbroad.

The ruling seemed to have settled the debate over the laws firmly on the side of those who argued that they violated free-speech rights, and for a while the very constitutionality of the remaining range of hate-crimes laws was in serious doubt. The concern was so widespread that the FBI was forced to send out letters to some 16,000 law-enforcement agencies to remind them that the ruling did not relieve them of the necessity to collect hate-crime data.

More significantly, other courts followed suit, declaring their states' hate-crimes laws unconstitutional because they created "thought crimes." One of these was the Wisconsin Supreme Court, which threw out that state's hate-crimes statute in its ruling on *Wisconsin v. Mitchell,* a case involving a black man who provoked a group of young black people to attack a white teenager, beating him unconscious and inflicting severe injuries. In 1994, however, the U.S. Supreme Court overturned the Wisconsin ruling, finding that the state's law—which was a "sentence enhancement" law allowing authorities to stiffen the punishment for bias-motivated crimes—only dealt with conduct (namely, violent crimes) that were not constitutionally protected as a form of free speech. Thus in its unanimous 1993 *Wisconsin v. Mitchell* ruling (authored by Chief Justice William Rehnquist), the Supreme Court drew a distinction between conduct and speech that would come to define hate-crimes laws in America—saying, in essence, that hate crimes were not a form of free speech.[33]

This simple concept came to inform nearly all ensuing efforts at passing hate-crimes legislation. The resulting model for constitutionally sound hate-crimes laws, as advocated by such groups as the Anti-Defamation League, follows essentially the same sentence-enhancement scheme. A number of states with constitutionally weak statutes (notably Texas) have in the ensuing years updated their hate-crimes statutes to reflect this. On the other hand, many states—such as Washington and Idaho—maintain constitutionally dubious "freestanding" hate-crimes laws that have not yet been challenged in court, in large part due to the fact that they are rarely enforced. The result is that, despite the definitiveness of court rulings to date, hate-crimes laws nationally are a hodgepodge of inconsistency, allowing a criminal to face charges in one state that would never be enforced in another.

The greatest weakness of the state hate-crimes laws, however, lies in their widespread failure to make enforcement a reality. Few if any of the state laws have included funding for education of law-enforcement officers and prosecutors about just what constitutes hate crimes, how to identify and investigate them and ultimately how to prosecute them. In a sense, hate-crimes laws became an unfunded mandate, forcing law-enforcement personnel to adapt to a new kind of law without giving them the basic tools for enacting them.

This has been particularly the case in rural districts, where budgets are often spread thin and the incidence of these kinds of crimes is perceived to be low, or at least at odds with most small towns' self-image as peace-loving communities. Indeed, because of that, there is a certain internal resistance to even recognizing a hate crime in rural areas—no one really *wants* to know if they're happening. It is possible for an entire rural police force to watch a hate crime unfold under its nose without a finger being lifted to stop it. This in turn contributes to an environment in which small towns become open territory for someone who wants to commit a hate crime.

This kind of milieu was what Minh Hong and his companions discovered that night in Ocean Shores, as had James Byrd that night in Jasper. Matthew Shepard encountered it, too.

CHAPTER EIGHT

THE TRIAL, DAY TWO:
RASHOMON REDUX

WHATEVER LEAKS MONTE HESTER MIGHT HAVE CREATED in Jerry Fuller's narrative on Wednesday did not seem to be bothering the prosecutor the next morning. He was jovial, chatting with reporters and people in the audience. He still had a parade of witnesses to present, and with them, he hoped to make his version of the events of July Fourth sail.

However, if the Rashomon effect had only briefly shown itself on the first day, it was the dominant theme throughout the second day, as some eleven eyewitnesses made their way to the stand and described the tragedy through their own eyes. Many of them had been drinking, and none of them was able to say they had witnessed the whole event. Some had better views than others, particularly at different stages of the unfolding drama. And some were clearly more reliable than others.

A large portion of them knew Chris Kinison from school or around town, and they were unanimous in describing Kinison as looking for trouble that night—some in more devastating terms than others. But there was wild inconsistency in the details, which seemed in many cases to be a product of each witness' limited view of events. One described Minh Hong as having gotten into the driver's seat of the car as they fled the fight, when it had been clearly established he was in the front passenger's seat; another witness insisted that the "man in the yellow coat" had jumped into the back seat. All this underscored many of the witnesses' basic confusion and the lack of cohesion in their stories—and because so many had been friends with Kinison, it also raised the question about the extent to which their natural bias might affect the accuracy of their testimony. In the end, only one prosecution witness could claim credibly to have had an unbiased and clear view of most of the fight itself—and his version of things nearly wrecked Jerry Fuller's narrative.

The day's first witness was Santana Deshazer, a twenty-six-year-old from Ocean Shores who'd seen the tail end of the fight between Minh Hong and Kinison. He seemed to corroborate William Keys's version of the fight, in which Hung Hong held back Kinison's arms while Minh stabbed him. But he said he saw only one arm being held "while the man in front was hitting him," and on cross-examination admitted he had seen this only briefly and that, moreover, he hadn't seen Kinison's arms being pinned back. He did say he had picked up a pair of glasses, walked over to the Asians' Honda and handed them to the driver (who he mistakenly, but understandably, identified as Minh Hong instead of his twin brother) and "told them to get the hell out of here."

Randy Deibel, the twenty-seven-year-old Ocean Shores carpenter who had given interviews to several reporters at the Texaco station in the days after Kinison's death, had been at the Texaco that night trying to get a malfunctioning pickup working and was at the back side of the building when he first saw Kinison harassing the Asians that night. "He was calling them 'gook,' 'slant-eye,' things like that," Deibel said, adding that he kept it up when they went inside, waving his Confederate flag and rapping on the window.

Deibel said he spotted a police cruiser coming by on Chance a la Mer and warned Kinison to cool it—which he did, albeit temporarily. Deibel said the gang of white kids mostly stayed subdued while the cop cruised through the parking lot of the grocery store across the street and then pulled away. Just about then, the Asians came out of the store, he said, and Kinison "started back up again." Deibel said he went back to work on the stalled pickup truck.

A short while later, he said, he heard the fight and came around the corner just in time to break up the confrontation between Minh Hong and Kinison. He said Kinison was clearly hurt, though he couldn't see any wounds at first. He said Kinison told him: "It hurts." Deibel helped him over to the side of his pickup, and watched as Gabe Rodda and Brock Goedecke pulled off his shirt to reveal the multitude of knife wounds from which he was now bleeding profusely. He said he watched as Chris' eyes slowly glazed over and the life seeped out of him.

Another longtime acquaintance of Kinison's was next on the stand: Zach Hoyt, a big nineteen-year-old with a linebacker's build who had been part of the crowd with whom Kinison was hanging out that night. He explained that he and another member of their crowd, Mike Corralis, had been quarreling throughout the day and it came to a head late that night, about an hour before the stabbing.

"Chris interceded," Hoyt testified. "He came up and put his arms around both of us and said, 'I love both you guys, I don't want you fighting.'" Hoyt wept as he explained that Kinison was someone he and the others looked up to: "He was like a big brother to me." Hoyt proceeded to minimize his role in the subsequent confrontation at the Texaco.

If all this testimony was intended to touch the jurors' emotions, then Fuller's next witness provided what he clearly hoped would be a knockout punch: Amanda Algeo, a young woman who had chatted with an Asian man she identified as Minh Hong while they waited in line to pay for their items inside the convenience store. Algeo, too, was a classmate of Kinison's.

Algeo said the Asian man had turned to her and asked if she knew the man outside. She said it was someone she had gone to school with.

"He asked, 'Does he have something against Asians?' And I said, 'Not that I know of.'" Looking at Kinison through the store window, she claimed, the man had said to her, while facing Kinison: "Well, he's going down."

"I told the cashier he needed to call the police," Algeo testified, but the clerk looked outside and, seeing things briefly quieted down, declined.

She said she walked outside and confronted Kinison. "I asked him what was going on," she said, "and he said he was trying to start a fight. I asked him why, and he said it was called racism.

"I said it's called stupidity. I said somebody was going to get hurt. And that's when I left."

Brett Purtzer's cross-examination of Algeo was relatively short and gentle. But he had Algeo admit she had only come forward several days after the stabbing when she was contacted by Gabe Rodda, who had urged her to make a statement.

Alyson Green, a twenty-one-year-old Olympia woman, was the first of the day's witnesses who hadn't gone to school with Kinison, but who knew him slightly from Olympia. She ran into him that night at the Texaco, apparently having pulled up while the three Asian men were inside the store. She said Kinison asked her if she wanted to see a fight, and then whipped off the Confederate flag from around his shoulders and began holding it up at the store window. She said she watched as the Hongs and Doug Chen emerged from the minimart and tried to make their way to their car, walking in single file, but were accosted by Kinison and about five of his friends, who were hanging out around the door. "There were words exchanged, but nothing I remember," she said.

Then, she testified, she saw one of the three Asians stop and pull up a pant leg. "Someone said, 'No knives,'" she said.

Hester and Purtzer objected to this testimony, and Judge Foscue agreed to limit Green's testimony on the point, since she was unable to identify which of the three Asian men had made the gesture, and which of the six white men had said, "No knives." Green went on to testify that the Hongs were not prevented from leaving by Kinison but rather stopped voluntarily—but then testified that she had departed just as the fight began to break out and didn't see everything.

The witnesses came and went throughout the remainder of the day, and the details of the stories kept shifting. Joel Kissner, a man from Medford, Oregon who had arrived in Ocean Shores with Alyson Green, said he had only watched Brock Goedecke fight with Doug Chen, and that had not lasted long: Goedecke "stomped him," he said. Mike Corralis, who'd been fighting with Zach Hoyt earlier that night, said he heard Gabe Rodda say, "Gooks go home." Stephanie Donohoe and Briana Dagnold, both classmates of Kinison's, added little new in the way of detail, except to offer more evidence that Kinison was crowing that he was "gonna kick some gook's ass." Dagnold, too, testified about the presence of the unidentified "mystery man" who was taking part in the verbal assaults. The man, she said, followed her to their car as she left with friends and asked for a ride, but they declined.

The most emotional testimony of the day came from Brock Goedecke, a shaved-headed Marine with a big, athletic build. Midway through his testimony he began weeping copiously and shuddering, something of an incongruous sight for someone so physically imposing. Kinison's death clearly affected him deeply, and his voice was strained and tight throughout his testimony.

Of course, there was no mention made of Goedecke's role in the weekend's events leading up to the stabbing, including his participation in the assault on the Filipino family. But Goedecke did say he had known Kinison for "four or five" years and had been hanging out with him that weekend. He also admitted he'd been drinking—seven or eight beers that night, "not that much."

Neither did Goedecke discuss his role in the verbal assaults that led up to the stabbing. But he was one of the participants in the fighting, and described much of it from his view. Goedecke said he was situated between the gas pumps at the Texaco, only a few feet from Kinison, when the three men in the gold Honda drove past them as Kinison waved his Confederate flag. He said no one blocked them, and that they stopped on their own and got out, and "words were exchanged from both sides—things like, 'White pride,' and 'Do you still want to go one on one, white boy?'"

Goedecke said he looked back and yelled for Zach Hoyt: "I turned back around and I was fighting some guy . . . Chris was getting jumped by the two males." As Goedecke related this, he took a tissue from Andrea Vingo and wiped his eyes, then wadded it and clenched it as he described his attempt to break free and help Kinison.

"I was trying to save my friend's life," he said, claiming that Kinison had backed away from the two Asians and into the street: "He was trying to get away."

For all the fairly transparent self-interest that infected much of the day's testimony, the prosecution's final witness turned out to be the most credible. Unfortunately for Jerry Fuller, he also directly contradicted key elements of the prosecution's narrative—and in some regards, shattered it.

His name was Matt Gonzales, a twenty-one-year-old from Olympia who also was in town to enjoy the holiday weekend—and who also had endured a race-baiting verbal assault from Kinison. Gonzales is tall and slender with a pleasant demeanor, and is not self-evidently Hispanic; his mother is white, and he appears decidedly Caucasian. Nonetheless, Kinison had singled him out that night as he walked out of the Texaco store, and "there was a racial aspect" to his threats: calling him a "spic," telling him to "go home" and shouting, "White power bitch!"

"He was very vulgar," Gonzales testified. "It was scary." However, he calmly told Kinison he was "picking a fight with the wrong guy," and walked away, across the street to the parking lot of the McDonald's on the other side of Point Brown Avenue. This was just before the Hongs arrived in their car, and was corroborated by other witnesses, one of whom suggested that the confrontation with Gonzales was what got Kinison wound up just prior to their arrival.

Gonzales told the jury he sat and watched the drama unfold from his seat across the street. The "Asian guys," he said, had appeared "scared," not angry. Most significantly, he said he watched as Kinison in fact walked in front of the gold Honda as it tried to drive past him, and he appeared to prevent the Hongs from driving away. He said, however, that he did not see anyone hem them in from behind.

The three Asians got out of their car, he said, apparently to talk: "They stood there. . . . The guy with the Confederate flag came up to the guy with glasses and was screaming, 'White pride!' and 'You gooks need to go home!' and nothing but racial slurs. . . . Thirty seconds into it, the guy with the Confederate flag punched one of the guys."

By then, Gonzales said, he had made his way back to the Texaco, and he quickly intervened in the fight between Brock Goedecke and Doug Chen, who he said had been knocked to the ground. When he looked up to see the fight between Kinison and the Hongs, he said one of the brothers was off to the side, away from Kinison, while the other was punching furiously as Kinison swung at him and wrestled him. Gonzales said that was when everything broke up, and when he next saw Kinison, he was leaning against the pickup, bleeding to death.

Gonzales was Fuller's own witness—and the last of the day—and, even though much of his more damaging remarks came during cross-examination, he contradicted the prosecution's own case during his initial testimony, particularly in describing how Kinison stepped in front of the Hongs' car. He also cast serious doubt on the claim that Hung Hong had pinned Kinison's arms behind his back.

Monte Hester and Brett Purtzer beamed as they left the courtroom. The jurors were going home for the night with serious doubts about the soundness of Jerry Fuller's narrative—and little doubt about the hellishness to which Chris Kinison had subjected the three young Asian visitors.

It was, after all, a particular kind of terror—a kind that had been making national headlines the past two years. Most of the jurors, like Minh Hong, knew all about James Byrd in Texas. And more recently, there had been Matthew Shepard in Wyoming.

CHAPTER NINE

THE HATE DEBATE

IN A PLACE LIKE SAN FRANCISCO, BEING GAY isn't likely to get you killed. But in a place like Laramie, Wyoming, it can, as Matthew Shepard found out one bitterly cold autumn night in 1998.

Shepard, a twenty-two-year-old student at the University of Wyoming, was openly gay, and was somewhat flamboyant about it, at least by Laramie standards. Hanging out in a local bar the night of October 6, he managed at least to attract the attention of two local rednecks, Aaron McKinney and Russell Henderson, who were looking for someone to rob, and picked Shepard because he was gay. They told Shepard they too were gay and offered to give him a ride home in their pickup truck, and Shepard accepted.

McKinney later gave multiple, conflicting accounts of what happened that night. He told a police detective that Shepard had not made any advances toward him at the bar, but that Shepard put his hand on McKinney's leg inside the pickup, at which point McKinney told him: "Guess what? We're not gay. You're gonna get jacked." From prison, he wrote to a friend that he started beating Shepard in the car because of an even more naked advance:

> "When we got out to where he was living, I got ready to draw down on his ass, and all of the sudden he said he was gay and wanted a piece of me. While he was 'comming out of the closet' he grabbed my nuts and licked my ear!! Being a verry drunk homofobic [*sic*] I flipped out and began to pistol whip the fag with my gun, ready at hand."[1]

Later, at trial, McKinney attempted to claim that Shepard had in fact made an advance on him at the bar, whispering a sexual proposition into his ear and then licking his lips suggestively. The humiliation he felt at the advance, he claimed, spurred a violent rage that made him want to beat Shepard. (The judge, however, struck down this testimony.)

Whatever the sequence of events and motivations, the three men wound up southeast of town in a remote area near the Sherman Hills subdivision. McKinney and Henderson robbed Shepard and tied him up with rope. As Shepard begged for his life, McKinney proceeded to beat him severely, ultimately pulling out a gun and pistol-whipping him over the head. They left him to die, in the freezing night air, leaned up against a wooden rail fence.

It was in that pose that two mountain bikers found him, some twelve hours later, at first thinking he was a "scarecrow" someone had propped up on the fence. (Their original description created a popular image of Shepard strung up on the fence like a crucified martyr, though in fact his arms were tied behind him and he was seated on the ground.) Though he probably should have either bled to death or succumbed to hypothermia, he was barely alive. He lingered for another five days at the Laramie hospital before he finally died of his injuries.

By then, however, a national firestorm had already erupted. And it transformed Matthew Shepard from an anonymous gay man into a tragic symbol in the rising debate over hate crimes.

✹

Perhaps it was that popular (though incorrect) image of the martyr's pose on the fence that struck a chord for so many people. Or perhaps it was the sheer brutality of the crime, especially the way he had been left to linger for so long. But it was, perhaps, timing more than anything that made Matthew Shepard a household name nearly overnight.

Certainly, there had been any number of anti-gay hate crimes committed over the preceding year that warranted the public's attention. The previous January in Springfield, Illinois, three men had kidnapped, robbed and assaulted a visiting man from Washington, D.C., because they believed (incorrectly) that he was gay.[2] In Honolulu that August, a group of teenagers beat a heterosexual man to death at a public shower because they thought he was gay.[3] In September in Fresno, California, a transgender woman named Chanel Chandler was stabbed to death with a broken beer bottle, and her apartment set on fire in an attempt to hide the body; two young men whose fingerprints showed up were questioned by police, but the prosecutor dropped charges when the pair refused to waive their right to a speedy trial and his evidence, including DNA work, had not arrived in time. Charges were never re-filed.[4]

For that matter, a steady drumbeat of news about vicious crimes directed against gays and lesbians had been getting increasing play in the nation's headlines for the previous decade. The sport of "gay bashing," in which groups of young men from rural or suburban areas would invade urban gay districts and commit brutal assaults, often with baseball bats, became something of a legend during the early 1990s; though the incidents were real enough, many of them went unreported because of gay men's reluctance to report the beatings to police.[5]

By 1998, even though only twenty-one states had hate-crimes laws against gays, lesbians, or bisexuals even on the books (Wyoming was one of seven states with no hate-crimes law at all), such crimes made up 11.6 percent of all hate crimes reported to the FBI, the third-highest such category. Since twenty-nine states were out of the picture, and many of the crimes went unreported anyway, the numbers could at best only hint at the levels of gay-bashing that were happening in reality. Indeed, one study, conducted in 1991, estimated that better than 50 percent of all gays and lesbians in America had been subjected to physical attacks motivated by their homosexuality.[6] As early as 1987, a Department of Justice report had observed that "homosexuals are probably the most frequent victims of hate crimes." The same report noted: "Many victims of bias crimes do not report incidents because they distrust the police, feel that the incident is too minor or that the police cannot do anything about it, have a language barrier, fear retaliation by the offender or—in the case of gays and lesbians—fear public exposure."[7]

What really stood out about these crimes was their viciousness. These weren't merely assaults: they entailed torture, mutilation, castration, sexual assault, and extremely severe beatings, and they were very likely to end in death. Gay-related homicides are notable for the "overkill" that pervades the attacks; a 1995 study found that in more than 60 percent of the homicides, there was evidence of "rage/hate-fueled extraordinary violence" that included "dismemberment, bodily and genital mutilation, use of multiple weapons, repeated blows from a blunt object, or numerous stab wounds."[8]

The violence, intended to intimidate, stirred a different response. Bolstered by increasing evidence of an epidemic of gay-bashing and the damage it was causing, a politically astute coalition of civil-rights groups began agitating in the late 1980s and early '90s for an innovation in federal and state hate-crimes laws that had already been instituted in a number of states, notably California; namely, adding "sexual preference" to the categories of bias motivation that would elevate a normal crime to "hate crime" status. By 1995, expanding the laws' scope was a top-level priority for such advocacy groups as the National Gay and Lesbian Task Force and the Human Rights Campaign, and their agenda had the endorsement of such mainstream organizations as the Anti-Defamation League and the Southern Poverty Law Center.

They ran full square into the American religious right, for whom the so-called "gay agenda" had been a favorite *bête noir* (and thus a significant fund-raising issue) since the late 1970s. As early as 1981, such large conservative-Christian political organizations as Jerry Falwell's Moral Majority, for instance, engendered national scare campaigns designed to frighten middle Americans about the threat to their well-being posed by homosexuals.[9] A handful of conservative special-interest lobbying groups—the Traditional Values Coalition, Gary's Bauer's Family Research Council, James Dobson's Focus on the Family, and Beverly LaHaye's Concerned Women for America—established themselves during the same time period by making their opposition to gay rights a loudly trumpeted feature of fund-raising drives.

For most of the 1980s, these efforts focused on attempting to blunt or reverse advances in gay rights that had been occurring on a number of fronts. This meant waging war upon anti-discrimination legislation and laws of various kinds, from housing and employment to civil-benefits laws, which were being passed by various states and cities in the 1980s and '90s. The most common argument raised by the religious right was that these laws, by purportedly granting gays and lesbians "minority" status, constituted "special rights" that they did not deserve.

The issue first raised its head in 1988, when Democrats succeeded in placing sexual orientation as a potential category of hate crime in the Hate Crimes Statistics Act (HCSA), the first attempt to pass a federal hate-crimes law of any kind. The law was very narrow in scope; it primarily enabled the FBI to oversee the compilation of data regarding hate crimes of various kinds around the nation and did not create any kind of federal law against the crimes themselves. Nonetheless, the inclusion of sexual orientation as a category of bias motivation incurred the wrath of various religious-right organizations and their congressional supporters. Sen. Jesse Helms, the arch-conservative North Carolina Republican, declared: "Studying hate crimes against homosexuals is a crucial first step toward achieving homosexual rights and legitimacy in American society. This Senator cannot, and will not, be party to any legislation which fuels the homosexual movement."[10] The legislation ultimately passed in 1990, but only after conservatives were assured that including the category did not represent an endorsement of such laws, nor did the bill create any gay-friendly anti-discrimination rights (and in fact a clause in the final version of the law states so specifically).[11]

By 1992, these same religious-right groups and their related local and regional offshoots (such as the Oregon Citizens Alliance) had organized a two-year, ten-state "no special rights" initiative campaign, aimed at rolling back or forestalling legislation that expanded anti-discrimination protections to gays and lesbians. The campaign, however, failed in nine of the ten states in which the vote was held, and the resulting law in the one state that approved the initiative, Colorado, was eventually overturned by the state's Supreme Court.[12]

There was a decidedly nasty side to the religious right's opposition, since much of the "gay agenda" in fact was aimed at confronting the effect of the AIDS crisis on their community; as a consequence, a great deal of anti-gay agitation during the 1980s by these supposedly Christian groups entailed cutting the funding for programs aimed at reducing AIDS infections and providing victims with adequate treatment. Some of their propaganda even portrayed gays and lesbians as "diseased" vermin worthy of "quarantine" in concentration camps, while the more conspiracy-inclined among them suggested that homosexuals played a key role in a sinister plot to enslave mankind and destroy democracy. They also explicitly associated homosexuality with pedophilia, and argued that the "gay lobby" wanted to open the doors of the nation's schools to open recruitment of American children into the "gay lifestyle," often portraying homosexuals as salivating at the prospect of having free rein to exploit tender children.[13]

With good reason, gay-rights groups began to point out that this kind of rhetoric helped fuel the rise of violent "bashing" episodes that plagued gay communities across the nation. Nonetheless, even as these same groups began organizing in the 1990s to address this violence by advocating, at the state level, hate-crimes laws that included sexual orientation as a bias-motivation category, their religious-right opponents mounted counterattacks on the laws that often reflected a continuation of the same rhetoric.

This marked the first concerted effort against hate-crimes laws generally, and proved a turning point in the national debate over the laws. In Maryland, the Republican minority leader in the House of Delegates, Ellen Sauerbrey (who in 1994 was the GOP's nominee for Maryland's governor), attacked a bias-crime reporting law by observing: "I just don't think we should be always separating out gays and lesbians. . . . I don't think we should be creating special categories for homosexuals for everything that comes along." The law was defeated.[14] In Indiana, an attempt to pass a bias-crime law (the state is one of four without one) foundered when its final version included a sexual-orientation provision; state Rep. Woody Burton, the brother of U.S. Rep. Dan Burton, offered an amendment to remove the provision by arguing that its passage would be "opening the door toward . . . teaching that kind of lifestyle to our children."[15] And in Texas, state Rep. Warren Chisum argued that a similar provision in a 1994 Texas hate-crimes bill "would give minority status to a human act, as opposed to being born black or brown or a woman, which are unavoidable indoctrinations into a minority group. [The legislation says] now you can opt to be minority by making a human thought." Chisum also contended that gays "put themselves in harm's way" because "they go to parks and pick up men, and they don't know if that someone is gay or not." The Texas bill also failed.[16]

Thanks in part to parliamentary maneuvering, though, the religious right was largely absent when the first federal hate-crimes law, the Hate Crimes Sentencing Enhancement Act (HCSEA), was passed in 1994. The sponsors of the bill included it as part of the Violent Crime Control and Law Enforcement Act (VC-CLEA) of 1994, which included measures much beloved by cultural conservatives, including a "three strikes" law mandating life imprisonment for three-time offenders. Under such political cover, the HCSEA, despite its inclusion of sexual orientation as a category of bias motivation, was approved and signed into law by President Clinton with scant debate. There was, however, a catch: the law's scope was extremely narrow, limited strictly to crimes that occurred on federal property or because the victim was participating in a federal activity, such as voting or mail delivery.[17]

Moreover, the inclusion of sexual orientation as a category was meaningless because the law was passed as an adjunct of the VCCLEA, which was an act of Congress, addressed to the U.S. Sentencing Commission to promulgate guidelines enhancing the penalties for any federal crime. The catch was that this requires an underlying federal crime. This is the reason the HCSEA is often thought of as a hate crime law for national parks, post offices and the like. In fact, it is a penalty enhancement provision for *any* federal crime committed with bias-motivation (including sexual orientation bias). As a practical matter, this restricts the statute because most bias crimes involve a parallel crime that is a state law crime (assault, arson, vandalism, etc.) and not a federal crime.

It also further restricts the scope of the law because the majority of federal hate crimes are prosecuted under the Civil Rights Act's Section 245, which is primarily concerned with federal activities—say, mail delivery and federal elections, as well as events on federal property. Section 245 also limits the Justice Department's authorization of an investigation to cases involving crimes motivated by bias against only the victim's race, color, religion, or national origin. Indeed, the majority of federal hate crimes are prosecuted under Section 245.

Thus any federal hate-crimes investigations involving gay-bashing were relegated to a tiny number of cases; in fact, the first prosecution under HCSEA's sexual-orientation provision did not occur until 2002, when Attorney General John Ashcroft, in a widely covered press conference, invoked it in charging a computer programmer for the brutal murders of two lesbian hikers in 1996 in Shenandoah National Park.[18] Nonetheless, the general weakness of the HCSEA as a prosecutorial tool was underscored the following year when Ashcroft's prosecutors quietly dropped the hate-crime charges from their case, arguing that they intended to seek the death penalty for Rice in any case.[19] (The charges against the programmer were later dropped altogether when the prosecution's DNA evidence did not match up.[20])

In other words, HCSEA was a reasonable first step, but it was wholly inadequate. Recognizing its weaknesses, civil-rights groups and gay-rights organizations began marshaling their forces in the late 1990s to broaden the scope of the laws. But at the same time, their foes on the Christian right began stepping up their own public-relations campaign against the "gay agenda," focusing particularly on the fashionable trend among entertainment stars to "come out of the closet," as well as increasing scientific claims that homosexuality was an innate trait in humans, perhaps genetically wired in. The right countered with its own public-relations campaign emphasizing self-described "ex-gay" ministries that claimed to be able to cure people of their homosexuality.

On Monday, October 5, 1998—two days before Mathew Shepard met Aaron McKinney and Russell Henderson—a broad coalition of national and state conservative Christian groups announced a "National Coming Out of Homosexuality Day," to be held three days later, featuring testimony from various "reformed gays" and harsh admonitions about the dismal reality of the "gay lifestyle." It was timed to counter the annual "National Coming Out Day" that had become an annual feature of gay-rights organizations. "The message from homosexual lobby groups is one of anger and despair," said Michael Johnston, national chair of the event and himself an "ex-gay" with AIDS. "They consistently blame everyone else for their misery and offer no hope to the adult or young person struggling with homosexual desires." In the *New York Times*, a key participant observed that the campaign was designed to "strike at the assumption that homosexuality is immutable and that gay people therefore need protection under anti-discrimination laws."[21]

The religious right was on the offensive, and their message was getting wide media play. A Focus on the Family press conference that Thursday at the National Press Club featured a prominent "ex-gay" whose story had already been featured on the covers of magazines like *Newsweek*. News stories ran on Fox News and in the *Washington Post*, which noted that the coalition planned a national blitz of sixty-second television ads. And it appeared to have an appreciable real-world effect as well.

In Lansing, Michigan, a campus gay-rights group painted a large rock that serves as a local landmark in honor of National Coming Out Day on that Wednesday. They woke Thursday morning to see that the rock had been repainted with crude gay-hating slurs: "No packing zone." "Fags." "Kill flames." "I kill fags."

That same afternoon in a remote corner of Wyoming, Matthew Shepard's half-frozen body was found tied to a rail fence. And then everything changed.

❋

Laramie is like a lot of medium-sized Western college towns—viewed as something of a "liberal oasis" in a sea of bedrock conservatism, and thus eyed with more than a little suspicion by the frequently anti-intellectual rural mainstream.

Indeed, Wyoming's widespread conservatism is so pervasive that Laramie could only be considered liberal by comparison to its surroundings; by nearly any other standard, its own politics run more in the centrist vein, with a strong dose of conservatism on the side.

The assault on Shepard shocked and appalled the town, and civic leaders from every walk of its political life came out and denounced the heinous hate crime that had suddenly blackened their community's name. Wyoming's Republican Governor, Jim Geringer, said he was "outraged and sickened" by the crime, and suggested that the state needed to enact hate-crimes legislation.

In Laramie, there was concern and soul-searching. "It's really hard to be gay and live in Wyoming because of the good-ol'-boy network," one Wyoming student, Kete Blonigen, told a reporter. "It's such a conservative state. I'm almost afraid and expecting someone to say, 'He was gay. What does it matter?' I can totally see that happening. I'm disgusted by this whole thing."[22]

Walter Boulden, a friend of Shepard's, had no doubt it was a hate crime. "There is no maybe," he told the *Branding Iron*, the campus paper.

A Democratic legislator from Laramie, Rep. Mike Massie, who had previously cosponsored hate-crimes legislation, accused his colleagues of dragging their feet. "Because of homophobic attitudes, every attempted bias crime bill so far to be proposed in the state legislature has been blocked. The viciousness of the attack on Matt clearly shows how critical this kind of legislation is. The attack was fueled by the kind of ignorance and intolerance that we as Americans must condemn in the strongest terms possible."[23]

That Saturday was homecoming on the University of Wyoming campus, and as the annual parade kicked off, a hastily organized gathering of about one hundred of Shepard's friends and local gay-rights supporters took the lead of the procession. Under the banner of the campus United Multicultural Council, they carried signs declaring "Hate is Not a Wyoming Value," "No Hate Crimes in Wyoming" and "Straight But Not Stupid." Football players wore the UMC's symbol on their helmets that day. Throughout both the campus and the town, there was a widespread grief and anger, though there was also a hint of fear at the cloud that was about to descend on the little college town.[24]

Whatever the reaction in Laramie, it was shortly overwhelmed by the nationwide flood of outrage that followed the widespread coverage the Shepard case provoked. It was a lead story on all three major networks and featured prominently on the front page of nearly every newspaper in the country. And with the coverage came denunciations from nearly every sector of the country: The House of Representatives passed a nonbinding resolution denouncing the assault. President Clinton issued a statement. Pundits and columnists from around the world weighed in on the Shepard assault.

When Shepard died five days after he was attacked, the outrage rose another level. By the following Sunday, the headlines were everywhere. The *Washington Post:* "Brutal Slaying Focuses the Nation on Violence Against Gays." The *New York Times:* "The Hate Epidemic" and "Hate Crimes Don't Matter, Except When They Do." The *Arizona Republic:* "Residents of Casper Reflect on Death of Shepard, Issue of Homosexuality." The *Atlanta Journal-Constitution:* "Gay Killing Renews Penalty Debate."

A national memorial vigil in Shepard's honor was held at the Mall in Washington, D.C., drawing high-profile celebrities and various national political figures. But perhaps its most eloquent speaker was Shepard's friend Walter Boulden, who spoke a great deal about Shepard's personal qualities and his belief that he was safe to have returned home to his native Wyoming:

> Matt's sense of safety was betrayed by every legislator in Wyoming and this nation who has opposed or voted against hate-crime legislation over the last years. These men and women represented the leadership of our state and Nation, and sent a clear and tangible message to the people of our state, and to the children of our nation, that it is okay to "Hate Gays and Lesbians." Through opposition to hate-crime legislation which clearly states we will not tolerate hate, our leadership has sanctioned an atmosphere of ignorance, prejudice, oppression, and hatred. Our children have been, and are still listening and watching. Alex and I stand here before you because some of our children heard that message and interpreted it to mean it is okay to savagely torture and murder one of our gay children.[25]

There were other vigils held in Shepard's honor around the country that week—in fact, there was one in nearly every major city and in many college towns as well. The need for hate-crimes laws that addressed violence against gays and lesbians was the focus of nearly each of these. Unsurprisingly, gay-rights groups like the Human Rights Campaign began beating the drums loudly for both state and federal laws: "Past opponents of the inclusion of 'sexual orientation' in hate crimes legislation argued that its passage would give 'special rights' to gays," remarked Rea Carey of the National Youth Advocacy Coalition. "It seems to me that Matthew Shepard could have used any rights the night he was tied to a fence and beaten. Anti-gay forces will have to be very creative in coming up with an argument for not passing hate crimes legislation next time around. Their excuses will fall on angry ears. It is time for the State of Wyoming and our country to right its past wrongs."[26]

The blame-laying, however, was helping to feed a media frenzy that reached feverish levels on a wave of stereotypes and misinformation. Bob Beck, Wyoming Public Radio's news director, recalled the first television story he saw about the case: "It was this woman reporter standing outside the Fireside doing what we call a bridge, a stand-up: "Hate: it's a common word in Wyoming." Beck encountered other journalists full of similar preconceptions, and it clearly colored their reporting. Most of all, much of it was a mishmash of unverified "facts" and half-truths. Not surprisingly, University of Wyoming president Phil Dubois protested: "Nothing could match the sorrow and revulsion we feel for this attack on Matt. It is almost as sad, however, to see individuals and groups around the country react to this event by stereotyping an entire community, if not an entire state."[27]

Wyoming officials were similarly defensive—and in fact, became simply defiant about the wave of approbation that had hit their state. Three days after indicating the state needed a hate-crimes law, the governor released a statement attacking hate crimes legislation, saying that "if hate is involved as a motive, it can make the penalty more severe. That helps little, if the victim is dead." Geringer criticized the national attention the case received and appeared to imply hypocrisy on the part of Shepard's supporters: "I note with irony that the national press didn't bat an eye when young Kristin Lamb was abducted from her grandparent's front yard, raped, murdered and dumped in a landfill. That action is just as repulsive as the loss of Matthew Shepard." At the same time, Geringer bemoaned the bad image the case had given his state: "Wyoming people are discouraged that all of us could be unfairly stereotyped by the actions of two very sick and twisted people."[28]

The next day, Geringer's spokesman told ABC News that "the governor says he's still not convinced the state needs [a hate-crimes law]." The same ABC report included footage of Geringer chastising supporters of hate-crimes legislation: "We shouldn't be running off as a lynch mob might trying to look for vigilante justice, because that would be just as wrong as the act we deplore already."[29]

In the end, Wyoming legislators refused to pass any of the four hate-crimes bills that were proposed that following year, in spite of (or perhaps because of) the national attention the matter brought them.[30] Just to the north, in Montana— where the Shepard killing received considerable attention—a similar attempt to expand its state's hate-crimes categories to include sexual orientation met the same fate, failing to make it out of committee.

Russell Henderson pleaded guilty to felony murder with robbery and kidnapping in April 1999 and was given two life sentences with no chance of parole. Aaron McKinney took his case to trial, where his lawyers attempted a "gay panic" defense arguing that McKinney, who had been sexually abused as a child, flew into an uncontrollable rage when Shepard allegedly propositioned him. But the judge struck down that defense, and McKinney was found guilty in November 1999. He too was given two life sentences with no chance of parole, after Shepard's parents requested he be allowed to escape the death penalty.

The case, officially speaking, was closed. But Matthew Shepard's murder would continue to ripple through the nation's political discourse for years.

In the weeks immediately following the beating death, anti-gay conservatives found themselves on the defensive, especially since their just-launched anti-gay campaign included television spots with questionable material that came under scrutiny in news reports. The Gay and Lesbian Alliance Against Defamation (GLAAD) in particular traced a direct link between the anti-gay campaign in the media and the rising tide of anti-gay violence. Jennifer Einhorn, the group's spokesperson, singled out the ads planned by the American Family Association and the Family Research Council, noting that the supposed depravity of homosexuality was a universal theme.[31]

"We invite those who are so obsessed with the lives of lesbians and gay men to examine the tone and tenor of their remarks well before they issue them," remarked GLAAD's executive director, Joan M. Garry. "Think of who will hear their words. Think of who will see these indelible images. If you think homophobic advertisements like those which ran in our newspapers this summer are devoid of repercussions—think again. These ads give people permission to hate. They are inciteful vehicles. They have a real impact on real people's lives."[32]

"The savage beating and burning of Matthew Shepard did not occur in a vacuum. Crimes such as these arise out of minds twisted and misinformed about lesbian and gay people. The leaders of the most powerful religious political organizations . . . have made a strategic, political decision to target gays and lesbians," said Human Rights Campaign education director Kim Mills.[33]

The religious right's image took a further beating with the appearance on the scene of the Reverend Fred Phelps, a fundamentalist preacher from Topeka, Kansas, whose ministry out of the Westboro Baptist Church is aimed almost singularly at denouncing gays in the ugliest language imaginable, assuring anyone within earshot that hellfire and brimstone await any homosexual after death. This, of course, included Matthew Shepard; and Phelps, whose extended family forms much of his traveling brigade of noisy protesters, made a splash in the media by showing up at Matthew Shepard's funeral service with signs announcing "No Fags in Heaven" and "Matt in Hell."[34] Most mainstream fundamentalists were horrified and made various pronouncements distancing themselves from Phelps's hatefulness—though the Family Research Council, while noting that it differed with Phelps over tactics, shared his dismay with the "homosexual agenda," adding moreover that "homosexuals . . . if unrepentant, will not inherit the kingdom of God."[35]

The religious right's nascent anti-gay campaign wilted in the face of public opinion, which had clearly turned against them. A poll released two weeks after Shepard's death found that some 75 percent of Americans believed that anti-gay violence was a serious national problem.[36] In response, the planned television-ad campaign was temporarily shelved, though the ads did begin resurfacing a year later.

The fight, however, was far from over.

✳

Nearly everyone, except Fred Phelps, denounced Shepard's killing, including those on the religious right. The latter, however, didn't believe it justified passing any new laws.

The Family Research Council (FRC), for instance, observed that "violently attacking a person is unconscionable, whatever the reason." FRC spokesman Robert H. Knight even suggested the assault on Shepard was connected to the abortion issue: "It is indicative of a culture that has become inured to violence and has lost respect for the human person."

But most of all, Knight contended, it did not form a rationale for new hate-crime laws. "Every crime is a 'hate' crime. Brutalizing a person is a reprehensible act, regardless of the motivation or the group affiliation of the victim. All citizens deserve equal protection under the law. 'Hate crimes' laws skew the legal system and afford unequal protection by design. This young man, no less than anyone else, should be protected, and his attackers should feel the full force of the law."

This argument—that "all crimes are hate crimes"—became the centerpiece of the opposition to bias-crime statutes in the debate that followed Shepard's death. It was heard not only from the religious right, but from mainstream conservatives and civil libertarians as well, who questioned both the constitutionality of the laws as well as the need for them. "There is no evidence that even a single crime would be prevented by new hate-crime legislation," wrote syndicated legal columnist Stuart Taylor. "Existing laws are entirely adequate to punish those who assault and murder, whatever the motives. . . . [T]he need for collective expressions of outrage can be (and has been) met by speeches, marches, services, vigils, congressional resolutions, and more."

The focus of the debate shifted from Wyoming to Washington, D.C., where a previously little-noticed piece of legislation—the Hate Crimes Prevention Act (HCPA) of 1998—had been wending its way through a series of committee hearings. The HCPA, originally sponsored in the Senate by Ted Kennedy, the Massachusetts Democrat, would in fact have created the first true federal hate-crimes law—amending the Civil Rights Act's Section 245 to include sexual orientation, gender and disability to the bias motivations of federal hate crimes, and to remove the severe limits on which hate crimes the Justice Department was authorized to investigate. If approved, it would have marked a significant step forward in the evolution of the laws.

James Byrd's horrifying murder earlier that summer had provided much of the impetus for Kennedy's bill, and consequently much of the debate surrounding it was relatively subdued. The usual opponents on the religious right spoke out against it by arguing that the bill would have done nothing to prevent Byrd's murder, and would have done nothing to enhance his killers' sentences, since they faced the death penalty anyway.

The FRC issued an "Action Alert" warning that the HCPA was a threat to the First Amendment: "Hate crimes legislation could severely restrict Americans' freedom of speech, freedom of thought, and freedom of religion. This legislation would give the government the power to interpret and classify certain speech, thought, theology, and moral belief as unlawful or contributing to crime. Will pastors, priests, rabbis, and other religious leaders who preach and teach against homosexual conduct be prosecuted for inciting a hate crime?"[37]

Nonetheless, the Christian conservatives' campaign against the bill was relatively quiet, indicating their intention to resort instead to conservatives' control of Congress to win. A parade of testimony from both sides—supporters included the NAACP, the American Psychological Association, the Anti-Defamation League, and various gay-rights organizations—was heard over the course of the summer. By that fall, however, it was becoming clear that the bill was fated to linger in the Senate Judiciary Committee, which was then controlled by Utah Senator Orrin Hatch, a longtime opponent of any kind of gay-rights legislation.

The Shepard murder appeared to change all that. Suddenly, in mid-October, both senators and representatives found their offices deluged with letters and phone calls urging that the bill be allowed to move to the floor for a vote. For awhile it appeared that public demand might force a vote. But, reportedly under pressure from the Christian Coalition, GOP Majority Leader Trent Lott announced on October 20 that the Senate would not have time to consider the bill before its annual November-December recess. The Republican leadership in the House, curiously, seemed to claim credit for the bill's demise; a memo from the House Republican Conference attacking hate-crimes laws as part of President Clinton's "big-government agenda" called the death of the legislation "a win for conservative priorities."[38]

Afterward, the Reverend Lou Sheldon of the Traditional Values Coalition tried to defuse the charge that conservative Christians were condoning violence against gays and lesbians with an incendiary countercharge: the hate-crime designation, he claimed, would increasingly be applied against religious believers who see homosexuality as a sin. "What Hitler began to build against the Jews is now being built against people of faith who believe the Scriptures are valid for today and their injunctions against certain sexual behaviors is correct," he said, adding that he had himself been the victim of gay activists' persecution, when they disrupted a conference of his in Sacramento. "But I didn't have the finances to get a lawyer. For a long time we were the target of their wrath. Now other people are surfacing against them, thank God. If you don't agree with [gay activists], they use Gestapo tactics to stop you."[39]

Despite the setback, however, the legislation was anything but dead. The following March of 1999, identical versions of the Hate Crimes Protection Act were reintroduced in both the House and Senate to great fanfare. The House version had 118 co-sponsors, while in the Senate thirty-one co-sponsors signed on. Vice President Al Gore and Assistant Attorney General Eric Holder both issued statements of support, along with the usual phalanx of civil-rights and gay-rights group.[40] The support for the legislation was even broader than before, including a coalition of law-enforcement officers and prosecutors who argued that the law provided them with vital tools for adequately coping with these kinds of crimes.[41]

Among the early witnesses offering supporting testimony for the bill were the family of James Byrd, as well as Matthew's mother, Judy Shepard, who observed: "There is no guarantee that these laws will stop hate crimes from happening. But they can reduce them. They can help change the climate in this country, where some people feel as though it is OK to target specific groups of people and get away with it."[42]

The battle thus joined, the religious right pulled out its big guns and began firing away. The Family Research Council (FRC) opined that "it is unconstitutional to elevate a category of sexual behavior to a legally privileged status," and argued that the law "punishes a criminal who commits a violent crime against a homosexual more severely than if he committed a crime against a non-homosexual."[43]

"We call it the Thought Crimes Act," said Robert Regier, a policy analyst at the FRC. "All people are equal under the law, and no one deserves more protection than another because of their sexual behavior. . . . Passage of this bill is nothing short of telling us what to think. In effect, it supercedes the jurisdiction of the church. They should leave the judgment of our minds and hearts to God, and let the government judge our actions and behavior."[44]

The opposition also became broader as secular conservatives began to chime in against the law. Officials from the libertarian Cato Institute, for instance, testified that they had constitutional concerns about the wisdom of expanding federal jurisdiction over crimes that traditionally were the purview of state and local officials, and suggested that the outcome of the Shepard and Byrd killings, in which the full force of the law came to bear on the perpetrators, "do not show the necessity for congressional action; to the contrary, they show that federal legislation is unnecessary."[45]

There was, however, a decidedly familiar ring to the arguments opposing the states' expansion of bias-crime laws. Many of them in fact replicated in form the arguments that had been raised sixty years before against anti-lynching laws—particularly the notion that the laws on the books already were adequate to the task.

This time around, the legislation did not stall in the Senate—rather, it proceeded out of the Judiciary Committee, and over the summer moved toward a floor vote. In July, it was folded into the Commerce, State, and Justice appropriations bill, approved by a wide margin, and forwarded to the House.

This set off alarms among its opponents, who began working feverishly to block passage in the House, where preliminary estimates suggested it would pass handily. On September 11, 2000, the Christian Coalition released an Action Alert urging its members to defeat the HCPA legislation, since it would infringe on the "free speech of Americans who view homosexuality as immoral." The Traditional Values Coalition chimed in that "the elevation of such a lifestyle into a protected group is a government endorsement of that lifestyle."

As it turned out, they had little to fear. Lying in wait for the bill were the Republican leaders of the House, particularly Majority Leader Dick Armey and Majority Whip Tom DeLay, both Texans with an oft-articulated animus toward the "homosexual agenda." Despite broad and bipartisan support for the measure even among their own ranks, they managed to maneuver it to death—removing it from the Senate appropriations bill and sending it to the House-Senate conference committee, where it was dropped altogether on a straight party-line vote. Later that month, President Clinton vetoed the appropriations bill in part because it omitted the hate-crimes legislation, but he eventually capitulated and signed a budget bill that did not include the HCPA provisions.[46]

It was as though the ghosts of the Senate's anti-lynching filibusters of the 1920s and '30s had taken up residence, instead, in the House—defying popular will to defend an order based on violence and oppression. If so, then the haunting would continue to manifest itself in the ensuing years, thwarting hopes for an effective federal hate-crimes bill for the indefinite future. They remain, to this day, unfulfilled.

✳

The hate-crime debate continued to rage on the state level, too—especially in Texas, where James Byrd's killing inspired another effort to pass an effective law. The key player: the state's moderate Republican governor, George W. Bush.

Texas already had a hate-crimes law, passed in 1993—which was in fact the source of the problem. Passed amid a rancorous debate over the inclusion of sexual orientation as a bias category, it was watered down so that the law defined a hate crime by referring to the selection of victims "because of the defendant's bias or prejudice against a person or group." This language was so vague as to render the law constitutionally unsound and virtually worthless; a similar Utah statute was thrown out in 1999 by a state judge who called the law "incomplete" and "unenforceable." Consequently, Texas prosecutors rarely used the law—and indeed, the cases pursued under the law in the ensuing years numbered exactly two.

Bush, however, had already made clear where he stood: "I've always said all crime is hate crime," he told a March 1999 news conference. "People, when they commit a crime, have hate in their heart. And it's hard to distinguish between one degree of hate and another."[47]

But the governor was on the verge of launching his ultimately successful campaign to capture the presidency, and he had already made clear he intended to present to the voters a vision of "compassionate conservatism"—a platform that suggested some moderation on social issues. At the same time, any bill approved in Texas that would expand hate-crimes categories to include gay-bashing, or might otherwise grant "special rights" to gays, was certain to attract the wrath of the Christian right, who constituted one of the Republicans' chief national constituencies.

So when State Sen. Rodney Ellis of Houston introduced a bill in the 1999 Texas Legislature to replace the state's weak hate-crimes law, Bush chose to take, officially, no position on its passage. Indeed, when it passed the House eighty-three to sixty-one, Bush said he would consider the bill if the Senate passed it. Then, quietly, his office went to work to kill it in the Senate, reportedly at the behest of Bush's political director, Karl Rove.[48]

The bill faced difficulties anyway; Texas legislative rules severely limit the length of time bills are allowed to linger between houses, and Senate Republicans promptly set about sidetracking the measure in the Criminal Justice Committee, where it remained. Supporters then turned to their trump card: James Byrd's family, who came to Austin in May to lobby Bush for his support.

Byrd's twenty-nine-year-old daughter, Renee Mullins, met with Bush on May 6 in his office. Accompanying her were a cousin, Darrell Verrett; state Rep. Senfronia Thompson, a Democrat from Houston; and a gay-rights lobbyist.

Mullins later described the meeting: "I went in there pleading to him. I said that if he helped me move it along I would feel that [Byrd] hadn't died in vain. . . . [Rep.] Thompson said, 'Governor Bush, what Renee's trying to say is, Would you help her pass the bill?' And he said, 'No.' Just like that.

"He had a nonchalant attitude, like he wanted to hurry up and get out of there. It was cold in that room."[49]

A week later, after a Bush staffer met with the Republican caucus, the Senate officially let the bill die in committee. However, the matter would continue to haunt Bush.

It returned in full force on October 11, 2000, during Bush's second presidential debate with Al Gore, moderated by Jim Lehrer, when Gore brought up the Byrd case:

GORE: And as for singling people out because of race, you know, James Byrd was singled out because of his race in Texas. And other Americans have been singled out because of their race or ethnicity. And that's why I think we can embody our values by passing a hate-crimes law. I think these crimes are different. I think they're different because they're based on prejudice and hatred, which gives rise to crimes that have not just a single victim, but they're intended to stigmatize and dehumanize a whole group of people.

MODERATOR [to Bush]: You have a different view of that.

BUSH: No, I don't, really.

MODERATOR: On hate-crimes laws?

BUSH: No, I don't, really, on hate-crimes laws. No, we've got one in Texas. And guess what? The three men who murdered James Byrd, guess what's going to happen to them? They're going to be put to death. A jury found them guilty. And I—it's going to be hard to punish them any worse after they get put to death. And it's the right cause, so it's the right decision.

No—well what the vice president must not understand is we've got a hate-crimes bill in Texas. And secondly, the people that murdered Mr. Byrd got the ultimate punishment.

MODERATOR: They were prosecuted under the murder laws, were they not?

BUSH: Well—

MODERATOR: In Texas.

BUSH:—all—in this case, when you murder somebody, it's hate, Jim.

MODERATOR: Mmm hmm.

BUSH: The crime is hate. And they got the ultimate punishment. I'm not exactly sure you enhance the penalty any more than the death penalty. But we happen to have a statute on the books that's a hate-crime statute in Texas.

GORE: Well—may I respond?

MODERATOR: Sure.

GORE: I don't want to jump in. (Laughter.) I may have been misled by all the news reports about this matter, because the law that was proposed in Texas, that had the support of the Byrd family and a whole lot of people in Texas, did in fact die in committee.

There may be some other statute that was already on the books, but certainly the advocates of the hate crimes law felt that a tough, new law was needed.

And it's important, Jim, not only—not just because of Texas, but because this mirrors the national controversy. There is pending now in the Congress a national hate-crimes law, because of James Byrd, because of Matthew Shepard, who was crucified on a split-rail fence by bigots, because of others. And that law has died in committee also because of the same kind of opposition.

MODERATOR: And you would support that bill?

GORE: Absolutely.

MODERATOR [to Bush]: Would you support a national hate-crimes law?

BUSH: I would support the Orrin Hatch version of it [omitting sexual orientation], not the Senator Kennedy version.

> But let me say to you, Mr. Vice President, we're happy with our laws on our books. That bill did—there was another bill that did die in committee. But I want to repeat; if you have a state that fully, you know, supports the law, like we do in Texas, we're going to go after all crime, and we're going to make sure people get punished for the crime. And in this case, we can't enhance the penalty any more than putting those three thugs to death, and that's what's going to happen in the state of Texas.[50]

A brief flap erupted in the press because Bush had clearly misstated the outcome of the Byrd murder trials—only two of the three men had been sentenced to death. Several commentators also noted Bush's apparent glee in talking about the death sentences; a member of the audience, in fact, asked Bush about this in the subsequent debate on October 17. And it was clear that Bush had misrepresented the debate in Texas and the state of hate-crimes laws there, adhering all the while to his "all crimes are hate crimes" mantra. But the Gore campaign focused on the factual mistake about Byrd's killers—for which Bush campaign officials issued a printed correction the night of the debate, with Bush adding at a post-debate press conference, "Listen, we all make mistakes"—particularly since, as constitutional lawyer Lawrence Tribe pointed out, Bush's remarks suggested a prejudice in a case for which he was still responsible for deciding any pending death-sentence appeals.[51] However, no one noticed Bush's other factual distortions. In the end, the issue gained little traction in the press, which had shown a marked preference for focusing during the campaign on Gore's alleged misstatements instead. Indeed, the conventional wisdom was that Bush, not Gore, had won the debate.

James Byrd's family was outraged but not surprised. Renee Mullins in particular was angry about Bush's performance, saying: "It was just another way of him misleading the public. He didn't have the statistics right."

The NAACP, which had supported the Byrd family's efforts in Texas, made a national campaign issue out of Bush's handling of bias-crime laws, with the family in a starring role. It prepared a series of television, radio and newspaper ads questioning the governor's commitment to racial justice, featuring Renee Mullins saying: "I went to Governor George W. Bush and begged him to help pass a Hate Crimes Bill in Texas. He just told me no."

The Bush camp responded testily: "Throughout the process, Governor Bush has treated the Byrd family with a great deal of respect," spokesman Ray Sullivan said. "He spoke to them prior to Mr. Byrd's funeral. He gave forty-five minutes of his time to meet with Miss Mullins. The governor's office helped to fund the prosecution of Mr. Byrd's killers."

But in truth, no one in the Byrd family could recall Bush phoning the family—and in fact, he had stayed away from the funeral by suggesting that the atmosphere was too "politically charged," even though other top state Republicans (including Sen. Kay Bailey Hutchison) had shown up. Nor was the contribution from the governor's office to the prosecution anything out of the ordinary—$100,000, or about an eighth of the actual costs (the federal government, in contrast, contributed about $250,000).[52]

Reality notwithstanding, Republicans in short order turned the NAACP's attack ads into a liability for Democrats, accusing the civil-rights group of "reprehensible" behavior for linking Bush to the Byrd killing. By the time the election rolled around in early November, conservative commentators offered as conventional wisdom the idea that the ads "implied that George W. Bush killed James Byrd." Right-wing pundit Ann Coulter featured the meme in her later book, *Slander: Liberal Lies About the American Right*, suggesting that Bush's support for the penalty should have mollified his critics, but instead, "they would not rest until the killers were found guilty of 'hate' and forced to attend anger-management classes."[53]

In the end, the hate-crime issue did no apparent harm to Bush's campaign. He won the campaign (though he did lose the popular vote) after the Supreme Court ruled in his favor at the culmination of the decisive Florida election dispute. And for the first nine months of his presidency, the matter of hate crimes receded to the national background.

The events of September 11, 2001, however, dramatically changed everything—including Bush's approach to hate crimes, at least publicly.

After Islamic radicals took more than 3,000 American lives with their coordinated hijacked-airliner attacks on the World Trade Center and Pentagon, concern immediately arose about the possibility of reactionary attacks on Americans of Arab descent and Muslims generally, since similar crimes had reared their head during the 1991 Gulf War against Iraq. Indeed, immediately after the 9/11 attacks, news reports carried accounts of various assaults on Arabs and persons believed to be of Middle Eastern descent. The Bush administration included several prominent Arab Americans (including Energy Secretary Spencer Abraham) as top officials, and moreover, the Republican Party had over the preceding years made a considerable effort to court the support of the Arab American voting bloc. Perhaps more importantly, it became immediately clear that American armed forces were going to be waging war against Middle Eastern terrorists, beginning with Afghanistan, and that the nation's military would be relying heavily on cooperation from such strategic partners as Pakistan, Saudi Arabia, and Turkey—all predominantly Muslim nations whose ties to the United States, and dependability as allies, would be severely undermined by the specter of unchecked assaults against American Muslims.

Suddenly, hate crimes were no longer just any crime.

In the days following the attacks, Republicans and Democrats in both the House and Senate jointly approved resolutions decrying any violence or bigotry directed at Arab Americans and Muslims. The administration bolted into action, too; Attorney General John Ashcroft and FBI Director Robert Mueller called a press conference announcing that the FBI was already pursuing some forty hate-crimes cases arising after the terrorist attacks. "Vigilante attacks and threats against Arab-Americans will not be tolerated," Mueller said. "Such acts of retaliation violate federal law, and more particularly, run counter to the very principles of equality and freedom upon which our nation is founded."[54]

Bush himself spoke out against the attacks, telling a gathering of Muslim leaders: "America counts millions of Muslims amongst our citizens, and Muslims make an incredibly valuable contribution to our country. Muslims are doctors, lawyers, law professors, members of the military, entrepreneurs, shopkeepers, moms and dads. And they need to be treated with respect. In our anger and emotion, our fellow Americans must treat each other with respect." (It is probably worth noting, however, that at no point in any of his speeches did Bush refer to "hate crimes.")[55]

Over the following year, the FBI aggressively investigated any anti-Muslim hate-crime cases that arose. By October 16, its list had grown to 170 cases, and by the following July, it had expanded to some 380 cases.

Unsurprisingly, not one of those cases was prosecuted under the 1994 federal hate-crimes law, largely because of its inherent weaknesses. The Justice Department relied instead largely on Section 245 civil-rights laws, as well as a variety of weapons- and arson-related laws, to crack down on the attacks. Neither did Ashcroft nor any administration officials at any time propose improving the federal hate-crimes laws to change this situation. And Bush, as was his wont, remained mum on the issue.

Indeed, if Republicans had undergone a genuine change of heart about hate-crimes laws, they continued to hide it well.

✳

The ignominious end of the Hate Crimes Protection Act of 1999 left its supporters stunned and shell-shocked. But the impetus they had gained, combined with how close to succeeding they actually were, kept their long-term hopes alive. They did not, perhaps, quite expect history to keep repeating itself. But it did.

Sporting many of the same bipartisan sponsors as the HCPA, a new piece of legislation, named the Local Law Enforcement Enhancement Act (LLEA), was introduced by Sen. Kennedy in the Senate in the spring of 2000. It featured the same amendments to federal laws as the HCPA, expanding hate-crimes categories to include sexual orientation and broadening the laws' investigatory scope. True to its name, it also contained language emphasizing the primary role of local and state agencies in handling hate crimes—and perhaps just as important, it included funding for federal grants to help local hate-crimes prosecutions, as well as for training law officers and prosecutors to identify and investigate the crimes.

In June, it passed the Senate by a wide margin, fifty-seven to forty-two, and proceeded to the House, attached once again to another appropriations bill, this time the Department of Defense Authorization Act. Again, it enjoyed broad, bipartisan support; House members in September passed a resolution by a forty-vote margin (232–192) instructing joint-body conferees to include the bias-crimes language in the DOD bill. But once again, the bill ran into the tandem team of Tom DeLay and Dick Armey, who succeeded on October 5 in stripping the legislation from the authorization bill.

Kennedy refused to give up, however, and reintroduced the LLEA the following March of 2001, replete with fifty-one original sponsors, even though its prospects in the narrowly GOP-controlled Senate appeared dim. But then, on May 24, Vermont Senator Jim Jeffords announced he was leaving the GOP and registering as an independent, which suddenly gave Democrats a one-vote majority in the Senate and control of both the committees and the legislative agenda.

For a time, it appeared that a bona fide federal bias-crime law was finally about to become reality. Since it was no longer forced to pass out of the Senate attached to an appropriations bill, it stood a far better chance of passage in the House as well. Kennedy pressed forward with the bill, gradually shepherding it through the Judiciary Committee to the Senate floor.

Faced with the prospects of the bill's passage, the religious right stepped up its rhetoric, denouncing the legislation again as "anti-Christian" and unconstitutional. Some of the fresh arguments raised against the legislation bordered on the bizarre. The Family Research Council, for instance, argued that its passage would lead inevitably down the slippery slope to the sanctioning of gay marriage: "Same-sex civil unions (which are marriage under a different name) came about in Vermont because they equated homosexuality to race and had extended special benefits to homosexuals in other areas of the law."[56]

In the Senate, the opposition—which knew it lacked the numbers to prevent passage—shifted tactics, choosing instead to amend the bill to death. Republican senators began filing numerous modifications ranging from Senator Bob Smith's attempt to add pregnant women to the class of potential victims to amendments regarding defense issues and human cloning. By June 11, some nineteen different amendments had been filed, nearly all of them frivolous in nature.

Democrats decided to hold a vote cutting off debate—which turned out to be a fatal move. Two of the Republican cosponsors of the bill, Arlen Specter of Pennsylvania and John Ensign of Nevada, reneged on their commitment and voted to allow the amendments to pile up, while another five Republicans who had voted for the bill in 2000 did likewise. In the end, the cutoff failed, and the bill returned to the Judiciary Committee, where it continued to languish.[57]

That November, Republicans retook control of the Senate, and the LLEA returned to the tender mercies of Orrin Hatch. The LLEA was revived in 2003 in the Senate, this time under bipartisan cosponsorship headed up by Gordon Smith of Oregon. But it remains bound inside the Judiciary Committee, and no prospect is in sight of its ever escaping—nor, for that matter, of its ever surviving the House in any event.

In the end, it may prove inevitable that a true federal hate-crimes statute will share the fate of its predecessors, the anti-lynching laws which fell victim to the same kind of maneuvering that thwarted the popular will of an earlier time. If so, it will be no less a moral failure, casting its long shadow over the nation's cultural landscape.

CHAPTER TEN

THE TRIAL, DAY THREE: REASON AND RAGE

EVEN THOUGH MUCH OF THE PROSECUTION'S EYEWITNESS testimony presented in the first two days bolstered Jerry Fuller's version of the events of July 4 was damning—especially Amanda Algeo's testimony that Minh Hong had said, "He's going down"—there was also a great deal of testimony that made abundantly clear just how vicious was the assault by Kinison and his friends that night.

Everyone heard the naked racism, the deluge of threats and obscenities that emerged from people's mouths—especially Kinison's—that night. Everyone heard about the finger running across the throat, something that a number of witnesses had remarked upon. All of these telling, and mounting, details were a serious problem for the prosecution.

The crime that Minh Hong was charged with, manslaughter, is defined in the law as having two characteristics: (1) the fact of a person's death at the hand of the suspect, and (2) the recklessness or criminal negligence of the suspect. Recklessness—which in Washington law arises when a person "knows of and disregards a substantial risk that a wrongful act may occur and his disregard of such substantial risk is a gross deviation from conduct that a reasonable man would exercise in the same situation"—is the defining culpability factor in first-degree manslaughter. For second-degree manslaughter, it is criminal negligence, or the failure to be aware of the risk inherent in an act, and that failure "constitutes a gross deviation from the standard of care that a reasonable man would exercise in the same situation."

At the outset of every manslaughter trial, jurors are informed about these key elements of the law. Thus in order to prove their case, all prosecutors have to

establish is that the alleged perpetrators acted beyond the realm of reasonable behavior. In Minh Hong's case, the question was: Was he being unreasonable when he
stole those knives and then wielded them? Did he act in anger or in self-defense?

In order to find that someone acted in self-defense, moreover, jurors are allowed to choose from any of a number of scenarios: if the defendant was protecting himself or herself, or family or property, or coming to the aid of another who
either was the victim of a heinous crime or in imminent danger of becoming one.
The prosecution's own witnesses gave jurors plenty of reasons to believe Minh
Hong had qualified on nearly all those counts.

If, on the other hand, jurors were to convict Minh Hong of manslaughter,
they had to be convinced "beyond a reasonable doubt" that he had acted recklessly or negligently in stabbing Chris Kinison. Again, the testimony presented so
far suggested much more than minor doubts whether he had done so. If jurors
were indeed putting themselves in Minh Hong's shoes, they were finding no reason to believe he was not utterly terrified—because nearly anyone would have
been, facing the situation most witnesses described. More to the point, there was
no evidence of recklessness or negligence on Minh Hong's part, even if there
might have been on his brother's, if the witnesses who said Kinison did not block
their exit, and who described Hung Hong as hankering for a fight, were to be believed; it was clear from all accounts that Minh Hong was not even driving the
car and only became involved after Kinison assaulted his brother.

The first two days of testimony from prosecutors had in fact presented at least
a reasonable case, based especially on the testimony of William Keys and Amanda
Algeo, that Minh Hong had acted out of vengeful anger—though this case clearly
was not without holes. However, the prosecution's own testimony had simultaneously, and perhaps unintentionally, made clear to what an outrageous extent Chris
Kinison had verbally and then physically assaulted the three Asians that night,
and to what extent he had put them in very reasonable fear for their lives. If prosecutors wanted the jury to believe that Minh Hong was not terrified of dying or
being severely injured that night, they still had a long way to go.

So on the final day of prosecution testimony, Jerry Fuller set out to prove that
Minh Hong was a liar—the point of which was to suggest that his claims of sheer
terror were fabricated. Fuller intended to demonstrate that Hong's self-defense
case was a sham.

The first few witnesses of Friday, the third day, were mostly evidentiary in nature: a pathologist from the state crime lab who described basic evidence in the
crime, and the two officers, including Sgt. David McManus, who submitted that
evidence. But the prosecution also called William Traversie, the clerk on duty
that night at the Texaco, to the stand. His testimony resurrected the spirit of

Rashomon in the courtroom, since it contradicted other witnesses' accounts, while it simultaneously was tainted by self-interest.

Traversie testified that he was slammed with customers that night—"probably one of the busiest nights we had all year up to that point." He said he remembered the three Asian men: "I thought at that time that they were very well-mannered. They didn't seem . . . you know . . . I just . . . they were . . . [they] got whatever they wanted. They used the bathroom, one or two of them did. . . . I just thought at the time I kind of wished everybody would behave like them or something."

But he said he never heard anyone knocking on the glass, though he did say there were large numbers of people milling around outside. "We were the only thing open in Ocean Shores at that time in the morning," he said. "It just seemed like they threw everybody there because there was nothing else—no place else to go." He estimated that there were at least twenty-five people milling outside, and later expanded this to say it may have been as many as fifty.

He said he decided to check outside when someone asked him to dial 911: "One of the customers had come in and said, maybe I should call the police or something like that. So I went out to check to see if I could see any kind of a problem, looked around the parking lot and saw the people, and everybody was standing around talking and I didn't see anybody misbehaving or any kind of problems, so I went back in because I was really busy."

He said, however, that this check occurred after the three Asians had left the store—which suggests that it occurred just as the Hongs were pulling out of their parking slip and trying to head out of the lot onto Chance a la Mer. (This contradicted Amanda Algeo's testimony that she had asked the clerk to phone police and had been refused.)

While most of the morning's testimony was interesting, it did little to advance the case of either side. But later that day, as he was wrapping up his case, Jerry Fuller called to the stand Dave McManus, who had interviewed Minh Hong after the stabbing, to explain what went on in those conversations. Fuller first played a portion of the tape from the second interview, before McManus had informed Minh Hong that Kinison had been killed. The tape showed Minh Hong clearly lying:

MCMANUS: We obviously have a very serious situation, OK? There's no doubt a knife was involved and you guys were cut, the other guy's been stabbed. You guys, from what you tell me, it's obvious you guys were defending yourselves. OK? You were outnumbered, it looks like these guys were definitely the ones starting everything.

HONG: And they also have us—they smell like beer when they come up to us. Then they start spitting at us and calling us "yellow" and I mean, it's not our fault that we're Asians.

MCMANUS: Absolutely. I understand that. I totally agree. You guys were defending yourself. If one of you used a knife to defend yourself, that is, you know, there's an argument of course for self-defense and all that. You know, it's not something I can give you any legal advice on, but the one thing I can tell you is that is if you guys lie to me about what happened, it doesn't make it look good. It's very important that you tell me really what happened. . . . I mean, if you think about it, it doesn't look like you're very innocent if you're lying about what happened. I'm not saying you are. I'm just saying you gotta think about that. . . . We're gonna find out the truth. It's very important that you tell me the whole truth. Do you understand that?

HONG: Yes, I do.

MCMANUS: OK. You want to tell me something else?

HONG: That's all I know. It just happened so quick.

MCMANUS: Do you know where the knife came from?

HONG: No.

MCMANUS: Do you know where the knife went?

HONG: No. . . .

MCMANUS: You understand how important it is that we get the whole truth because we're gonna know it. OK? So if you tell me, and you know, you gotta tell me you did it to defend yourself, you know, there's certainly an argument there, but if you don't tell me the truth, it doesn't look good. Do you remember stabbing him?

HONG: No, I don't. Like I say, there's so many of them coming towards us. I mean, I don't even . . . the only thing I saw was when they were hitting my brother, then I, uh, pushed them away and that's when I got hit and my glasses are gone. I was pretty much just getting thrown around and these guys were like two to three times the size of me.

MCMANUS: I understand that, which again, would make an argument that if you used a knife to defend yourself, would make sense. I mean, you're outnumbered and they're bigger than you guys. But you need to tell me if you did. Do you remember having a knife in your hand at any time?

HONG: I don't remember any . . .

MCMANUS: OK.

HONG: No.

Jerry Fuller spent quite a bit of time going over the details of the interview with McManus, stressing throughout Minh Hong's obvious dishonesty. They also discussed Hong's ultimate revelation, while lying in a hospital bed, to McManus that he had indeed stolen the knives and used them to attack Kinison.

"He said that when Kinison attacked his brother he ran over and began stabbing Chris Kinison to stop him from fighting with his brother," McManus testified. "He said he did not intend to kill Chris Kinison, but he wanted to stop him."

He explained that Hong had told him that they had thrown the knives out the window somewhere while they were driving but officers were never able to track them down: "Lieutenant Fitz and other officers checked the downtown area. Checked all the garbage receptacles that were in the downtown area. Walked the sides of the roads in the downtown area. But Ocean Shores is very spread out; even in the downtown business corridor there are heavily wooded areas. For instance, behind the car wash, there is a slough that runs through there—just all kinds of places that something like that can be disposed of where we would never find it."

The combination of the tapes and McManus' testimony left little doubt that Ming Hong had lied that morning, before the gravity of the situation had sunk in. But the tapes particularly stressed a point central to the defense's case: That, regardless of what they told the officer, *even the police* believed there was abundant evidence that Minh Hong had acted in self-defense. Indeed, McManus had stressed this repeatedly on the tape.

Monte Hester zeroed in on this during cross-examination. "You told him, [you] understood why he would arm himself before facing Kinison and his friends, correct?" he asked McManus.

"I'm not sure that I remember it being worded like that," McManus said. "Yes, I told him I still understood why he would arm himself before facing Kinison and his friends."

"On several occasions, you indicated words to the effect that you understood why they would be defending themselves, or that he would be defending himself under the circumstances, correct?"

"Yes," McManus answered. "Under the circumstances he had described them to me, yes."

Shortly thereafter, the state announced that it was resting its case. The ball was now in Monte Hester's court.

❇

As hard as Jerry Fuller had tried to establish that Minh Hong had killed Chris Kinison out of reckless anger, nearly all of the testimony his witnesses had provided also underscored the defense's case: that Minh Hong had more than adequate reason to fear for his well-being and even his life, and the steps he took to defend himself were those any reasonable person would make in that situation.

Thus in many regards, by the time the defense came to present its side, most of its work was already done. At that point, Hester and Purtzer had only to make clear in the minds of the jurors just how grave a threat was posed by Kinison. Matt Gonzales had already testified that the Asian men were justifiably frightened (other witnesses had also said they looked "scared") and that Kinison had prevented them from leaving. Numerous witnesses had described the throat-slashing gesture Kinison made. And the prosecution's own pathologist had discredited the idea that Kinison's arms had been pinned behind his back.

The defense's first witness was another forensics pathologist who debunked this contention altogether: Dr. Emanuel Lascina of Tacoma had been hired by Hester to examine both Minh Hong's and Chris Kinison's wounds. First Lascina noted that Hong's wounds were consistent with a person trying to ward off an assailant, not of a person attacking. He also noted Chris Kinison's arm wounds, saying: "In general, if a person is restrained, say for example being held or being tied, he will not sustain this defense-type of wounds that Mr. Kinison had sustained."

Lascina also said there was nothing unusual about the number of wounds Kinison sustained: "During this brief interval the assailant is inflicting injuries, really, without probably any intent rather than actually wanting to kill somebody, probably just intent on trying to defend himself. . . . At that point the person is probably just trying to survive and trying to ward off the other person who is trying to hurt him."

Jerry Fuller attacked Lascina's conclusions vigorously. Suppose, he suggested, someone was only briefly held. Suppose someone was hitting him from the back and the front. Suppose he was on the ground. Fuller offered a handful of situations in which the pathologist's findings were consistent with someone still being restrained or attacked unfairly. "You can't tell me just how these wounds happened, can you?" Fuller demanded.

"I suppose you can create all kinds of scenarios and it would be consistent," Lascina dryly responded. Fuller, of course, obliged by proceeding to do just that, again emphasizing: "You just don't know, do you?"

Next up was the day's last witness: Rhyanna Von Kallenbach, a young Gig Harbor woman who was in Ocean Shores for the Fourth of July festivities and happened to be down at the Texaco station that night. When she arrived, she told Brett Purtzer, she saw Kinison and his crowd milling around outside.

"There was about four or five of them, and they were white males and they had—all of them had shaved heads and they were just looking, and one had a cane," she testified.

"Did you see any individuals with a Confederate flag?" Purtzer asked.

"Yes, there was."

"Did you go in the Texaco station itself?"

"Yes, I did."

"And while you were in the station, did you notice anybody pounding on the windows?"

"Yes, I did."

"Who was the individual that you saw?"

"One of them was the male with the Confederate flag, and there was another male that was next to him that was in the group."

"Were they saying anything?"

"They were banging on the glass telling whoever was in the building—I wasn't sure who it was directed to—to leave the town, that they were not wanted in the town. You know, this was their town, pretty much just 'white power.'"

"And did you notice any Asian boys in the store as well?"

"Yes, I did."

"How did they appear to you at that time?"

"At the time the men were banging on the windows they appeared nervous."

"Did that escalate?"

"Yes, it escalated, and therefore not only myself but them, they looked terrified."

Purtzer had no more questions. Andrea Vingo, on cross-examination, pointed out that Von Kallenbach had only identified one person rapping on the window in her initial statement. But in questioning her further, the witness emphasized that not only did the men have shaved heads, she thought they were "skinheads."

The jurors would have those words ringing in their ears throughout the weekend; defense attorneys wrapped things up shortly thereafter and everyone headed home. On Monday, they would all get to hear Minh Hong's own version of what happened.

CHAPTER 11

THE MYTHOLOGY OF HATE

IT HAD ALL THE INGREDIENTS OF A GREAT STORY: LURID SEX, grotesque death, children and gays. To the religious right, the murder of Jesse Dirkhising seemed like a perfect fit: their own version of Matthew Shepard in reverse.

Dirkhising was a thirteen-year-old boy from Prairie Grove, Arkansas, who was brutally raped and murdered in September 1999 at the apartment of two gay men who were charged with the crime. Local media covered the murder, as they would any such crime, and the story gained coverage on a few national media outlets.

That wasn't enough for anti-homosexual conservatives, who began playing up the case in hopes of making Dirkhising's murder into a national *cause célèbre*. Arguing that the case constituted a gay hate crime, they loudly questioned why the major media outlets hadn't seized upon it as they did Mathew Shepard's brutal murder in Wyoming. "I wonder why?" queried the far-right *WorldNetDaily*'s Joseph Farah. "I wonder if it's because the victim is not a part of some politically protected sub-group, a special class deserving of extra government privileges? I wonder if it is because the suspects are, indeed, members of such a group."[1]

Religious-right groups voiced similar arguments. Louis Sheldon of the Traditional Values Coalition claimed that "liberal journalists" spiked the story: "Could it be that liberals place a higher value on the death of a homosexual, than on the brutal murders committed by homosexuals? How many other acts of rape and violence committed by homosexuals are being spiked by a journalistic community co-opted by radical sex groups?"[2]

One of the country's most prominent conservative gay writers, Andrew Sullivan, raised the same specter in his column in *The New Republic*. Comparing coverage of the Shepard and Dirkhising cases, Sullivan described the discrepancy as "staggering" and concluded that "the Shepard case was hyped for political reasons: to build support for inclusion of homosexuals in a federal hate-crimes law." Meanwhile, he contended, editors buried the Dirkhising story because they feared they might excite anti-gay bigotry. "I think there is clearly evidence that many in the media decided we're not going to go there because we know it will feed anti-gay prejudice," Sullivan told ABC News.[3]

There was just one problem: the killing of Jesse Dirkhising was not a hate crime.

The boy's parents were friends with one of the gay men, Davis Carpenter, who wound up killing him. The boy spent weekends with Carpenter and his partner at their home with his parents' consent; they reportedly believed he was working for them at their hair salon. It was during one of those visits to his home that Brown—who told police he and Jesse had frequently tied each other up, though not for sexual purposes—decided to "play a game" by sneaking up on Dirkhising from behind, binding his hands, and shoving underwear in his mouth, then wrapping it all with duct tape and then placing a T-shirt over his head. (Carpenter was present and had apparently encouraged the acts.) Brown then proceeded to rape Dirkhising multiple times with various objects, and then left him lying on the bed while he went to eat lunch. When he returned, the boy had stopped breathing, and attempts to resuscitate him failed.[4]

There was, however, no evidence anywhere that the two gay men had acted out of a bias motivation against straight children, nor that Dirkhising had been intentionally selected because of his sexual preference. Neither Brown nor Carpenter had ever evidenced any animus toward straight people, and there was no indication of any desire to terrorize the straight community or "put them in their place."

In reality, Dirkhising's death was a relatively simple if appalling case of child murder—and indeed, Brown was eventually convicted of, and Carpenter pleaded guilty to, murder charges and both were sentenced to life in prison without parole. There were 1,449 such murders committed in 1999—and though the media report such cases locally, they rarely make national headlines, largely because even though every child murder is by nature horrifying, there is no national debate over the wrongness of pedophilia or assaults on children, nor the propriety of stiffer penalties for them. These murders in fact are perpetrated by all kinds of people, though predominantly by heterosexuals who attack young girls. And while some are horrendous enough to catch national attention, there are too many of them to all receive splash coverage. Indeed, in the same month following Dirkhising's killing, there were noteworthy murder/rape stories in Kansas and Wisconsin involving young girls that received about the same amount of media coverage.

The only conceivable reasons a national editor might have for calling out the case would be either a taste for salacious details or to deliberately portray gays in a grim light (as, indeed, did Farah and the religious right). Focusing on a case like Dirkhising's while comparatively ignoring a thousand other heterosexual child murders reflects a genuine bias, not an imagined one. Farah, Sullivan, and their cohorts essentially chastised their colleagues in the media for their failure to participate in their own rather spectacular display of gay-bashing (which, in the case of Sullivan, is also bizarre).

By seizing on the Dirkhising case, the opponents of gay hate-crime laws rather starkly demonstrated either their own failure to grasp the requisite components of bias-crime laws, or their willingness to trade in outright misinformation about them, or perhaps both. By suggesting that the killers had perpetrated a "gay hate crime," they confused the basic concept of the crimes themselves.

The highly charged racial and religious context in which hate crimes have been portrayed generally to the public has given birth to one of the most basic misconceptions about them: that is, **the notion that any kind of crime involving intergroup conflict, especially different identity groups**—interracial crime, for instance, or the Dirkhising case—**constitutes a "hate crime."** Thus when a black-on-white crime—or a gay-on-straight crime—occurs, observers will sometimes wonder why it is not treated as a hate crime, even though there is no evidence the crime was motivated by bias.

And, of course (as detailed in Chapter 7), it is precisely the presence of a bias motivation, and nothing else, that makes a crime a "hate" crime. This certainly is reflected in the fact that the word "hate" at best appears only in the title of any hate-crime law; the laws themselves uniformly refer to them as "bias-motivated."

The federal and state laws dealing with these acts all are built around a basic concept: providing longer and tougher sentences for crimes in which certain kinds of bias are the motive. Racial, religious, and ethnic biases are universally addressed in both federal and state laws; some states also include gender, sexual orientation, or disability.

The laws, as such, are universal for all citizens. Any race, any religion, any ethnicity is protected by hate-crime laws. There are no "designated groups"—rather, there are only categories of bias. The laws are focused on the motive of the criminal, not on the group identity of victim. Their purpose is less to protect any "groups" than to focus approbation on a recognizable social pathology in its expression as a crime.

They arise out of a basic reality: bias-motivated crimes create more harm than the parallel crimes that they resemble. They are intended to victimize not only the actual subjects of the crime but the entire community that is the object of the criminal's bias. A swastika scrawled on a synagogue wall, as such, is not mere graffiti—it's intended to threaten and intimidate all Jews within its reach, to "send a message" and "keep them in their place." At the same time, studies have shown that hate crimes are more likely to cause great physical harm to their victim—and the long-term psychological effects are far greater, resembling often the trauma associated with victims of rape.

In this sense, these laws are very much like those against terrorist acts—they recognize that the motive underlying the crime can cause much greater damage beyond the mere crime itself, and so deserves stiffer punishment. For that matter, they are structured similarly to anti-terrorism laws as well. They typically don't create new crimes; instead, they give prosecutors, judges, and juries the ability to punish (with longer sentences) only those acts that are already crimes. In the case of terrorism, the requisite motive is the desire to force political or social change; in the case of hate crimes, it's a desire to harm anyone belonging to the group against which the criminal has a bias.

There has previously been relatively little public debate over the value and propriety of most anti-terrorism laws, particularly in the wake of September 11— even though, as bias-crime legal expert Frederick Lawrence points out, there are actually far more significant First-Amendment issues raised by anti-terrorism laws, particularly those passed since the Al Qaeda attacks of 2001 (and those laws have, in fact, stirred some controversy in civil-liberties circles).[5] But their cousins the hate-crimes laws have been derided and attacked from the start, which may be why the nation still has no effective federal hate-crimes law on the books.

Confusion over the meaning of the term "hate crime" is probably the most obvious reason for this. Many advocates of the laws, in fact, argue strenuously for dropping any kind of reference to "hate" because of the tremendous confusion it creates. And legally speaking, they are probably right. While it is true that, almost without exception, any bias-driven crime has a kind of hatred at its core, many non–bias crimes—especially violent crimes such as murders, assaults, and rapes—unquestionably also can be driven by hatred. In other words, contrary to the popular aphorism, not every crime committed in hatred is a hate crime. Nor is hate necessarily a component of a bias crime, though it is rare that it is not; most such cases involve cold-blooded sociopathic or psychopathic personalities, though their acts were clearly bias-motivated.

On the other hand, "hate crime" has become so embedded in the cultural lexicon that it is probably by now indispensable as a generic reference to bias crimes, and it is moreover entirely accurate when describing the heart of the bias motivations themselves. Building a broader understanding of the laws is perhaps a more effective way of eliminating the confusion.

And it is difficult to conclude that it is anything besides utter confusion that could drive someone like Andrew Sullivan to compose the following exercise in sheer nonsense, in the course of an exhaustive essay on hate crimes, for the *New York Times Magazine* (let alone for the *Times* to publish it):

> For all our zeal to attack hate, we still have a remarkably vague idea of what it actually is. A single word, after all, tells us less, not more. For all its emotional punch, "hate" is far less nuanced an idea than prejudice, or bigotry, or *bias* [emphasis mine] or anger, or even mere aversion to others. Is it to stand in for all these varieties of human experience—and everything in between? If so, then the war against it will be so vast as to be quixotic. Or is "hate" to stand for a very specific idea or belief, or set of beliefs, with a very specific object or group of objects? Then waging war against it is almost certainly unconstitutional.[6]

If hate-crime laws actually were **an attempt to outlaw hate**, then there might indeed be real cause to oppose them. As Sullivan suggests, it's highly unlikely they'd have passed constitutional muster with the Supreme Court. However, the laws currently on the books certainly have done so, and the federal legislation proposed so far hews closely to them. More to the point, even though Sullivan mentions "bias" several times in the 7,657-word piece, nowhere does he evince any kind of awareness that the laws he is addressing deal solely with bias-motivated crimes.

This kind of fundamental confusion, unfortunately, has characterized nearly the entirety of the national debate over hate crimes and the laws to combat them. A whole mythology built on misconceptions and false assumptions has grown up surrounding hate crimes, and it has prevented a healthy debate about the realities that the crimes present and the right way for an American society built on free-speech rights to address them. Some of these myths have been promulgated by the laws' proponents; some of them are the product of bad reporting in the media; but the lion's share have been propagated by opponents of the laws in their efforts to combat them—suggesting, perhaps, that even their positions could be brought to change by the force of factual reality. Not all of the arguments against the laws, of course, are quite so groundless—and in fact, several of them have at least a reasonable level of merit. But even these, upon close examination, do not hold up.

✳

MYTHS AND REALITIES

Many of the myths about hate-crime laws simply fly in the face of the facts we know about them. This is especially the case, as we have just seen, with the two most prominent myths about hate crimes—**(Myth No. 1)** *they criminalize* *intergroup conflict*, or that **(Myth No. 2)** *they are an attempt to outlaw "hate."*

It's equally true of many others as well. Let's look at them.

• Myth No. 3: All crimes are hate crimes.

This retort—favored by critics of the laws from President George W. Bush and other Republican Party leaders to religious-right organizations like the anti-gay Traditional Values Coalition to white-supremacist organizations—is a product of the same confusion regarding "hate" as the central component of the laws. This only underscores how irrational the debate has become, because it is even more transparently baseless than others. Only a little reflection can produce a long list of crimes that lack anything resembling a hateful element—embezzlement or securities fraud, say, or insider trading.

In reality, the recognition that not all crimes are alike is a basic tenet of law. Bias-crimes statutes recognize, like a myriad of criminal laws, that motive and intent can and should affect the kind of sentence needed to protect society adequately—that is, after all, the difference between first-degree murder and manslaughter. Intent and motive can be the difference between a five-year sentence and the electric chair.

Attempting a sort of zero-sum analysis that makes the outcome (in the case of homicide, a dead person) the only significant issue in what kind of sentence a perpetrator should face (the death sentence vs. a prison term) would overthrow long-standing legal traditions of proportionality in setting punishment, effectively eliminating the role of culpability—or *mens rea*, the mental state of the actor—as a major factor.[7] Or, as Justice Oliver Wendell Holmes famously put it: "Even a dog distinguishes between being stumbled over and being kicked."[8]

• Myth No. 4: The laws on the books now should be adequate to punish hate crimes.

This myth arises from one of the realities about hate-crime laws: they only exist on the books as laws dealing with a special category of crimes with which we already are well familiar (murder, assault, threatening, intimidation, vandalism, etc.)—that is, a hate crime always has a well-established "parallel" crime underlying it, upon which is added the layer of motivation by bias (racial, ethnic, etc.). Thus, opponents argue, the laws for those parallel crimes should be adequate for punishing perpetrators. (If this argument sounds familiar, it is; the identical points were raised in the 1920s and '30s by opponents of the anti-lynching legislation that was the NAACP's *raison d'etre* during its early years.)

Are hate crimes truly different from their parallel crimes? Quantifiably and qualitatively, the answer is yes.

The first and most clear aspect of this difference lies in the breadth of the crimes' effects. Hate crimes attack not only the immediate victim, but the target community—Jews, blacks, gays—to which the victim belongs. Their purpose today, just as it was in the lynching era, is to terrorize and politically oppress the target community. Hate-crime laws resemble anti-terrorism laws in this respect as well—adding, in effect, punishment because more than just the immediate victim is targeted and affected, and thus greater harm is inflicted.

But this is only one aspect of the greater harm inflicted by hate crimes than their parallel crimes. There are several more, and they are substantial.

The violence quotient. Hate crimes are much more likely to be violent than other crimes, on two levels. First, bias crimes involve physical assaults at a significantly higher rate. A study based in Boston found that out of all hate crimes reported to police, fully half of them were assaults—well above the average of 7 percent of all crimes generally. Second, serious physical harm is far more likely to be inflicted on hate-crime victims; the same study found that while physical injury occurred in only about 30 percent of all assault cases nationally, they were present in almost three-quarters of bias-crime cases.[9]

The personal trauma levels. There is also a singularly greater level of harm from bias crimes' impact on the emotional and psychological well-being of the victim. As Frederick Lawrence observes in his *Punishing Hate: Bias Crimes and American Law:*

> The victim of a bias crime is not attacked for a random reason—as the person injured during a shooting spree in a public place—nor is he attacked for an impersonal reason, as is the victim of a mugging for money. He is attacked for a specific, personal reason: his race [or religion, or sexual preference]. Moreover, the bias crime victim cannot reasonably minimize the risk of future attacks because he is unable to change the characteristics that made him a victim.
>
> A bias crime thus attacks the victim not only physically but at the very core of his identity. It is an attack from which there is no escape. It is one thing to avoid the park at night because it is not safe. It is quite another to avoid certain neighborhoods because of one's race. This heightened sense of vulnerability caused by bias crimes is beyond that normally found in crime victims. Bias-crime victims have been compared to rape victims in that the physical harm associated with the crime, however great, is less significant than the powerful accompanying sense of violation. The victims of bias crimes thus tend to experience psychological symptoms such as depression or withdrawal, as well as anxiety, feelings of helplessness, and a profound sense of isolation.[10]

Harm to the community: All crimes, of course, harm the broader community in which they occur. They create fear and uncertainty about citizens' personal security, and add to a climate of civil distrust. However, bias crimes create, in addition to these harms, a further level of injury to a community in a democratic society: They violate the underlying egalitarian principles of equality for all citizens, and they profoundly disturb whatever harmony may exist in a modern, heterogeneous society. Hate crimes may not be as profound an offense in a non-democratic society, but they represent a gross violation of basic American legal and cultural institutions.[11]

This harm is especially evident in small rural towns—such as Ocean Shores, or Jasper, or Laramie, or Hayden Lake—which are often dependent to some extent on tourist dollars, and whose names can be permanently blackened by a hate crime committed in their backyards. Not only can the economic effect be widespread, the community itself must grapple for years with questions about its basic integrity; the cloud may lighten, but it never completely goes away. Small towns are especially vulnerable because they rarely have a law-enforcement department capable of adequately handling such crimes, which can create conditions in which a series of incidents can escalate into full-blown violence, as they did in Ocean Shores.

• Myth No. 5: The laws create "protected groups."

They do no such thing. Every citizen, regardless of race, religion, ethnicity, gender or sexual preference, is protected equally. Indeed, the most significant test case for hate-crime laws—*Wisconsin v. Mitchell,* a unanimous 1993 Supreme Court ruling—involved a white victim and a black perpetrator. Meanwhile, a quick glance at annual FBI statistics reveals that anti-white bias crimes, for instance, are among the most common hate crimes reported, averaging 1,094 such cases annually between 1991 and 2001.[12]

In truth, the actual race or sexual preference of the victim is not centrally germane to the laws as they are structured. What matters is the motivation of the perpetrator and whether he or she is driven by an identifiable bias that is a recognized social pathology. Thus, an assault on someone merely for being *perceived* to be gay or Jewish or Arab is a hate crime—they don't in fact have to *be* any of those things. (Indeed, anti-gay hate crimes in which the victim turns out actually to be heterosexual are not uncommon.) Likewise, a gay man who assaults a straight victim simply because he is motivated by a bias against straight people would likely face charges under any hate-crime law including sexual orientation.

Even though this myth is one of the more readily debunked, it maintains a peculiar hold on the thinking of opponents of bias-crime laws. It forms, for instance, the core of many of the arguments raised by James Jacobs and Kimberley

Potter in their 1998 book, *Hate Crimes: Criminal Law and Identity Politics*. While Jacobs and Potter raise any number of worthwhile points in their analysis of the laws, it is undergirded throughout by characterizations that are simply wrong: "Unlike modern-day hate crime statutes, which cover only those victims who fall within the groups listed in the hate-crime statute, the post–Civil War statutes apply to everyone," they wrote at one point.[13] In reality, of course, they *do* cover everyone—white or black, straight or gay, Christian or Jewish—equally.

Much of the confusion creating this myth arises out of the way the laws have come into being—namely, through the advocacy of various special-interest groups who wish to see hate crimes committed against their constituents punished. Indeed, opponents of the laws are not alone in misapprehending their structure—many proponents likewise believe that the categories of bias contained in them represent categories of "protection" for various groups.

In most respects, however, it is almost nonsensical to refer to the laws as offering protections of any kind. The laws hinge entirely on the *mens rea* of the perpetrator, not on the victim's real or imagined status; the victims, for the most part, are almost incidental, though obviously their minority or other identity status can play a significant role as evidence. Certainly the laws do not create a protection in which a certain class of citizen is given special status that converts any assault or other crime against him or her into a hate crime—even though this is the portrait drawn by many of the laws' critics.

More to the point, all hate-crime laws take effect *ipso facto:* Whatever preventative effect they might have arises purely out of any deterrence that the laws' presence on the book may create, a factor that can be only guessed at. The laws instead give communities and their law-enforcement officials the proper tools for coping with these crimes when they occur—simply because, as we have seen, they are indeed special crimes. If there is any protection offered by the laws, it is only from the sense of the targeted communities that their law officers are equipped to deal adequately with the crimes.

- **Myth No. 6: Hate crimes are usually committed by "skinheads" and other members of so-called hate groups.**

This is an image favored especially by filmmakers and television scriptwriters, and it has had an unfortunate effect on how well law-enforcement officers can identify hate crimes when they happen. In reality, only a small portion of hate crimes are committed by members of white-supremacist or other violence-prone racist organizations, such as the Ku Klux Klan. One study, for example, found that as few as

5 percent of the hate crimes in the Los Angeles area were committed by members of organized hate groups.[14]

The vast majority of hate crimes, in fact, are committed by otherwise law-abiding people who generally harbor a prejudice that renders their victims in a starkly dehumanized light. While most of the victims are chosen randomly, many of the crimes themselves are planned out and relatively organized, and in many cases are the products of an escalating spiral of bias crimes that begin with threats and vandalism and gradually turn to violence—which is what occurred in Ocean Shores. They often can be fueled further by drinking and "thrill-seeking" impulses and, as in Chris Kinison's case, a desire to start a fight. [Chapter 5 follows this analysis with further details.]

- **Myth No. 7: Hate crimes arise in times of economic hardship, which leads to a scapegoating of victims.**

Regional or even national economic downturns were for many years assumed to be one of the chief sources of outbreaks of racist violence and bias crimes. But a 1996 study co-authored by Yale hate-crimes expert Donald Green examined the premises underlying this thesis and found it severely wanting.

Green and his co-authors compared monthly unemployment rates from the U.S. Bureau of Labor Statistics with monthly bias-crime statistics compiled by the New York Police Department for the boroughs of Queens, Manhattan, Brooklyn, and the Bronx. Jobless rates and bias crimes were examined separately for black, Asian, Latino, gay/lesbian, Jewish, and white victim groups. The study found no statistical link between rates of bias crime and economic fluctuations. Moreover, when they applied the same comparisons to a historical example—analyzing historical statistics that related cotton prices to the lynching of blacks in the South prior to World War II—no such connections were to be found.[15]

Instead, subsequent studies by Green and others have concluded that demographic change, especially dramatic shifts within previously homogeneous societies, are more likely to produce the conditions that give rise to hate crimes. Economic downturns have, if anything, a dulling effect on the actual levels of violence.

- **Myth No. 8: Including sexual orientation as a hate-crimes category creates special civil rights for homosexuals.**

It should already be clear, of course, that hate-crimes laws only create categories of bias motivation, not victim identity; a victim need not actually be a member of the group against which the perpetrator is biased to be assaulted because the attacker *perceives* him or her to belong to that group. By way of example, many of the people assaulted in anti-Muslim hate crimes after the terrorist attacks of September 11, 2001, were in fact Sikhs, and, as noted, a number of "gay bashing" assaults are actually carried out against heterosexuals merely suspected of being gay.

More to the point, however, is the fact that homosexuals are not granted any kind of protected or "special" status by including sexual orientation in hate-crimes laws. These kinds of laws simply guarantee that *any* citizen, regardless of sexual orientation—straight, gay, lesbian, or transgender—will see society able to bring the full force of the law against anyone who threatens violence against them merely for their sexual identity, perceived or otherwise. Neither does the existence of these laws create any kind of precedent that could be construed as granting a special right to homosexuals that is not available to everyone else.

The existence of laws against such crimes essentially recognizes their reality as a social pathology—a reality underscored by the statistics showing that violence against gays and lesbians constitutes the second-most common kind of hate crime.

- **Myth No. 9: Gays shouldn't be considered for hate-crime protections because their status is based on a personal choice, while race and ethnicity are not.**

This myth at first appears to offer a neat distinction, and it is one that has been adopted by many blacks and other minorities who are opposed to adding sexual orientation to the categories of criminal bias. Of course, there has been considerable debate over whether or not homosexuality is in fact an innate characteristic and not a matter of choice; a number of biologists have cited increasing evidence to suggest that sexual preference indeed is part of our hard-wiring, though naturally this evidence has been voluminously contested by conservatives and the anti-gay lobby.

But even if this is not the case, this argument runs quickly aground on the hard rock of reality about hate-crime laws. The most basic of these laws includes *religion* as a key category of bias motivation. And though for many Americans, religion is not really a choice but an ineluctable part of our heritage, nonetheless most of us deeply cherish the principle of the freedom of religion. We would no sooner suggest a Catholic or Jew should change their religion just to avoid discrimination than we would suggest a rich man give up his money to avoid being robbed.

When it comes to deciding what constitutes a hate crime, the victim's ability to choose whatever status provoked the crime has no relevance. And denying that the violence endured by gays and lesbians constitutes bias-motivated crimes of the same essence as those perpetrated by racists and anti-Semites is, frankly, not dealing in reality.

- **Myth No. 10: *Including gays for hate-crime protections could threaten conservative Christian pastors with conspiracy charges if they preach nonviolently against homosexuality and one of their flock later commits a hate crime.***

There has never been such a conspiracy charge, and for good reason: The preachers' free-speech rights in this case are fully protected by the First Amendment. One might only face charges if he had in fact advocated violence against gays, and even then the speech would have to be specifically connected in detail to the act that followed—that is, the preacher would have had to tell them who, where, and how to attack. Hate-crime laws do not expand a prosecutor's purview in this regard, nor do any of the laws being proposed attempt to do so.

Hateful speech, of course, remains a fully protected part of American society. But, as we will explore shortly, neither threats nor actual criminal conspiracy constitute protected speech.

✳

It has already been observed that proponents of hate-crime laws are themselves somewhat prone to misunderstanding the nature of bias crimes, frequently lapsing into language describing the laws as creating "protected categories" when advocating their passage. But though they have the weight of most of the facts on their side, hate-crime activists are known to descend into their own mythologies about bias crimes. In particular, they are prone to believing two provably false notions:

- **Myth No. 11: *Hate crimes represent a new phenomenon that has hit the nation with an epidemic of violence.***

This myth has become one of the bedrock themes beloved by advocates of hate-crime laws, painting a picture of a nation suddenly overwhelmed by an outpouring of hate-filled violence. The very title of one of the first books to address the issue—*Hate Crimes: The Rising Tide of Bigotry and Bloodshed,* by Jack Levin and Jack McDevitt—suggested just such a scenario (the authors, in the most recent edition of the text, have revised both the title and the argument),[16] and civil-rights groups like the Southern Poverty Law Center were known to refer to this "rising tide" and a hate-crime "epidemic" in their fundraising material; journalists too have been prone to write about a "recent explosion" of hate crimes and a national "epidemic." This was especially so during the early 1990s, well before criminal-law officials were able to get any kind of firm grasp of the actual breadth and depth of the problem.

As the years have passed since 1990, when the FBI first began gathering statistics on the crimes, it has become increasingly clear that there is no "epidemic," and neither is the tide of hate crimes rising. What in fact has been remarkable about the crimes, from the numbers gathered so far, is their relative steadiness, clocking in annually with roughly the same percentage in each respective category. Even the total numbers have been stable in recent years; between 1991 and 1995, when the apparatus for gathering hate-crime statistics was still in its formative stages, the numbers fluctuated widely. But since 1996, the total numbers of hate crimes have averaged about 8,000 per year, a rate that shows no sign of increasing or diminishing. (Some of this uniformity is undoubtedly the product of serious problems with the statistics-reporting system itself, as we shall explore at length in Chapter 13; but there is some likelihood this trend would continue even with more accurate accounting.)

What hate-crime statistics clearly reveal is that racial, ethnic, anti-religious, anti-homosexual and anti-gender violence occurs at a steady pace in America, and the trend strongly suggests that this pattern has been in place for a long time—a point that is quickly confirmed by a review of history. As Jacobs and Potter trenchantly observe, "it is preposterous to claim that the country is now experiencing *unprecedented levels* of violence in all these categories." As they proceed to describe in detail, this kind of violence dates back to the nation's origins during the Spanish exploration and subsequent European settlement of the continent, and includes the long and bloody histories of slavery, Nativism, the Indian wars, and the lynching era.[17]

The nature of this violence has changed along with the makeup of society, as has society's response to it. As sociologist and hate-crimes expert Valerie Jenness observes, the very idea of a "hate crime" was impossible in the context of pre-1960 American society, because the concept of racial and religious prejudice as a serious social pathology was not broadly accepted before then. Before civil rights, racial and religious equality, and equality of opportunity became broadly cherished social values, our society did not think of violence targeting individuals because of a bias against their minority group as a problem in need of a solution, especially not one based in the law. The notion of hate crimes came from a coalescence of interests between the Civil Rights movement and the crime-victim movement of the late 1960s. Their analysis of the nature of racial, ethnic, and related interpersonal violence as erupting from the same base impulse to terrorize "outsiders" led to the basic concept of bias-motivated crimes as a special social harm requiring greater punishment.[18]

This latter core concept, however, is clearly descended from those previous if sporadic efforts to combat racial violence, particularly the anti-lynching legislation battles of the 1920s and '30s. And it is important to remember that those efforts failed not because of principled opposition (though that did exist) but because of the triumph of the forces of bigotry to thwart overwhelming popular will. The failure of those laws to be enacted is not endorsed by history.

In this sense, hate-crime laws are the clear descendants of the legacy of those fights, and their enactment and enforcement ultimately is a reflection of a society dedicated to equal protection of its citizens and their rights of equal opportunity and access—as well, it must be added, of their free-speech rights.

The lack of a "rising tide" does not militate against the passage of hate-crime laws, as Jacobs and Potter argue. Rather, the constant presence of these kinds of crimes argues for taking them seriously and addressing them properly. What the laws take into account is their outsize harm for everyone involved: the victims, the target community, and the broader community. Our past failures to address them should not be any kind of argument for our continued failures to do so.

- **Myth No. 12: Hate-crime laws are the most effective way of combating hate.**

This myth is much beloved among the laws' advocates, for clear reasons: Why else promote them if they are not the most effective way to prevent these crimes? But the evidence that the laws have a strong preventative effect is only anecdotal and circumstantial. For example, many "hate groups"—white supremacists, skinheads, neo-Nazis and the like—are vehemently opposed to hate-crime laws. This is particularly true of such groups with a strong presence in the prison system (and by extension, among the violent criminal element), where the effect of the laws is felt directly in the form of longer terms behind bars. However, there is no statistical evidence to indicate that the laws prevent crimes from occurring, and the steadiness of the national rate of hate crimes over the past decade suggests that they have been ineffective—though of course, these statistics may also be affected by increasing awareness and understanding of hate crimes, and thus increased reporting. Also, the lack of coherent laws, both at the federal and state levels, could very well affect their efficacy negatively.

The reasons for passing hate-crime laws have much less to do with their ability to prevent hate crimes than with their ability to give communities and states—and their law-enforcement personnel—the tools to deal adequately with these crimes when they do arise. Moreover, the laws send an important "message"—one that has a more than salutary effect beyond merely the perceptions of various minority groups that they are now being "protected" by the laws. They are, in fact, an important statement for any society that cherishes civil rights and equality under the law.

Ultimately, however, the most effective means of preventing hate crimes involves much harder work than merely passing laws and enforcing them. It will require eliminating the conditions from which they arise: social disenfranchisement and the belief that "the Other" is to blame; bigotry and scapegoating; and glorification of a culture of violence. Clearly, these will take much longer to address, let alone dismantle.

If we look to the lynching era as an example, it becomes clear that lynching came to an end in the South and elsewhere not merely because of any laws passed against them, though a number of states did have anti-lynching laws on the books, and some did effectively enforce them in the 1920s and 1930s, especially in the Midwest. But what was most effective in the end was the gradual and utter stigmatization of lynching as even a remotely acceptable way to treat American minorities—which was an important transformation from a society that had for years celebrated lynching as a form of "community justice." This change occurred on a real grassroots level, through the efforts of organizations like the Association of Southern Women for the Prevention of Lynching. These groups believed, perhaps rightly, that real social change began by altering individual attitudes, and set about doing so through a program of outreach and education about lynching and its many harms. In the end, this method worked: By the 1950s, popular attitudes about lynching had completely reversed, and that sensibility has never changed. A similar program for hate crimes, in the end, would be every bit as effective for turning the tide against them.

✳

REASONED DEBATE

Of course, not all of the arguments raised by opponents and proponents of hate-crime laws are grounded in the loose sand of these myths. In fact, many on the opposing side raise reasonable concerns about free speech rights, the role of the federal government, and the real-world value of the laws. These opponents include not just the religious right (who, to be frank, only occasionally revert to these arguments, preferring instead the comfortable habit of their mythology) but also civil libertarians, free-speech advocates, and legal specialists. These well-grounded arguments come from sources ranging from the conservative/libertarian Cato Institute to the liberal National Association of Criminal Defense Lawyers, and include Jacobs's and Potter's thoughtful if problematic text, *Hate Crimes: Criminal Law and Identity Politics*.

However, most of these arguments do not bear up well under close scrutiny. Many raise points that should remain in mind of the laws' advocates, particularly the concerns about intruding on free-speech rights. But in the end none present a fatally convincing case against the laws—and in fact suggest deeper reasons for passing and enforcing them.

• **Hate-crime laws constitute "thought crimes"—the unconstitutional punishment of thought deemed to be offensive.**

This begins with a seemingly reasonable and simple argument: A simple assault will bring, perhaps, a two-year sentence; an assault committed with a bias motivation may bring as many as five. The only difference is in the thoughts of the perpetrator; therefore, the laws punish him for his or her thoughts. This, they argue, is in clear violation of the First Amendment protection of free speech.

Of course, as we have seen, the perpetrator's *mens rea,* or mental state, in fact is a fundamental feature of determining the severity of punishment for a broad range of crimes. The hate-crime laws currently on the books no more create thought crimes than do tougher sentences for first-degree murder.

The Supreme Court indeed dismissed in 1992, with its *R.A.V. v. St. Paul* ruling, an earlier version of some hate-crime laws for violating First Amendment principles. But the now commonly accepted form of bias-crime laws was endorsed unanimously by the Court a year later in *Wisconsin v. Mitchell,* an opinion authored by Chief Justice William Rehnquist. That ruling explicitly found that the laws, by focusing on criminal acts that are not protected the First Amendment, are perfectly constitutional:

> Mitchell argues [via the First Amendment] that the Wisconsin penalty-enhancement statute is invalid because it punishes the defendant's discriminatory motive, or reason, for acting. But motive plays the same role under the Wisconsin statute as it does under federal and state antidiscrimination laws, which we have previously upheld against constitutional challenge. . . . Title VII, of the Civil Rights Act of 1964, for example, makes it unlawful for an employer to discriminate against an employee "because of such individual's race, color, religion, sex, or national origin." . . . In Hishon, we rejected the argument that Title VII infringed employers' First Amendment rights. And more recently, in R.A.V. v. St. Paul, . . . we cited Title VII (as well as 18 U.S.C. 242 and 42 U.S.C. 1981 and 1982) as an example of a permissible content-neutral regulation of conduct.
>
> Nothing in our decision last Term in R.A.V. compels a different result here. That case involved a First Amendment challenge to a municipal ordinance prohibiting the use of " 'fighting words' that insult, or provoke violence, 'on the basis of race, color, creed, religion or gender.' . . . But whereas the ordinance struck down in R.A.V. was explicitly directed at expression (i.e.,

"speech" or "messages"), . . . the statute in this case is aimed at conduct un-
protected by the First Amendment."[19]

Put simply: The First Amendment protects speech, not conduct—thoughts,
not crimes. One cannot commit a crime and simply claim it as an act of free
speech. An assassin cannot kill the president and pretend he is protected by First
Amendment rights to political speech.

Indeed, underlying many of the arguments offered by opponents of hate-crime
laws (reflected, for instance, in the Traditional Values Coalition's charge that they
are "anti-Christian") is the notion that criminal behavior (such as assaulting or
threatening a gay person) somehow deserves First Amendment protections. But
crimes are not a form of free speech. Gay-bashing is no more a right than is lynching or even, say, assassinating the president. Political thought may motivate all of
them, but that doesn't mean the Constitution protects any of them.

However, it is worth noting that the speech-conduct distinction drawn by
the Court is not without its problems, in no small part because speech and conduct are so often inextricable. As Frederick Lawrence observes, "applying the distinction between conduct and expression requires a process that assumes its own
conclusions. That which we wish to punish we will term 'conduct' with expressive
value, and that which we wish to protect we will call 'expression' that requires
conduct as its means of communication."

On the other hand, Lawrence points to the distinction between bias
crimes and their underlying parallel crimes, which in effect create two tiers of
evidence for any kind of hate-crime prosecution to succeed. At both tiers, the
criminal's *mens rea* is an essential component. In the first tier of a crime—say,
an assault—the intent to commit the crime still must be established; at the second tier, both the first-level intent and the second-tier bias motivation must be
proven. For a bias-crime prosecution to succeed, it must establish both tiers of
mens rea. Thus someone who merely partakes of hate speech, with no intent to
intimidate, is guiltless of a hate crime, because the first tier of motivation is absent. But because menacing and intimidation, all of which in fact take the form
of words alone, are punishable crimes in every state, anyone using hate speech
to terrorize his neighbors has partaken of a bias crime.[20] The courts have *always*
recognized that First Amendment rights are not limitless, and established
crimes of violence indeed have always been one of their most significant
boundaries.

Consider, for instance, the example of cross burning. A white supremacist
who burns a cross at a private rally is undoubtedly voicing a kind of racial hate,
but there has been no attempt to intimidate or menace anyone, and no crime
has been committed. Likewise, someone who, say, dumped garbage on a black

neighbor's lawn would only be guilty of harassment or intimidation, not a bias crime (unless, of course, evidence existed that he had done so because of the neighbor's race). But someone who burns a cross on his neighbor's lawn has clearly committed a hate crime, because both the intent to intimidate and the motivation of racial hatred are clearly established. In this sense, hate-crime laws avoid running afoul of the First Amendment in the same fashion as any other of the myriad sentence-enhancement laws, including anti-terrorism statutes, because they all reflect the differences in *mens rea* among acts that are already established crimes.

And indeed the Supreme Court recently has moved in this direction in upholding the constitutionality of hate-crime laws. A cross-burning case, *Virginia v. Black,* produced a March 2003 ruling (authored by Sandra Day O'Connor) that followed this logic closely. The state of Virginia, the Court said, was well within its rights to outlaw cross-burnings meant to intimidate:

> The protections the First Amendment affords speech and expressive conduct are not absolute. This Court has long recognized that the government may regulate certain categories of expression consistent with the Constitution. . . . For example, the First Amendment permits a State to ban "true threats," . . . which encompass those statements where the speaker means to communicate a serious expression of an intent to commit an act of unlawful violence to a particular individual or group of individuals. . . . The speaker need not actually intend to carry out the threat. Rather, a prohibition on true threats protects individuals from the fear of violence and the disruption that fear engenders, as well as from the possibility that the threatened violence will occur. . . . Intimidation in the constitutionally proscribable sense of the word is a type of true threat, where a speaker directs a threat to a person or group of persons with the intent of placing the victim in fear of bodily harm or death.[21]

At the same time, the court threw out the provisions of Virginia's law that would have made *any* cross-burning a de facto attempt to intimidate and thus proscribed. This is, again, consistent with the logic proposed by Lawrence (who, as it happens, helped advise the attorneys arguing the Virginia case).

Hate-crime statutes are still evolving as a matter of law, and will continue to do so for years. What the body of these rulings makes clear, however, is that the bias-crime laws now on the books do not create "thought crimes," nor do they chill or suppress anyone's right to speak and think freely. They simply punish the decision to act inappropriately upon those thoughts—by committing what is already a crime. As such, they just remove the fig leaf of "free speech" from crimes that clearly harm both individuals and society.

- *The underlying criminal activity of a hate crime, such as robbery, assault, or murder, traditionally falls under state jurisdiction. There is growing concern that by passing federal hate crime laws, there will be a mass federalization of crime that should and could be adequately handled at the state level instead of overburdening our already overwhelmed federal courts.*

This concern, while legitimate, is not very well grounded. Neither the current federal hate-crimes laws, nor the latest federal bias-crime legislation currently making its way through the Senate, step into state jurisdictions in any form.

The federal hate-crimes laws, either on the books or proposed, so far restrict themselves to sentence enhancements for federal crimes committed with a bias motivation. In this respect, they closely resemble federal anti-terrorism laws, at least structurally; these laws, too, deal only with federal crimes committed with a terroristic intent.

The current federal law, passed in 1995, in fact is extremely limited (and nearly useless) because it restricts federal law enforcers from filing a hate-crime charge unless the crime is committed on federal property or as a disruption of a federal activity (including voting). The new version, currently making its way forward in the Senate, largely eliminates this limitation, but is even more explicit about maintaining state and local prerogatives, and restricting the federal government primarily to the role of financier, coordinator and helper. The 2001 version of the bill, named the Local Law Enforcement Enhancement Act, contains even more explicit language carefully limiting the role of federal authorities vis à vis local and state officials, and carefully defining the precise roles of each, with the latter being given the lion's share of control of these cases.

Hate-crime laws do raise important questions about federalism—but then, all federal criminal legislation raises them. These include their antecedents in the Reconstruction (particularly the Civil Rights Act of 1866 and the Enforcement Act of 1870) and in the anti-lynching legislation of the 1920s and '30s. And of course, the federal hate-crimes laws on the books (as well as those proposed to date) are very circumspect and limited in scope, largely for just this reason.

- *In many cases, it is very difficult to prove a hateful motivation for the criminal act. The FBI, for example, includes gestures and other body language in its hate crime statistics. Prosecutions to date in some cases have been based upon bigoted statements made several years before the act in question.*

There is no doubt that the main point here is true: Establishing a bias motivation is unquestionably the most difficult aspect of prosecuting these cases. Indeed, the bar is extremely high, since proving this motivation requires relying on both previous statements or associations and with establishing the perpetrator's state of mind, or *mens rea*, at the time of the act.

Most prosecutors in fact are reluctant to file such charges for precisely these reasons. That being the case, most hate-crime prosecutions occur only when the evidence is clear and substantial. In other words, the well-established structure of the criminal courts provides the strongest insurance against abuse or questionable prosecutions. At times this barrier may fail, but not often. This is frankly no different than in any other area of criminal law.

- *The gender provision of the proposed federal expansion bill could make run-of-the-mill rape and domestic violence incidents "federal hate crimes." The disability provision could result in basic crimes against disabled victims—such as mugging a person in a wheelchair—being prosecuted as "federal hate crimes." The result is a trivialization of the federal criminal sanction.*

This is simply so unlikely to happen as to border on being simply false. Establishing a bias motivation—which is at the core of filing a hate-crimes charge—is, as already noted, an extremely high bar that requires more than simply a few words uttered during or before the commission of the crime. Prosecutors typically must prove several aggravating factors; they must demonstrate a pattern of behavior consistent with the bias, as well as a willingness or desire to use extreme or criminal means to act upon it. A simple mugging or rape does not meet this standard; but a gang of youths who systematically attack handicapped people over the course of a night, or a rapist who delights in terrorizing not just his victims but the community with misogynist taunts—these do.

Moreover, even though the federal government may possess the authority to engage in dual prosecutions, the U.S. Justice Department in fact employs a standing bar to double jeopardy called the "Petite Policy," which restricts federal prosecutions in the wake of a state trial to cases in which "substantial federal interests" remain "demonstrably unvindicated." This, in practice, is only a handful of cases, and is likely to remain so, considering the severity of the limits.[22]

- *In many cases, enhanced penalties are not even possible. In most states, the penalty for murder is life in prison, and in many, the death penalty is already available.*

This is both true and untrue. It is certainly true that at the upper end of the criminal spectrum—particularly with murder—there is very little sentence enhancement to be obtained by trying the case under hate-crime laws (though, as already noted, hate-crime elements can in fact help prosecutors raise the penalties they pursue to the death-sentence level). Indeed, because the bar is so high on those laws, it is extremely rare to see a prosecutor even attempt it, especially if the evidence related to the parallel crime is overwhelming.

The most prominent example of this, of course, was the Jasper case—James Byrd's killers were not tried under a hate-crime law, but rather under Texas's murder law. (Because it was clearly a hate crime, the federal government was able to chip in and assist the state prosecutors who were handling the case with some $250,000 in grants, nearly a third of the trial's cost to the county. This in fact is the reality of how hate-crimes laws currently work vis-à-vis the federalism issue.) However, it's worth recalling that Buford Furrow, the neo-Nazi who shot up a Jewish day-care center and killed a postal worker in Los Angeles in the spring of 2000, in fact faced both local and federal hate-crime charges, despite the fact that his crimes neared the upper end of the spectrum.

But it is simply not true that these constitute "many" cases. In fact, murder, as we have noted, is probably the least prosecuted of all hate-crime charges. There are annually only a tiny handful of such cases at best. The vast bulk of bias-crime cases involve assaults, intimidation, property crimes and vandalism. In the end, this argument does not pertain to them—because clearly, in those cases, there is considerable room for sentence enhancement.

- *These are simply message laws—there is no evidence to suggest that hate crime laws will have a deterrent effect upon hate crimes.*

There's very little evidence, actually, that laws against murder have a deterrent effect on would-be killers, either. This does not mean we should not have laws against murder. Indeed, deterrence is often the weakest argument for or against any kind of law that affects punishment.

Hate-crime laws, as we have seen, exist for a panoply of sound reasons, the main one being that they provide communities with the tools to confront these crimes, which are clearly different in nature and intent than their parallel crimes. Moreover, their value in sending a "message" is not merely ephemeral, but in itself presents a different kind of real deterrence.

The "expressive value" of punishment as form of social approbation has always been a fundamental feature of modern criminal law, as Lawrence argues in detail.[23] The British Royal Commission on Capital Punishment, in a report for the Parliament, put it this way: "[The] ultimate justification for any punishment is, not that it is a deterrent, but that it is the emphatic denunciation by the community of a crime."[24] Laws against murder are surely on the books as much to make clear society's utter proscription of such acts as to protect itself.

Laws against hate crimes are not mere measures to send a message to various special-interest groups that their constituencies are being "protected"—they are an important element of law for any democratic society that is serious about protecting its values of equal opportunity and access and racial/religious harmony. On a fundamental level, hate-crime laws combat the conditions that give rise to this violence by creating a social base line, much like the line against any other kinds of crimes. They embed in the larger society the core values of fair play in a democracy, and help instill a basic awareness of the wrongness of such acts. This is not simply a matter of sending a message, but of establishing a basic, and deeply American, value.

- *The laws only exist on the books because of agitation from special-interest groups, and as such they really are only feel-good measures that do little good, and may create more harm along the way.*

There can be little doubt that advocacy by a variety of special interests—civil-rights groups, victim-rights organizations, ethnic and racial associations, gay and lesbian advocates—played major roles in the passage of hate-crime laws across the country, including at the state level. As sociologist Valerie Jenness describes, "the hate crime policy domain was built upon a foundation laid by the anti-hate-crime movement, which, in turn, was made possible by a handful of earlier social movements that provided its central discursive themes and strategies," notably the civil-rights and victims-rights movements, which originated respectively on the political left and right in America.[25] Moreover, it is equally true that those advocates, particularly in the early years, created a false portrait of a "rising tide" of violence that in fact was a fairly constant feature of American life.

But focusing on the movements somewhat distorts the larger picture, which included those many states—like Idaho, Washington, and California—who were at least partially, if not largely, driven to pass hate-crimes laws out of a grassroots demand for them. This demand was created by communities who were being confronted with hate crimes and their awful ramifications for the first time and were desperate in many cases for adequate tools to prosecute them, since it was clear in many cases that the standing laws for the parallel crimes (intimidation, vandalism, and assault especially) were inadequate for pursuing and punishing these cases.

Recall, if you will, the local prosecutors in northern Idaho who traveled to the capital to lobby for a hate-crimes law because their communities were demanding the help. This phenomenon occurred throughout the country, though in many cases their efforts were overshadowed by the advocacy groups' campaigns. Nonetheless, local law officers, prosecutors, and a variety of regional and local church-based organizations have also played vital roles in the passage of the hate-crimes laws at the state and federal level, and that continues to be true today. The Local Law Enforcement Enhancement Act currently before Congress counts among its supporters both law enforcement and prosecutors' associations.

As in Idaho, many other states had found that even though white supremacy, culturally speaking, had been relegated to the fringes of society, its remaining adherents were every bit as willing to resort to violence, or to advocate it, to achieve their ends as they were in the days of the lynch mob. And it was also clear that the violent crimes that resulted were not ordinary assaults and murders and threats, but had several special qualities to them. For one, they were inherently more violent, and much more likely to result in severe harm. More significantly, they clearly victimized not just the immediate sufferer but the larger racial, ethnic or religious community to which that person belonged—and that in many cases, this was exactly what the perpetrators intended, as a way of "putting them in their place." This not only extended the reach of these crimes, but it made clear that they were perniciously anti-democratic, and clearly destructive in a society supposedly dedicated to racial justice and equality.

While special-interest advocacy played a lead role in passing hate-crimes laws in America, the laws gained broad support on both the right and left because communities at the base level recognized the need for them. They arose, as it were, from the kind of common-sense decency that has always been an embedded element of American law.

Thus it is simply not true—or at best, only partially true—that, as Jacobs and Potter contend, "[t]he passage of hate crimes laws . . . did not occur because of a lacuna in the criminal law, or because some horrendous criminals could not be ad-

equately prosecuted and punished under existing laws. Insufficient or unduly lenient criminal law is not a problem that afflicts that United States."[26] There are
literally thousands of hate-crime victims and their families who, before the passage of the laws, would have watched their tormentors get off with a slap on the
wrist who would beg to differ. And there are hundreds of prosecutors who likewise
can attest to the inadequacy of ordinary intimidation, vandalism, and assault laws
in confronting hate crimes.

Jacobs and Potter carry this flawed argument to its logical conclusion and beyond, contending indeed that instead of helping to heal the racial divide, bias-
crime laws make things worse:

> Our concern is that rewriting criminal law to take into account the racial, re-
> ligious, sexual, and other identities of offenders and victims will undermine
> the criminal law's potential for bolstering social solidarity. By redefining
> crime as a facet of intergroup conflict, hate crime laws encourage citizens to
> think of themselves as victimized and besieged, thereby hardening each
> group's sense of resentment. That in turn contributes to the balkanization of
> American society, not to its unification. [27]

This particular passage is riddled with the problems that plague Jacobs and
Potter's arguments throughout. Again, as elsewhere, their description of hate
crimes laws is derived from the idea that they create special "protected groups."
Moreover, they turn on its head the reality of what hate-crime laws achieve, and
what conversely is the effect of the failure to pass or enforce them.

Bias-crime laws do not redefine crime as a mere facet of intergroup conflict—
they specifically recognize that certain crimes are in fact *a direct cause* of intergroup conflict, and indeed worsen the divide between us. The laws are intended to
close the divide, or at least prevent it from worsening. Indeed, it is specifically the
failure to enact and enforce hate-crime laws throughout history (and this includes
their antecedents in the filibustered-to-death anti-lynching laws of the 1920s and
'30s) that encourages minority citizens to "think of themselves as victimized and
besieged," and there is little doubt it hardens their resentment when these crimes
are treated generically.

Hate-crime laws are clearly intended to heal the racial divide, not widen it.
And it is equally clear that failing to recognize the differences inherent in the
crimes quantifiably worsens the gap.

But do they make a real difference? As we will shortly explore, that all depends—largely on how well the laws are enforced. And that, in turn, ultimately
depends on how well they are understood, and how thoroughly the myths surrounding them are dispelled.

✳

Hate-crime laws are relatively new laws, and understanding them in some regards requires rearranging our traditional ways of thinking. Certainly, it requires dispelling many long-favored myths. But in the final analysis, they represent something that, given the perspective of history, is a long thread running through American culture, something many of us almost instinctively understand—that is, the ethical imperative to stand up against the bullies and the thugs and the nightriders, because their whole purpose is to terrorize, oppress and disenfranchise the people they deem different or "not American." Hate-crime laws at their core draw on Americans' sense of decency and fair play, and to the extent they are enforced fairly and adequately, they are an important reflection of those traits.

The old anti-lynching laws from which hate-crime laws are descended were never approved, mostly because of the vehement opposition of the Deep South. But the spirit that drove them has remained alive and resurfaced in more congenial times.

Frederick Lawrence, perhaps, sums it up best in *Punishing Hate:*

> If bias crimes are not punished more harshly than parallel crimes, the implicit message expressed by the criminal justice system is that racial harmony and equality are not among the highest values in our society. If a racially motivated assault is punished identically to a parallel assault, the racial motivation of the bias crime is rendered largely irrelevant and thus not part of that which is condemned. The individual victim, the target community, and indeed the society at large thus suffer the twin insults akin to those suffered by Ralph Ellison's *Invisible Man.* Not only has the crime itself occurred, but the underlying hatred of the crime is invisible to the eyes of the legal system.[28]

Hate crimes in recent years have come to the nation's attention in large part through the outpourings of rage and anger inspired by the murders of James Byrd in Texas and Mathew Shepard in Wyoming, as well as the respective rampages of Benjamin Smith in Illinois and Indiana and Buford Furrow in Los Angeles. But the reality is that the mass of hate crimes occur without such fanfare, and in fact may strike our communities at times without our even being aware of them. Dealing with them at that level—in the sometimes mundane daily world of small towns especially—requires an awareness of the real harm they can bring . . . and lacking such knowledge can have disastrous consequences.

In Ocean Shores, the Fourth of July hate crimes did not occur out of the blue. They grew in an environment in which no one was even capable of recognizing a bias crime when it stared them in the face. It took several days of buildup to finally burst into a bloody event no one could ignore.

But when the dust finally settled six months later in the Grays Harbor courtroom, the community managed to pick itself up, collect its breath and do the right thing. In the end, that core of American decency prevailed.

CHAPTER 12

THE TRIAL, DAY FOUR: IN FEAR

THE DAVID DUKE FACTOR, LONG DREADED BY THE GRAYS HARBOR police, finally made its appearance on Monday: David Jensen, the operator of the western Washington chapter of Duke's National Organization For European American Rights (NO FEAR) arrived that morning. As disturbances go, it wasn't much.

There was understandable concern about the white supremacists. They had been agitating loudly for murder charges against both Hong brothers, and were using Chris Kinison as a martyr figure in their propaganda for the "white cause." Rumors had flown that Duke—a rather notorious national figure as a former Ku Klux Klansman and Louisiana politician with a penchant for the spotlight— would put in an appearance himself. Jensen had likewise intimated that a whole squadron of fellow supremacists would be appearing at the trial and perhaps even protesting outside.

In reality, Duke had been in Russia organizing white supremacists there since January of 2000, and was still in Moscow at the time of the trial. He remained overseas proselytizing among fellow anti-Semites in Russia, Africa, and the Middle East for a total of three years, in no small part because FBI agents had charged him, just about the time he departed, with mail fraud and income-tax invasion stemming from what was revealed to be Duke's penchant for big-stakes gambling, which he had underwritten with money donated to his nonprofit organizations. (He eventually returned and plea-bargained his way into a fifteen-month prison sentence and a $10,000 fine.) There was literally no chance he would show up in Montesano, not unless he wanted the town to be a stage for his arrest.[1]

Instead, only Jensen himself showed, in fairly subdued fashion. He chatted with a couple of reporters briefly outside the courtroom, complaining that the county clerk had misled him about the dates of the Hong trial. He said the clerk's office had told him it didn't begin until December 12—that day.

(David Scheer of the Aberdeen *Daily World* checked with County Clerk Cheryl Brown, who said no one in her office would have intentionally misled Jensen. She noted that a trial for a man named Horn was set to begin December 12.)

Though a murmur crossed the courtroom when Jensen first entered, he took a seat toward the back of the room and scribbled notes quietly. Kinison's family and friends, still seated near to the jury at one corner of the room, occasionally cast dirty looks in his direction. Minh Hong's family and his few supporters, seated mostly on the other side toward the front, just ignored him.

It was clear that Molly Kinison especially was upset by his presence. She stiffly ignored him throughout the proceedings and brushed past him during a break in the trial. The counselor who was at her side for much of the trial, Michaelan McDougal, told reporters that Jensen was not a welcome sight: "I don't think she is happy about [his presence] at all," she said. "They don't want him here. They don't even know him."[2]

I talked outside for awhile with Jensen during one of those breaks. He is a stocky fire plug of a man, about five-foot-eight, with graying blonde hair and a ready smile, though he has a diffident, offhanded demeanor that may be intended to project a cynical air. He smiled a little when I asked him whether Duke himself was going to show.

"I don't know where that rumor got started," he said.

He complained to me about the alleged "screwing" he got from the county clerk. He insisted that NO FEAR wasn't "a hate group." "I checked these guys out before I ever joined them," he said. "They're not into all that racist talk. They're genuinely about advancing white rights. That's what I care about. The endangered white male."

On our way back in, he saw Molly Kinison coming out of the courtroom. He walked up and tried to talk to her. She turned on him coldly and said, "You're not welcome here."

Jensen left quietly a little while later. It didn't matter. He wasn't the show that day, or any day in the near future. That day, the spotlight was on Minh Hong.

✳

If there was a hidden side to Minh Duc Hong—a cold-blooded killer, quick with a knife—then prosecutors had done little to persuade anyone it really existed. And when Hong himself took the stand, the notion largely evaporated.

The man who sat quietly on the witness stand with his hands folded, peering out through a pair of thick glasses, was exactly as any number of witnesses had already described him: polite, well-mannered, a little shy. Those who already knew him saw the gentle, thoughtful young man they had always known. He was soft-spoken and hesitant at times, but never nervous—and in fact, remarkably calm and steady throughout. Even when he was being pressed by prosecutors, his voice never lost its steel or evenness; he exhibited a reservoir of courage, or something like it, beneath the timid exterior. By the end of his testimony, many in the audience had a better idea why he had survived that night and Chris Kinison had not.

The nightmare began, Hong said, when they arrived at the store and got out of their car and were confronted by the group of "five or six" white men. "They looked like skinheads to me," he said. And they were standing between them and the door. He and his friends tried filing by in single file and were promptly subjected to verbal assaults.

He said "a man with a Confederate flag" shouted slurs in his face, and the entire group of white men mocked them: "Ching chong!," "Slant-eyes!" But Hong said the trio made it inside the store without physical contact.

Once inside, the three of them milled about and found the noodles they had come for. Kinison, though, started peering at them through the store window behind the clerk. Minh Hong said that Doug was the first to notice.

"Doug told me. . . . And then we looked over at someone with a shaved head and the flag and he pointed to us, did the slicing-the-neck"—at this, Minh ran his finger across his throat—"and then pointed to the door." Hong said the gesture's meaning was clear: "He wanted to cut my throat when I came outside." He said he made it "several times."

That was when Hong saw the two paring knives on the store shelf. He took them out of their packaging there and stuffed them deep in the pockets of his puffy yellow coat. Then they went back outside, because "it seemed quieter."

But only for a moment. Kinison's group sat on the sidewalk next to the convenience store when they came out, Hong said, and so the three Asian men walked out into the driveway to get around them. They weren't getting off so easy: Kinison, he said, was suddenly in his ear, taunting him, spitting on him, shouting loudly in his face: "You don't effing belong here. Go back to your country," was how Hong described it.

They made it safely to their car, Hong said—"I was very relieved"—and, with Hung Hong behind the wheel, they tried to drive away through what looked like the nearest exit. Kinison, Hong said, stepped into their path, raising and waving his Confederate flag, as they tried to pass the pumps. When they stopped, he said, "something hit the car," and they saw others standing about nearby. They concluded that they were trapped. Hong testified that he reached for his cell phone:

"I dialed 911 but my carrier, VoiceStream, they don't have any service down here." He held the phone up, he said, so their assailants could see it, but it had no apparent effect.

At that point, they decided to just abandon their car and flee, Hong testified: "My brother said, 'Just make a run for it. Leave everything.'" Hung Hong got out first, and then Doug Chen climbed out of the back seat. Kinison, he said, kept shouting racial slurs, especially at his brother. As he sat in the front passenger seat, Minh Hong said, he saw Kinison punch his brother, twice, knocking him to the ground. He saw another man attack Doug Chen. That was when he decided to move.

"I came out of the car and I wanted to push [Kinison] away," Hong said. "Before I got to the person with the flag, I got hit in the face." He said the blow knocked his glasses off, rendering him essentially sightless.

That was when Kinison grabbed him by the throat, Hong said, and started hitting him. "I did not pull the knife out at first," he said. He felt a sharp pain in his hand and arm, and that was when he reached for one of the knives in his pocket. He said he used only the one blade, and that he only blindly slashed in Kinison's direction: "I know I had used the knife, I didn't know I had stabbed anyone."

"I was trying to get away from the attack," Hong explained. "At that point, I was in fear for my life. He made me believe my life was in danger."

He lost track of Hung Hong during the fight, he said, and had no idea where his brother was until they got back to the car and someone handed his glasses to him. However, he also insisted that he didn't take the knives with him. He denied ever telling police that he had thrown them from the window.

Jerry Fuller, sensing an opening in cross-examination, began harping on Minh Hong's recorded falsehoods during his initial conversations with police. But Hong explained that he was simply frightened at the time: "I didn't know anyone got hurt," he said. "I felt terrible that I lied to the cop about the knives. I told him that I had never stolen anything before."

"I see," said Fuller. "What you're telling me is that you were concerned about shoplifting a $1.98 knife."

"Yes," said Hong, somewhat perplexedly. "I was still in shock at what had happened."

Hong also denied ever having spoken with Amanda Algeo—"I wouldn't say anything like that"—adding that he didn't even recognize her. He said he did chat with another woman inside the Texaco, but he was only asking whether any restaurants were open that late at night.

His brother, he pointed out, was the member of their group who had stood in the line to pay for their things.

No one emphasized this point much, but it blew apart the relevance of Algeo's testimony, which was suddenly revealed as a case of understandable mistaken identity. If she had spoken with anyone in line at the store, it wasn't Minh Hong. If anyone had said, "He's going down," it was more likely his identical twin. But it was Minh, not Hung Hong, who was on trial.

In the end, Fuller's depiction of Minh Hong as a liar ran headlong into Hong himself. His testimony may have been riddled with the taint of self-interest that infected most of the stories told in the courtroom, but the quiet simplicity of it, and the understated integrity of the person telling it, revealed more than any confused knifing scenarios. If Minh Hong was fabricating, he was exceptionally good at it. By the end of his testimony, no one was weeping. But there was a breath of silence, as the audience and jury digested his story, and as some placed themselves in his shoes, and wondered, perhaps, whether they would have handled the events of that night as well.

The defense then announced, to everyone's surprise, that—three witnesses into its case—it had rested. The day had already run late, so the trial was called to an end for the day. Closing argument would wait for the morning.

CHAPTER 13

WALL OF SILENCE

EVEN THOUGH MOST PEOPLE HAVE SOME CONFUSION about what constitutes a hate crime, at times it can be unmistakable: They know it when they see it. In Grays Harbor County, it was almost a matter of common sense that what happened on the Fourth of July in Ocean Shores was something well out of the ordinary, and if any act deserved the name, this did. "Of course it was a hate crime," says Aberdeen *Daily World* editor John Hughes. "I think most people in town understood that it was."

Yet, even though the Ocean Shores case clearly involved all the elements of a hate crime—the racially biased motivations, the threats and intimidation and ultimately the assaults—no bias-crime prosecution ever emerged from it. Of course, the FBI investigated, and found it did not fit the parameters of federal law. Both the Ocean Shores police and the Grays Harbor County Sheriff's Office briefly investigated the incidents (including the assaults on other minorities in the days leading up to the Fourth of July) as hate crimes, and concluded that because the participants were so tight-lipped, it would be difficult to proceed with a case. However, as we will see, clear evidence of a hate crime involving people beyond just Chris Kinison was produced (by the prosecution, no less) at Minh Hong's trial. In spite of this, the Grays Harbor County prosecutor never considered filing hate-crime charges against the other participants in that day's events.

Yet oddly enough, the Ocean Shores incidents did turn up that year in the state's Uniform Crime Reports for bias crimes, and they appeared in the FBI's annual hate-crime statistics as well. What that means is that officers in the Ocean Shores PD and the sheriff's office filed reports with the state (they appear in the statistics as one anti-black incident, and two separate anti-Asian incidents). In other words, police recognized the cases as hate crimes—but the prosecutors did not.

If Minh and Hung Hong (or, for that matter, the Filipino family terrorized by Kinison's friends) felt victimized by this, they at least had one consolation: they weren't alone. Indeed, there are many more hate crimes reported than prosecuted every year, which suggests statistically something that in-depth studies have corroborated—namely, that there is a serious disconnect among police, prosecutors regarding how bias crimes are pursued and reported. The result is frequently the same as in cases of rape: What has befallen the victim is treated as unimportant, or worse, as deserved.

Many victims have it far worse. Their cases are never reported or treated as hate crimes at all. And when we examine these gaps closer, we can see just how deep the chasm truly runs.

❋

Every year, literally thousands of bias crimes—the estimates run as high as 40,000 annually—go unreported and uninvestigated in America. Many times the crimes in fact result in charges, but only those arising from the parallel crimes. The hate-crime aspects of the acts go unnoticed—a fact which has many far-reaching effects, both in terms of policy and society at large. Among these are the real-world effects of leaving the victims' greater trauma unrecognized, as well as ignoring the terror the crimes may inflict on the targeted minority community.

The problem, of course, is not one of mere numbers, but of real flesh and blood, death and life. Consider the following cases, which are typical of the failures of the system:

BILLY JACK GAITHER

Gaither was an openly gay thirty-nine-year-old textile factory worker who lived quietly in the small town of Sylacauga, Alabama. On the night of February 19, 1999, two other local men—Steven Eric Mullins, twenty-five, and Charles Monroe Butler, twenty-one—drove Gaither from a local drinking spot to a boat ramp and beat him badly with an ax handle, then threw him in the trunk and drove fifteen miles to remote Peckerwood Creek. Once there, they proceeded to beat him to death, then threw his corpse on a pile of tires, doused it with kerosene and lit it aflame. They later told police they had plotted Gaither's death for two weeks because he allegedly had made an advance at Mullins.[1]

Both men were eventually convicted of murder, but were spared the death penalty at the request of Gaither's family. However, Gaither's murder was neither prosecuted as a hate crime (for reasons similar to the James Byrd case; the state's murder laws were more effective in a capital case such as this one) nor was it ever reported as one. Indeed, the state of Alabama has not filed a hate-crimes report for years—and Gaither's murder was never reported to FBI statistics-gatherers as a hate crime.

DANNY OVERSTREET

On a relatively calm evening on September 22, 2000, a man wearing a black trench coat approached another man in a Roanoke, Virginia, alleyway and "asked where the gay bar was, because he wanted to waste some gay people," as a police spokeswoman later described it. The man pulled aside his coat and flashed his gun—but thinking the man was joking, the other man pointed him in the general direction of a local gay bar.

Instead of heading there, however, the man in the trench coat—a fifty-five-year-old drifter and Vietnam veteran named Ronald Gay—showed up a few minutes later in a different gay and lesbian tavern and ordered a beer at the bar. Danny Overstreet was among the patrons there that night.

Overstreet, a forty-three-year-old gay man, was enjoying a quiet evening at a table near the door of the tavern. After Overstreet hugged a friend at the table with him, Ronald Gay stepped away from the bar, drew aside his trench coat, pulled out a nine-millimeter handgun and began firing. He hit Overstreet in the chest with the first shot and killed him almost instantly, then continued firing. Five other people were wounded, three of them seriously, before Gay walked outside and tossed the gun. Police apprehended him two blocks away.

In an interview with police, Gay said he was angry about the meaning the word "gay" had acquired, and was humiliated that four of his sons had changed their names. The following March, just before his trial, Gay composed a rambling letter to the *Roanoke Times* calling himself a "Christian Soldier working for my Lord" and contending he was told by God to kill gays. "Jesus does not want these people in his heaven," he wrote, adding that homosexual "meeting places and bars" should be "burnt to kill" the AIDS virus, "or slow it down." He added, ominously: "When I am gone another will take my place."[2]

Gay pleaded guilty to murder and multiple counts of malicious wounding, and was sentenced to four life terms in prison. But the crimes were never reported or prosecuted as hate crimes. Roanoke's official entry in the 2000 FBI statistics shows one hate crime in the year 2000—but none under "sexual orientation."

PRIVATE BARRY WINCHELL

Winchell was a twenty-one-year-old Missouri boy who was stationed at the Army base in Fort Campbell, Kentucky, who found himself rudely awakened from his sleep the early morning of July 5, 1999. Two of his fellow recruits forced him outside the barracks and then one of them—an eighteen-year-old private named Calvin Glover, who just two days before had been knocked down by Winchell—proceeded to beat him to the verge of death with a baseball bat. Winchell died of his injuries the next day.

At first, Army officials treated the case as a result of drunken youths becoming violent, saying only that Winchell's injuries were the result of a "physical altercation." But news reports, spurred by information provided by the Service Members Legal Defense Fund (a Washington-based organization devoted to providing support for gays and lesbians in the military), began revealing that the murder may have been motivated by anti-gay bias.[3] And it may have been encouraged by the conduct of camp officers.

It emerged that, earlier in the year, Winchell had begun dating a transvestite dancer from Nashville. Subsequently, his sergeant had made inquiries about Winchell's sexuality that were well known throughout the platoon. For months, his fellow recruits had taunted and abused him with epithets ("faggot," "queer," "homo"). When asked at the subsequent trial why he didn't intervene, the sergeant responded: "Everybody was having fun." It became clear that Winchell had run afoul of the Catch–22 inherent in the military's recently adopted "Don't Ask, Don't Tell" policy regarding gays within their ranks: Winchell was unable to report the abuse without revealing his own homosexuality.

Eventually, the Army acknowledged that the murder probably was a hate crime. Nonetheless, Winchell's attackers were never charged accordingly, nor were their sentences enhanced for the bias elements of the crime. Glover was found guilty that December and sentenced to life imprisonment with the possibility of parole; his cohort, twenty-six-year-old Justin Fisher (Winchell's former bunkmate) was given a twelve-and-a-half-year sentence for obstructing the investigation and lying to officials about the killing.

The following July 21, Army officials released a report exonerating all the officers at Fort Campbell of any misconduct in the case (though it admitted that "there were some incidents where violations of policy occurred"). And the Winchell murder was not included among Kentucky's hate crimes reported to the FBI in 1999.

SASEZLEY RICHARDSON

Sometimes being a crime victim comes down to bad luck, and nineteen-year-old Sasezley Richardson couldn't have had it any worse. Walking home from a trip to buy diapers for a friend's infant at a local mall in Elkhart, Indiana, on November 20, 1999, Richardson had the misfortune to be on the sidewalk when Jason Powell and Alex Witmer, ages twenty and nineteen, drove up looking for a black man to shoot.

Both men sported the shaven "skinhead" look and a full complement of hate toward minorities. Witmer was a reputed member of the Aryan Brotherhood, a white-supremacist organization based largely in the nation's prison system; Powell wanted to join, and was told by Witmer he would have to kill a black man. So the pair drove up alongside Richardson as he strolled down the sidewalk, and at Witmer's urging, Powell pulled out a handgun and fired twelve shots, two of which hit Richardson, one of them in the head. They drove off and left him bleeding by roadside. He died three days later.

Powell eventually pleaded guilty and was given a life sentence with no chance of parole. Witmer received an eighty-five-year prison sentence. The cases were not tried as hate crimes, and Elkhart police failed to file reports with the state to include the Richardson case in its annual bias-crime statistics. According to FBI reports, Elkhart had no hate crimes in 1999.

✴

These, of course, are all higher-profile cases, the ones that made headlines. And because they all involve murders, bias-crime laws were unlikely to be in play— though it must be observed that because they were not, several of the perpetrators of these killings got off with relatively lenient sentences. In any event, all were bias-motivated murders, of which there are actually only a handful of cases annually. As such, they do not really embody the larger problem, except for the vivid colors in which they illustrate the nature of hate crimes and the failures of law enforcement to handle them adequately.

Far more representative are the thousands of assaults, threats and vandalism incidents that are clearly bias-motivated but are neither prosecuted as hate crimes nor reported to the FBI as such. A mere sampling:

- **A building** and car in Amenia, New York, are spray-painted with neo-Nazi graffiti, but police do not report it as a hate crime, and only briefly investigate it, because the case "was not of a level that the FBI would get," a police spokesman tells the Southern Poverty Law Center (SPLC). Nonetheless, the two suspects are tried and convicted for felony criminal mischief.[4]

- **While committing** a series of home-invasion robberies in Indianapolis, three men break into an apartment occupied by two men whom they come to believe are gay. They force the men to strip at gunpoint, tie them together and begin torturing them with a hot iron, all the while kicking and beating them with various household items, including a small baseball bat; taunts and homophobic remarks accompanied the attack. One of the victims is forced to drink a combination of urine and bleach. Finally, after more than half an hour, the three men leave, and attempt to set the building afire on their way out—though, strangely enough, they return to douse the fire and give the victim who had been forced to swallow bleach a drink of water. Only one of the assailants is caught and charged. Indiana has no hate-crimes law, so no such charges were ever considered.[5]

- **Someone paints** anti-Semitic, anti-black, and anti-Hawaiian slurs on some fourteen cars in a student parking lot at the University of Nevada, Las Vegas. But campus police decline to investigate it or report it as a hate crime, contending later that they "thought it was just juveniles playing a practical joke"—and besides, a spokesman tells the SPLC, "it wasn't on a Jewish person's car." However, at least one black student reports that his car was covered with anti-black graffiti.[6]

- **Three young men** spend forty-five minutes or more threatening and assaulting gays in Salt Lake City, Utah, on February 7, 1999. They begin by standing outside a well-known gay bar and threatening people who leave. They ask one man, "Are you a faggot?" When he fails to respond, one of the trio shouts, "He is a faggot!" and all begin chasing him. The man reaches his car safely, but his assailants pound on it until he darts back out and runs back to the bar, where he calls police. The three men then cruise about town and throw a beer bottle at two other men in a car they decide are "queers." Then they return to the bar and physically assault two men just leaving. They later tell police they were "just out for a good time." They are charged under Utah's bias-crime statute, which (like Texas' law) toughens penalties for crimes committed "because of the defendant's bias or prejudice against a person or group." When the case proceeds before a state judge, he throws out the hate-crimes charges, ruling that the law's unconstitutionally vague language renders it "incomplete" and "unenforceable." The two later pleaded guilty to misdemeanor assault charges.[7]

- **A lesbian woman** who, along with her partner and eleven-year-old daughter, had endured months of harassment from her neighbors in Germantown, Maryland (including rocks thrown at their home), is allegedly assaulted by a local man and his twelve-year-old son on April 15, 2000. She claims that the pair kicked her repeatedly as she lay on the ground, the

youngster shouting, "I'm going to kill you, dyke bitch!" When police arrive, the victim is bleeding on the ground, footprints on her shirt and
marks on her neck, for which she is hospitalized overnight. Nonetheless,
Germantown police decline to arrest the man because they did not witness
the crime, although he later is charged. The county attorney later observes
(angrily) that he could not charge the man with a hate crime because
Maryland's bias-crime law does not include sexual orientation as a category.[8] However, the case is eventually dropped because witnesses disagreed
about the nature of the attack.[9]

- **Racist graffiti** is painted on the home of Dennis "Oil Can" Boyd, the one-
time pitching star for the Boston Red Sox who retired to his hometown of
Meridian, Mississippi. The vandals sign their work, "KKK." The
ballplayer's son, a seventh-grader, discovers the signs. Nonetheless, Meridian police decline to investigate the matter as a hate crime, and eventually
the case is dropped.[10]

- **A pleasant** overnight outing in an idyllic setting turns nightmarish for a
group of gay campers at Kaua'i, Hawaii's Polihale Beach State Park on May
25, 2001. Between 3 and 4 A.M., while most of the campers slept in their
tents, two local young men named Eamonn de Carolan, eighteen, and
Orion P. Macomber, nineteen, begin assaulting the men, first pouring
kerosene on two tents and setting them on fire, then breaking into their
cars at the road nearby. Confronted by the campers, who douse the fires,
the two assailants throw rocks, swing clubs and issue threats, shouting,
"Die, faggot, die," and "Jesus told me to kill you." The pair eventually runs
off. When police arrive, they find the two men sleeping not far away. However, neither is charged with hate crimes—since, as the county's deputy
prosecutor notes, Hawaii at the time had no bias-crime law in the books
(one that had passed the state legislature was at the time still awaiting the
governor's reluctant signature, which was finally granted a week later). Instead, the two men are charged with attempted murder and terroristic
threatening, though they later plea-bargain reduced charges and end up
with five-year sentences. And since Hawaii does not participate in federal
hate-crime reporting, the incident never appears in the FBI's statistics.[11]

Cases such as these, and many others like them, provide anecdotal evidence
that something is amiss with the nation's hate-crime reporting system. They suggest that within the ranks of law enforcement itself there is widespread misunderstanding of just what constitutes a bias crime; that many law officers and
prosecutors are dismissive of the very concept of hate crimes; and that many of
these same officials not only resist using the laws, but are strongly disinclined to

investigate incidents as hate crimes. And since the majority of these incidents in which bias crimes go unreported or uninvestigated occur in small towns and rural areas, the collective weight of the stories suggests that the problem is especially acute in America's less-populated heartland.

The evidence that all these problems exist, however, goes well beyond mere anecdotes. In 2000, the Justice Research and Statistics Association released a report conducted under the aegis of the Department of Justice titled "Improving the Quality and Accuracy of Hate Crime Reporting." This report—coauthored by Northeastern University's Center for Criminal Justice Policy Research—provided statistical and empirical evidence that the problems suggested by anecdotes are not only real but fairly widespread.

In other words, the nation's hate-crime laws are not working, for one main reason: Across a broad cross-section of America, but particularly in the rural heartland, they are not being enforced.

✯

There is one very good reason for gathering statistics on hate crimes: Doing so will give the nation a clearer understanding of their scope and nature, which in turn will help policymakers decide how much to spend pursuing the problem and how best to spend it. When the government recognized the rising problem of teen crime in the mid-1980s, for instance, studies and statistics it compiled over several years provided the impetus for policies that created after-school programs, community centers, and a system of mentoring in local schools. Likewise, the hope has been that a firm handle on the hate-crime phenomenon will eventually generate a broader response to the problem beyond law enforcement, enacted in proportion to the real levels of the problem.

Initiated in 1990 with the passage of the Hate Crimes Statistics Act, the project under the care of the FBI was largely understood in its early years to be nascent and problematic at the outset, for a variety of reasons: many law-enforcement agencies were slow to participate; the initial numbers of hate crimes were likely to be skewed by the sharp increase certain to result from increased awareness of the crimes; and uncertainty and confusion reigned regarding the need to report and how to do it. It was hoped that, given enough time, the reporting system's flaws would self-correct and begin providing a clearer picture of the phenomenon. That was largely what happened. As already noted, by 1996 the wild fluctuations in numbers that occurred early on had largely disappeared, and the statistics began indicating a fairly stable phenomenon indicating about 8,000 bias crimes reported annually, and largely stable percentages of the kinds of the different kinds of hate crimes.

However, what closer examination—particularly the Department of Justice study—revealed was a reporting system that was deeply flawed, with statistics distorted by widespread failures to report the crimes and moreover, confusion about the differences between the absence of a report and the active reporting of zero hate crimes. The DOJ study, which surveyed 2,657 law-enforcement agencies, reported a "major information gap" in the data: It estimated that some 37 percent of the agencies that did not submit reports nevertheless had at least one hate crime. Worse yet, roughly 31 percent of the agencies that reported zero hate crimes did, in fact, have at least one; about 6,000 law-enforcement agencies (or one-third of the total of participants) likely dealt with at least one unreported bias crime.[12] All told, the Southern Poverty Law Center estimates that the total number of hate crimes committed annually in America is closer to 50,000 than the 8,000 found in statistics.[13]

"The overall numbers are worthless," says hate-crime expert Donald P. Green, a Yale University professor whose work includes debunking the notion that tough economic times increase the likelihood of hate crimes. Green says that bias crimes are especially likely to arise when minorities, for a variety of economic reasons, begin moving into communities that were previously homogeneous (that is, for the most part, predominantly white, such as the Midwestern communities that are currently experiencing a large influx of Hispanics); or when previously oppressed minorities, such as homosexuals, begin asserting themselves in public fashion.

Green observes that the fear of negative publicity, especially the kind that can damage a community's reputation, significantly affects hate-crime reporting—particularly in places like Ocean Shores that rely on tourist dollars. "Especially as demographic change is moving into suburban and exurban areas, there is even less attention to the issue of reporting," he told the SPLC. "They don't want to do it. . . . And that only exacerbates the problem. We need to address this embarrassment factor."[14]

But there are other factors too, all cited specifically in the Department of Justice study:

- A hostility to, or ignorance about, the concept of hate-crime laws, and a general over-eagerness to dismiss the bias aspects of crimes as a mostly "political" determination.
- Confusion about the definition of hate crimes and which acts need reporting, particularly arising from the many differences among various state laws and the murky federal statutes.
- Miscommunication between local and state reporting agencies, with the latter often reporting a bias crime simply as its parallel crime.
- False zeroes or the reporting of zero crimes within a jurisdiction that in fact failed to report at all, which further skews the data regarding the actual rate at which hate crimes occur.

- The natural reluctance of victims to report hate crimes or pursue charges, and the common failure of law-enforcement officials to either recognize or deal appropriately with this reluctance.
- A significant lack of training in identifying and investigating hate crimes, as well as in handling victims of the crimes. The smaller the department, the less likely it is to offer such training, which generally translates into severe undertraining in rural areas.

Perhaps unsurprisingly, many of these problems begin with the pervasiveness of the most enduring myth about hate-crime laws: a "crime is a crime."

✵

"I always had a problem with hate-crime laws, anyhow," Ken Delacerda, the police chief in San Augustine, Texas, told the SPLC when two researchers for the *Intelligence Report* tried following up on holes in the hate-crimes law. "I mean, you don't shoot people because you love them."

The "all crimes are hate crimes" mythology promoted by opponents of the law in fact is quite common in law enforcement. The DOJ study's authors, Northeastern University professor Jack McDevitt and Joan Weiss of the Justice Research and Statistics Association (JRSA), reported: "Indeed, some academics and officers perceive the difference between bias and non-bias crimes as solely political; and hate crime, for some, represents the popular culture *cause celeb* of the 1990s. The skepticism is captured in one officer's quip in the mail survey, 'Since I have yet to see a 'love' crime, every crime I investigate is a hate crime.'" These attitudes were particularly notable in precincts that either did not participate in hate crimes reporting or reported none, and were similarly common in agencies with little training in recognizing or investigating hate crimes.[15]

At times, these attitudes originate at the upper levels of state law enforcement. Of course, in four states (Wyoming, Indiana, Arkansas, and South Carolina), there are no bias-crime laws, and as such there exists no official support for the concept of the laws. Many other states either do not participate in hate-crimes reporting or barely do so. Even though it passed a bias-crimes law in 2000, Hawaii has never reported any hate crimes to the FBI, and apparently has no intentions of doing so. "We likely won't be participating in the FBI program," Paul Peron of the Hawaii attorney general's office told the SPLC, in spite of the fact that Peron had been helping the state implement its new law. He decried the FBI's definition of a hate crime as "very broad and very subjective and it's hard to know what somebody had in their heart when they beat somebody up."

Likewise in Alabama, there is a hate-crimes law on the books, but it has gone unused for years, reflected in the paucity of reports of any kinds of bias crimes from

Alabama since the HCSA passed in 1990; in most years, it is not listed as reporting, even though the state has a separate law requiring law enforcement to report hate crimes to the Alabama Criminal Justice Information Center. "For five or six years, we have had this form available and no one has filled it out," says Carol Roberts, a center spokesperson. "There is a reluctance on the part of law enforcement to determine the motive of the offender." Billy Jack Gaither's murder was not reported, she told the SPLC, because Alabama's hate-crime law does not cover sexual orientation—even though state law has no direct bearing on which crimes are supposed to be reported to the FBI.[16]

※

Reflected in this kind of hostility, confusion and reluctance, the DOJ study uncovered a great deal of misunderstanding about the definition of hate crimes both in state and federal statutes, as well as a frequent failures to grasp the federal reporting requirements. However, this is in many regards also a product of the hodgepodge of seemingly conflicting laws that have been passed on every level.

There are in fact four different kinds of bias-crimes laws, depending on the kind of wording upon which they are enacted:

- **Criminalization of the interference with a person's civil rights.** These statutes outlaw the threat or use of force to prevent or intimidate others from the proper exercise of their civil rights, and then go on to specify categories of bias that may motivate such acts (race, religion, ethnicity, sexual orientation, etc.). California, New York, Tennessee, and West Virginia all have such statutes; and the most commonly used federal "hate crimes" law, the Civil Rights Act of 1968's Section 245, fits this category.
- **"Freestanding" statutes.** These laws create new categories of crime (typically "malicious harassment" or "ethnic intimidation"), which are enumerated in detail as to types of intimidation and injuries that fall within the statute, and they again specify the kinds of group biases that constitute the crimes. These laws are on the books in Colorado, Idaho, Louisiana, Maryland, Massachusetts, Michigan, Montana, Nebraska, North Carolina, Oklahoma, Oregon, Rhode Island, South Dakota, and Washington.
- **"Coattailing" statutes.** These create new crimes of "malicious harassment" or "ethnic intimidation" by adding them to criminal codes that already exist, and creating enhanced sentences for them. Such laws can be found in Delaware, Illinois, Iowa, Kentucky, Missouri, New York, Ohio, Pennsylvania, Utah, and Vermont.
- **Modification of a pre-existing statute.** By reclassifying a crime already on the books to a higher penalty level if committed with a bias motivation,

these laws also simply alter a pre-existing statute, and a separate crime is not created. These laws are on the books in Minnesota, New Jersey, New York, and Virginia.

- **Penalty-enhancement statutes.** These bolster the sentences for crimes already on the books if motivated by one of the categorized kinds of bias, and require prosecutors to produce evidence regarding both the parallel crime and the second-tier bias motivation. These are the most popular kind of hate-crimes law, in no small part because the Supreme Court explicitly validated them in *Wisconsin v. Mitchell,* and the Anti-Defamation League offers one as its "model" law. The federal Hate Crimes Sentencing Enhancement Act of 1994 was this type of statute, as are the laws on the books in Arizona, Alabama, Alaska, California, Connecticut, Florida, Illinois, Maine, Mississippi, Montana, Nevada, New Hampshire, New Jersey, North Carolina, Rhode Island, Texas and Wisconsin.[17]

The laws also vary widely from state to state by the categories of bias they cover. All of the forty-six states (plus the District of Columbia) that have bias-crime laws universally identify race, religion and ethnicity (or national origin) as proscribed bias motivations. Of these, some twenty-nine include sexual orientation as a category of bias, while another seven of these add "gender identity" (that is, bias against transgender persons). Seven other states identify gender itself as a potential bias motive; and a total of seventeen states enhance the sentences for crimes motivated by bias against persons with disabilities. Some five states add political affiliation to the list, while an age bias can be found categorized in another thirteen state hate-crimes laws. The federal laws, meanwhile, include race, religion, ethnicity, national origin, gender, disability, and sexual orientation. And these statutes, as we have observed, are currently so limited as to be useless as well. Consider, for instance, that the Justice Department has charted some 300 hate-crime cases being either investigated or prosecuted related to anti-Muslim bias after the events of September 11, 2001. Yet none of these so far have been charged under the 1994 federal hate-crimes law.

Finally, there is the issue of the relations of all these laws to each other, particularly the federal to the state statutes. Both the DOJ study and the SPLC found that a number of local officers operated under the misimpression that "hate crimes" were primarily the purview of federal investigators, and as such did not pursue them as hate crimes unless they reached "that level." Yet in reality, of course, the federal hate-crimes statutes are extremely limited in scope, and even the proposed improvements to the laws carefully prescribes the federal role as clearly secondary to that of state and local law enforcement.

Negotiating all these contrasts and intersections can be mind-boggling, particularly in those states that lack statutes matching the federal laws. Confusion somewhat naturally arises when law officers try to determine whether or not an incident should be reported as a hate crime in such cases—and for the most part, these officials err on the side of caution and choose not to file at all.

✳

The information gap between reporting agencies manifests itself in other ways. The DOJ study uncovered a recurring trend: Senior law-enforcement officers would report hate crimes to state agencies or the FBI, only to discover later that the crimes did not show up in FBI statistics. "Very often, these [officers] were disturbed to find out that their jurisdiction was listed as not having reported or reporting zero information about hate crimes to the Uniform Crime Reports *because they personally had been involved in the investigation of one or more incidents of bias crime.*" They noted that "one capital city in the South reported on our survey that it had (and reported) twenty hate crimes; the official UCR reports indicate this city had zero incidents."

The researchers tried to get to the bottom of these "procedural pitfalls" by recontacting the participating agencies. They found, in addition to confusion over jurisdictions and misconceptions about bias-crime laws, a peculiar gap between state and local law enforcement agencies. Hate crimes, the study found, are often coded by the local investigating officers for categorization both as the parallel crime (such as intimidation or assault) and the bias crime, but then the latter notations are ignored when the crime is reported to the state, or in some cases by the state itself.

A similar gap in the lines of communication occurs with the reporting of "false zeroes"—that is, cases where a jurisdiction appears in the statistics as having reported zero hate crimes, when in fact it hasn't reported at all. This has the effect of skewing the data by making the participation rates higher than they actually are, making states that submit false zeroes look better by comparison to those states that don't. As the SPLC observed in its follow-up to the DOJ study, "The dimensions of this problem may be enormous; fully 83 percent of jurisdictions that reported in 1999 said they had no hate crimes."

Indeed, the SPLC found at least seven states that filed false zeroes. The state agencies responsible in many of those cases admitted that they filled in zeroes for non-reporting agencies. But in only one state, North Carolina, was the false reporting brought to the public's attention and later corrected; following a television station's in-depth report that found hundreds of false zeroes in the state's hate-crime reports, Congressman Mel Watt called the misreporting a "flagrant disregard for common sense" and urged congressional hearings to get at the bottom of the problem. None were ever held, however.

✳

Of all the factors that cause law-enforcement officers to fail to identify and investigate bias crimes, the most significant, the DOJ study's authors found, was the gap between the victims and the police. The less trust that exists between minorities and their local law enforcement, the greater the likelihood that hate crimes will go unresolved.

The Filipino family that encountered Chris Kinison and his friends in Ocean Shores was a textbook example of how hate crimes can go unresolved this way. Many of the victims spoke poor English and had difficulty communicating with the police officers who came to their rescue; even though some of them later reported that they had wanted to pursue harassment charges against the men, the officers either failed or refused to register this. And the officers, little trained in dealing with hate crimes, clearly did not recognize that they had come upon the scene of a felony, which in most other such cases would require a careful and serious investigation and specialized handling of the victims.

By seeming eager to simply break up the potential violence and send everyone on their respective ways—and particularly by escorting the family to the town's borders—the officers communicated to the victims the message that the harassment they had endured was insignificant. This in turn feeds the distrust that any outsider (particularly a minority) in a strange town is likely to feel.

Moreover, the incident vividly illustrates that the problem of letting hate crimes go unresolved extends well beyond the mere statistical issues, and that the stakes can be very high indeed, especially for small towns. The result, as it was in Ocean Shores, is that these crimes can escalate from simple harassment to outright violence. Perpetrators, as some studies have observed, see their escape from the arm of the law almost as an invitation to step things up.[18]

Other studies have likewise observed that the most common cause of this cascade of crime is the failure of police to proactively bridge the gap between themselves and the victims. The JRSA's Joan Weiss, in earlier research, found that the reluctance of victims to report crimes was significantly higher for hate crimes than for other crimes.[19] The DOJ study reiterates this point: "For a multitude of reasons, hate crime victims are a population that is leery of reporting crimes—bias or otherwise—to law enforcement agencies."[20]

Most hate-crime victims are minorities in the communities where the crimes occur. In many cases, they have poor English skills and have difficulty asking for assistance; in others, they may simply be unaware that what has happened to them is a serious crime. This is particularly true for immigrants, who may be reluctant to even contact police because of their experience with law enforcement in their homelands, where corruption and indifference to such crimes are not uncommon. Likewise, hate-crime victims may be confused about or unaware of the bias motivation involved, interpreting a threat or assault as a random act when other evidence suggests it was not. At other times, they may be reluctant to tell police about the bias aspects of the acts against them, fearing the police won't believe them or that they simply won't do anything about it anyway.[21] And in the case of gays and lesbians, many are reluctant to report the crimes out of fear they will be forced to reveal their own identities as homosexuals; many more fear (sometimes with good reason) that they will wind up being humiliated and victimized further by police.[22]

Likewise, many minorities in certain communities—blacks in the South or Hispanics in the Southwest, for example—have long histories of built-up distrust of law enforcement in their communities, and may simply refuse to participate in an investigation without proactive efforts on the part of police to bridge that gap. Indeed, this level of involvement was almost unanimously the chief factor reported by advocacy groups when queried by the authors of the DOJ study about what most affected hate-crime victims' decision to call or cooperate with police.[23]

✳

To their credit, most law-enforcement officials who participated in the DOJ study recognized the gap within their communities, too; a large majority (over 60 percent) believe that the most important factors in discouraging victims from reporting to police arise from the established relations between the victims (and their respective communities) and law enforcement. Yet in other respects, there are significant gaps in perceptions; while most minorities emphatically say hate-crime victims are *less* likely to report crimes against them, a large majority of police believed bias-crimes victims either were *more* prone to reporting or that the matter was neutral. This disconnect, as well as skepticism about the victims' abilities to correctly identify a bias motivation, was widespread across all sizes and kinds of agencies, but was particularly pronounced in departments that did not offer hate-crime training for its officers.[24]

Indeed, while most officers agreed that training was an essential component of overcoming both the gap between minorities and their departments, as well as the misconceptions and miscommunication that create massive underreporting of bias crimes, the level of training being offered was minimal at best. Though nearly 67 percent of the participating agencies indicated they offer some training on hate crimes, some 35 percent actually provided only two hours or less. This indifference is also apparent at the upper levels of government: Only eight states have laws that mandate training for law-enforcement personnel in hate crimes, and a mere handful of others have state regulations that do the same.

Perhaps the most significant feature of the DOJ's study's findings, from a larger cultural perspective, was that there was a close correlation between reporting of hate crimes and the level of training provided (some 75 percent of agencies that reported hate crimes also offered training, while less than 60 percent of the non-reporting and zero-reporting agencies offered any)—and simultaneously, found a correlation between hate-crime training and the size of the agency. The smaller the department, the less likely it is to provide such training—and likewise, less likely to report hate crimes.[25]

Obscured by the numbers are their real-world ramifications for the American cultural landscape: the smaller the town, the smaller the department. This means in turn that, geographically speaking, the problem of hate crimes going not only underreported but uninvestigated and unprosecuted is most widespread in *rural America*. This coincides with the prevalence of anecdotes of unpursued bias crimes emanating from rural precincts. This in turn, makes the problem even more acute, since these same small towns may be the communities most vulnerable to suffering severe damage at the hands of hate-crime perpetrators.

Most significantly, this phenomenon in fact reflects the perceptions many minorities have of small, rural towns: that they are not safe for people of color or for gays. That if trouble were to erupt, there would be no one to help them, and law enforcement officers would be unsympathetic. That if someone were to commit a hate crime against them, there is a reasonable likelihood the perpetrator would get away with it.

The fear and suspicion with which rural denizens regard cities and their dwellers is a well-established American archetype. What is often less observed, but is equally true, is the sheer dread that rural America raises in the minds of those minorities whose populations are largely centered in urban areas. When they leave their familiar surroundings for the so-called heartland—where some 83 percent of the population nationally is white—it is often with real fear about what might befall them.

It is a mistrust bred partly of myth and partly of reality. Its consequences, whatever its cause, are profound on a broad scale, because its chief effect is to widen the already formidable cultural gap between white America and the rest of us.

CHAPTER 14

THE TRIAL, DAY FIVE:
IN CLOSING

THE AUDIENCE FOR THE FIRST FOUR DAYS OF MINH HONG'S TRIAL had at first been small—there were only about twenty people in the courtroom the first day—but had been slowly building as the case progressed, until Tuesday, when about fifty people filled the courtroom to hear the closing arguments. It wasn't crowded, but the seats were filling up.

Nearly half of the Tuesday crowd was constituted of Asian Americans, over twenty of them. It was clear that the Seattle community that knew the Hongs was there to let Minh Hong know he wasn't alone. They were quiet and respectful, but the message was clear. Later, outside, Minh told me he was "amazed" at how many people drove down to watch. He was obviously grateful.

Many were there too because there was at least an outside chance that there might be a verdict that day, at least if closing arguments were short. Monte Hester's decision to close up shop and send the case to the jury after only three witnesses had taken everyone by surprise. A quick verdict, which Hester clearly believed was likely (he had briefly moved to have the case dismissed after the prosecution rested, which Judge Foscue had denied), was suddenly a real possibility.

Nonetheless, the move surprised many of the trial's observers. It meant, for instance, dropping some potentially potent testimony. During pretrial hearings, Brett Purtzer had fought hard to win approval for the testimony of a Seattle psychologist, Dr. Gary E. Connor, who was going to explain to the jurors the phenomenon of "hyper-vigilance." (Fuller had fought this testimony, referring to it as "mumbo jumbo," but Foscue had allowed it.) The jury, however, never heard him.

However, Hester had good reasons for the short defense—namely, the prosecution clearly had not cleared its own bar. Fuller and his team had needed to demonstrate beyond "reasonable doubt" that Minh Hong acted out of anger—and thus recklessness—and not out of fear or self-defense that night when he stole those knives and wielded them. Yet those doubts were aroused by the very testimony presented by prosecutors. And Minh Hong's subdued but powerful testimony had, if anything, confirmed them. If the prosecution has not made its case, then there is no reason to continue, since doing so could only wind up muddying the issue.

It was evident, however, from Jerry Fuller's closing statement that he was convinced he and his team had succeeded. He referred specifically to the jury instructions, insisting: "Hong's act was criminally negligent beyond a reasonable doubt."

"We've tried to give you everything you need to reach a guilty verdict," he told the jurors. "We just want you to use your common sense."

He said there was no doubt Chris Kinison was "making an idiot of himself that night. He was looking for a fight.

"There was no excuse for Kinison's conduct. It was rude, it was obnoxious, it was obscene. But he did not deserve to be the victim of this savage assault," continued Fuller. "He did not deserve to die."

It was the first time in the trial anyone had referred to Kinison as a "victim."

Fuller wondered aloud why the Hongs had exited from the Texaco from the door nearest where Kinison was instead of the "back door." He pointed to testimony saying no one had blocked their exit. Minh Hong and his group, he said, deliberately decided to "take out" Chris Kinison because he had angered them: "There was no reason for them to stop unless they wanted a confrontation. No. They decided that they were going to take advantage of this rube, this drunken rube who had insulted them.

"Why did they stop the car? Because Kinison was out there alone."

Minh Hong, he argued, stole the knives because "he was getting ready for a fight. He was preparing for an opportunity to sandbag Chris Kinison."

Kinison, he said, thought he was getting into a fistfight, and came unarmed accordingly. Minh Hong, he said, did not.

"It is not yet the law in the state of Washington that fatal force can be brought to a fist fight," Fuller reminded jurors.

Monte Hester's response underscored the weakness of Fuller's argument: What Minh Hong was being invited to was not a fistfight. It was a hate crime, with all its attendant threat of serious and imminent harm. When Chris Kinison ran that finger along his throat, it was not unreasonable to interpret that as statement he intended to kill Hong. Nor, for that matter, was it beyond reason to conclude from such a gesture that Kinison in fact was armed with a knife himself, and intended to use it.

"The conduct of Mr. Kinison and his confederates convinced Minh and his associates they were in danger of serious injury or death," Hester emphasized, echoing the requirements of a self-defense argument. "The only evidence of recklessness was the testimony of the doctors who examined both men, and they found they were only 'consistent with self-defense.'"

Hester said that Hong was frightened mainly because Kinison was motioning for Hong to step outside and intimating he was going to slit the man's throat. Hong was secretive about taking the paring knives because he didn't want to "escalate the situation," Hester argued.

He also lingered on Fuller's suggestion that the Asians could have avoided a confrontation by leaving another way. "Why didn't they use the back door? Why didn't they use the back door?" repeated Hester, letting the words linger. That same suggestion, he argued, was the kind you used to hear justifying laws that required separate drinking fountains for minorities or that forced them to ride in the back of the bus.

"It boils down to racism," said Hester. "A person who is a minority approaches social settings differently than people from the white majority. When you or I see someone with a Confederate flag, it may seem innocuous. But if you are a minority, you see it as a symbol of white supremacy. You see it as a symbol of a person who thinks of you as a minority as less than a human being."

If possible, he said, jurors need to think about what it is like to be in the position of a person of color: "I know you're not minorities, but you need to do that."

Put yourself in Minh Hong's shoes, he urged jurors. Think about what it would be like to encounter people like Chris Kinison, alone and in a vulnerable situation: Men who threaten you and degrade you for your race, and a crowd of faces who seem content to let you endure it. "They appear not to care whether you live or die," said Hester. "So what do you do? Do you submit? Or do you look for a way to defend yourself?"

He recalled Rhyanna Von Kallenbach's testimony: "They looked terrified." And, he emphasized, they had reason to be: "Kinison recognized that these little Asian fellows were easy prey," he said. "They were small, they acted scared, there were only three of them. They were vulnerable."

Minh Hong, he said, was desperate because he believed Kinison and his friends were going to subject him to severe harm and perhaps death: "Because," said Hester, "he knows that is what happens to people like him."

A little while later, the two sides had finished. The jurors were reminded of their instructions, and sent off to decide Minh Hong's fate.

As they filed out of the courtroom, Hong watched them silently. Twelve white people from a small rural town were going to decide whether he would spend the next decade of his life in prison for having had the audacity to fight back. The look on his face was that of someone stranded on a strange highway in the middle of nowhere: alone, naked, vulnerable. Waiting for whatever comes next.

CHAPTER 15

THE GREAT DIVIDE

DAVID SOLOMON HAD SEEN A LOT OF AMERICA in his forty-seven years. The son of sharecroppers who had witnessed his share of racial hatred over the years, he wasn't the kind to let it stop him or frighten him. Then again, he probably didn't expect to encounter it in broad daylight at a roadside stop along a Montana highway.

Solomon ran a little mail-order computer-parts company in Spokane, Washington, that provided him with a decent living. As a black man with a white wife living in a city about forty miles from the Aryan Nations compound in northern Idaho—and living in a city that had its own history of battling hate crimes and various violent expressions of bigotry, including a recent bombing and bank-robbing spree by a gang of violent white supremacists—he had no doubt experienced his moments of discomfort, if not fearfulness. But he had lived all over the country: Born in North Carolina, he had bounced around with his company from Boston to St. Louis to Philadelphia before landing in Spokane. He was the kind of man, his son later said, who was comfortable and happy and made friends wherever he was. He led a good life with his wife, Kathleen, their little four-year-old boy, Andre, and David's nineteen-year-old son, Adam.

In 1999, he decided to bounce one more time. He decided it was time pack up the company and move to Arizona, mostly so he could be closer to his chief clients. So on June 29, David packed up their belongings in a station wagon and a U-Haul and headed down the road with Kathleen and Andre; Adam stayed behind to finish up a few things on the house.[1]

A few hours eastward on Interstate 90, the family pulled over at a rest stop near Gold Creek in western Montana to stretch their legs and use the facilities. That was when they encountered Douglas Zander.

Zander was a twenty-six-year-old former homecoming king from Mandan, North Dakota, who was drifting through Montana and happened to have arrived at the rest area at the same time. As it later turned out, Zander was suffering from a severe psychotic episode and was hallucinating. He had just broken up with a girlfriend—he later told police he had lost her to a new love interest, a black man—and had been bouncing around from town to town around the Pacific Northwest, driving aimlessly from Seattle to Olympia to Salem to Boise and then to Helena. Trying to get to Mandan, he took a wrong turn at the Garrison Junction and started heading west again, then pulled over at Gold Creek to try to get his bearings. Considering where he had been driving, David Solomon may well have been the first black man he had encountered in awhile.

David Solomon had pulled into a truck parking spot large enough to accommodate the car and trailer, and the family had just begun to get out of both sides of the car. Zander allegedly backed his red Ford Mustang alongside Solomon as he got out of the station wagon, stuck his eight-millimeter Mauser rifle out the driver's-side window, and fired once point-blank into David Solomon's chest. Then he turned around and drove off, while young Andre and Kathleen, having witnessed it all, ran to the aid of their fallen father and husband. David Solomon died there.[2]

State patrolmen picked up Zander without incident a short time later. And initially, news reports indicated that the shooting was a hate crime. The first affidavit filed by the Powell County prosecutor stated that Zander shot Solomon because of his race: "'I shot him,'" the affidavit quoted Zander as telling their investigators. "Zander said he was mad and said something about 'racial.' . . . He indicated that he intended to 'probably kill' the individual he shot, and that he shot him, in effect because he was black."[3] The case sparked a few outraged letters to the editors of local papers, and the Montana Human Rights Network, which voiced concern about the case, set up a trust fund for the family that eventually netted $2,721.

But when Zander's case went to trial the following spring, the picture had changed dramatically. Psychiatrists who examined him concluded he was mentally ill and suffering an extended psychotic break, replete with hallucinations and voices from nowhere, when he shot David Solomon. He entered a no-contest plea that prosecutors accepted, and District Judge Ted Mizner sentenced him to a sixty-year term in the state mental hospital "because I believe it's the rest of your life, Mr. Zander, and I believe there has to be supervision over you for the rest of your life."

In spite of the earlier evidence to the contrary, the psychiatrists insisted that Solomon was chosen randomly and not because of his race. His plea, and the resulting sentence, thus bore no indication that Solomon's murder was committed with a bias motive (and indeed, Powell County reported no hate crimes that year to the FBI). David Solomon's family was satisfied that Zander was being put away, but was not so sure about the outcome: "What really matters is there is no doubt and no shadow that he killed my father," Adam Solomon testified. "This," he said of the psychiatrists' testimony, "is just theories."

The family had returned to Spokane for awhile to try to piece their lives back together. Adam told the court he was concerned about Andre, who he said was acting out murder scenarios at times, trying to cope with having watched his father die before his eyes. "I don't want my father's murder to make up what's the rest of his life because there's so much of his life left," Adam Solomon said.[4]

✳

Whether or not David Solomon's murder was a hate crime, it was the kind of story that reverberates throughout minority communities that already have reasons to fear traveling to rural districts.

Minorities in the Northwest do not have to look far to find reasons for being fearful when they leave the known dangers of urban life behind and venture into the region's vast wide open spaces. The presence of a white-supremacist enclave in northern Idaho called the Aryan Nations—cradle not merely to the neo-Nazi criminals The Order, whose murderous 1984 rampage made national headlines, but also to dozens of hate crimes, bombings, assaults and would-be acts of terrorism over the past twenty years—is well known to virtually everyone in the area. So is the presence of far-right militiamen, like the Noxon-based Militia of Montana, whose connections to the white-supremacist Christian Identity movement (the "religion" that is practiced at the Aryan Nations) have been well documented.[5] And then there are the crimes like Matthew Shepard's and David Solomon's murders that are never resolved to anyone's satisfaction.

An editorial writer for the *Seattle Times*, Lynne Varner, discussed this at length in an October 2000 op-ed piece for the paper, describing the fear many black people have of even traveling into Idaho: "To the average black person, something smells in Idaho and it's not the skunk hiding behind the ponderosa," she wrote.

> There are scores of Idahoans who have come out in opposition to the hatred their neighbors spew. Some have risked physical harm. But there are many more who said nothing. Their silence becomes tacit acceptance, making Idaho attractive to those who prefer to do their dirty work in rural darkness.
>
> . . . I sometimes dream of visiting Idaho. My mind runs fleetingly over the region's green landscape. Its myriad lakes and the largest stand of western white pine trees anywhere. Then fear sets in.

Varner described how she once tried to drive into Idaho, flying into Spokane—twenty-five miles inside the Washington border—renting a car and then getting as far as the interstate exit before giving in to her fear and staying on the Washington side. "If I ran out of gas or needed some other emergency assistance, how could I tell the friendly houses from the ones that shelter racists?" she wondered. "What are my chances of being physically harmed for simply visiting Idaho? The answer is that I don't know and I don't care to find out."

And, as Varner suggests, this has real-life ramifications for people like herself and how they view their place in America: "I open the newspaper and read that hate groups are expanding. And I pore over a map of the United States and draw lines through areas where I'm afraid to travel. Suddenly, the country seems a lot smaller."[6]

Commentary like this is painful for native Idahoans (myself included), because we know very well that the reality is rather different—that someone like Varner is probably more likely to get real help, and real human warmth, from people in Idaho than she ever would in a place like Seattle. Certainly, that is the view Idahoans have of themselves. Their homes and their towns are safe and welcoming places. Most see themselves as racially tolerant—even if, just as an aside, they may not think much of all the Mexicans moving into town, or the way those drunk Indians cause trouble, or think gays have no business flaunting their sexuality in public. Still, they don't *hate* anyone.

At the same time, many of us are perfectly aware that her fears are not entirely groundless, because we know too well that those haters are out there in our woods and our small towns—in tiny numbers, perhaps, but still potent in their capacity for violence. We all know about the local kids who drive around in the black pickups with the Confederate flags in the rear window, the ones who like to get into fights. We like to think that they are held in check by the basic decency endemic to small-town life.

That is not, however, the view from the outside.

Ken Toole, a native Montanan (and state senator) who runs that state's Human Rights Network, knows all about the fear minorities have of rural places like his home state. "I've experienced that firsthand, in talking with African American people on airplanes, et cetera, and their perception that Montana's not a safe place. And I think that stems from hate-crime incidents, but is more heartily reinforced by the presence of Militia of Montana, Aryan Nations, and things like that. It all feeds together.

"Here in Montana, in lily-white Montana, we spend all this time engaged in a debate whether or not these groups are white supremacist. Your average person of color doesn't even have that debate. They just know it."

Toole says that when the image of a place as a haven for haters is combined with news stories of real-life hate crimes, the result is a widespread desire by minorities to avoid that place at all costs. "What you end up with is, we've heard about African American people being transferred to Montana and rejecting the transfers," Toole says, noting that it is something of a commonplace that rural people avoid the cities out of an irrational fear of crime committed by minorities: "There's very little question in my mind that, yeah, we rural folk maybe get a little nervous about the deep colors of the inner city, but that is very much a two-way street."[7]

Perhaps of equal significance are the real-world ramifications of this fear for both minorities and the places they fear to visit: an impoverishment of the nation's democratic underpinnings. As expert Donald Green points out, hate crimes succeed in making the nation indeed a smaller place for people like Lynne Varner.

"I think if you had to kind of step back and ask, 'Does hate crime pay?,' you'd say yes," Green says. "If the point of hate crimes is to terrorize the population into maintaining boundaries between these perpetrators and the victimized populations, at least in some areas—certain parts of town, certain parts of the country, et cetera—you know, certain kinds of romantic relationships, whatever—then it does succeed in that. Because people really do feel that they have to constrain their behavior lest they open themselves up for attack. You know, gay men don't often hold hands in public. Black and white couples don't form spontaneously to the extent that you might expect based on their daily interactions.

"There are a lot of instances like that—and you know, we all probably have interactions with people who, when they're invited to a certain part of town, say, 'Oh, I better not go there.' From my standpoint, you tend not to attract much notice from policymakers, but I think of that as a massive dead-weight loss of freedom.

"Even if you say, 'Ah, well, they would have spent their money in this restaurant, maybe they'll spend their money in some other restaurant,' and so it's a wash, just the fact that people feel less than free in a free country is a tragedy."

Green also argues that even seemingly insignificant incidents—the kind police are prone to ignore or de-emphasize—can contribute to the cumulative effect. "If you see a swastika on an overpass, you say, 'Well, you know, it's just a bunch of kids blowing off steam, it doesn't really mean anything,' but when you start to think about the kind of cumulative effects that that would have on a variety of people, both perpetrators and victims, then the result is considerable.

"And that's why I think that, while there's a segment of the law-enforcement community—and even people like me in an unguarded moment—that will say that in some respects the hate crimes laws have been a flop, the laws in fact have a substantial basis in theory. And that theory is that if you could somehow put a value on that dead-weight loss in freedom, it actually would be a significant sum. And therefore it does pay society to deter this kind of activity."[8]

✳

The idea that their homes and neighborhoods are seen as threatening in any sense runs deeply counter to rural dwellers' self-image. Most would be shocked at the idea of someone fearing even to step out of their car in their hometowns or along their highways. They see their lives as the portrait of tranquility and decency, and possess a deep belief that their places in the country are the safest places on Earth. But not everyone does.

"I think that's only if you're white," Toole observes. "I think that people of color in our communities don't feel the same level of safety that white people do. And this cuts across classes of hate crime, too. I think this is also very true of the gay community—you and I feel safe and secure in Boise and Billings, but if you're a gay man, you're not feeling safe and secure. You're thinking about Matthew Shepard. And reasonably so. And feeling particularly unsupported by police."[9]

These feelings came back to the surface a year and a half after David Solomon's murder, when there was another apparent hate crime in western Montana that not only went unresolved, but it became a classic case of law-enforcement officials compounding the victimization of the injured parties. This time, it involved a lesbian couple.

Carla Grayson was an assistant professor in the University of Montana's psychology department who, along with a UM biological-sciences staff member named Carol Snetsinger, filed a lawsuit in early February 2002 against the university over its refusal to provide health-care and other benefits to the partners of same-sex couples employed by the school. The suit was well-covered in the local press and garnered a few cries of outrage from local conservatives.

Two days later, a Wednesday, Grayson and her partner, Adrianne Neff, received a hate letter ("Die Dykes!" and "Anthrax") in an envelope containing white powder, as did Carol Snetsinger and her partner, Nancy Siegel. Both turned out later to be benign, but the threat was clear.

That Friday, while sleeping in their home on Rimrock Road, Neff awoke and thought she heard someone moving around on the main floor below, then smelled gasoline. Moments later, their home's fire alarm went off. Smoke and flames were pouring upstairs from the ground floor. Neff and Grayson grabbed their two-year-old son and ran to the master bedroom, whose window was a relatively short distance above the ground. Grayson dove out the window, Neff handed the boy to her, and then managed to clamber out herself. They ran to get help from their neighbors and then had to watch as their home was gutted by the flames. Firefighters managed to put it out before it burned to the ground, but their belongings were destroyed and the house ruined.

It was immediately evident that it had been an arson. Gasoline had been spread throughout the ground floor. And initially, police investigated it as a hate crime. But within a week, rumors began flying in Missoula that Grayson and Neff had set the fire intentionally, as a ploy to gain sympathy for their lawsuit. Investigators told the *Missoulian* that they were pursuing that angle as well; and though they explained that this was standard for any arson investigation, it was also clear that the couple were the police's chief suspects. Indeed, the head of the state gay-rights organization, PRIDE, was named as a "person of interest" in the investigation.

Toole's Human Rights Network protested that the police were engaging in a classic case of "blaming the victim," and a variety of gay-rights organizations and community activists stood to protest the police behavior; many were simultaneously angry with the *Missoulian* for running the stories. County prosecutor Fred Van Valkenburg put the clamps down and told investigators to stop talking to reporters about the case; but the damage was already done.

In August, police filed an application for a search warrant of Grayson and Neff's home, implying that the arson had been an "inside job." Van Valkenburg later suggested to reporters that there was "evidence there that causes one to have suspicions as to whether they are truly the victim in this incident." The couple issued a statement heatedly denying they had set the fire, and later—after moving away from Missoula to Ann Arbor, Michigan—gave an interview to the *Missoulian* describing both the fire and the investigation in detail, reasonably debunking most of the investigators' alleged evidence against them.

And they cast serious doubt about the likelihood that police would catch the arsonist: "They just take our comments and spin them to suit their ideas," Neff said. "But it's scary, because they're not going to catch this person."[10]

Indeed, ten months later, the investigation had reached a dead end: A police captain told the *Missoulian* that the case was "officially inactive from our perspective." Van Valkenburg denied that the trail had gone cold because investigators had focused on the victims as potential perpetrators; in any event, he said, there wasn't enough evidence to charge anyone in the arson.

Carol Snetsinger and her partner chose to stay in Montana and continue her legal battle (which lost its first-round battle in state courts, but is being appealed to the state Supreme Court). But she said the mystery of the Grayson/Neff arson, and the fact that neither the person who set the fire nor the one who sent the anthrax threats has been caught, remains an open wound among gays and lesbians in Montana.

"Part of it is that we still, as a lot of gay people do in this community, live in fear," she said. "Though the urgency of that has subsided, it's still a factor in our lives."

Especially chilling, she said, was what happened to Grayson and Neff at the hands of police. "I realized how quickly victims of any kind of violence—especially if you're a minority—how quickly you can be revictimized," Snetsinger said.[11]

This kind of scenario, says Ken Toole, is exactly what crosses the minds of minorities of all kinds when they choose to avoid places like Montana (or in the case of native Indians, confine themselves to reservations): "It is one thing when hate crimes are not prosecuted, which is a problem in itself. But the police reaction is also an important component.

"It is a very common and accurate perception in the Indian community, the black community and the gay community, that: 'If we have an encounter with law enforcement, they ain't there to help us. They're there to suspect us.'"[12]

✯

There is a deep irony that resides in the typical response of small towns like Missoula and Ocean Shores to the phenomenon of hate crimes: Even as they run in terror-stricken denial from facing up to the crimes—what Donald Green calls "the embarrassment factor"—they are themselves chief among the victims.

The main theoretical justification for hate-crime laws—which typically enhance punishment for crimes committed with a bias motivation—is that the acts cause greater harm than the simple crimes (say, assault and battery or vandalism) that they resemble. Most of the time, this expanded harm is viewed in the context of the direct victim (who is usually traumatized to a considerably greater extent), the target community (that is, the minorities who typically are terrorized by the crimes), or society at large, which finds its goals of racial equity and social justice undermined by these kinds of acts.

What often goes unremarked, though, is that the communities in which the crimes occur are victimized by them as well. "It is one thing when groups are rightfully identified with the immediate offenders, for example, the association of a bias crime offender who is a member of a Skinhead organization with other members of that organization," observes Frederick Lawrence in *Punishing Hate: Bias Crimes Under American Law*. "It is quite another when groups [or communities] are wrongfully identified with the immediate offenders. . . . In addition to generating concern and anger over lawlessness and the perceived ineffectuality of law enforcement that often follow a parallel crime . . . a single bias crime may ignite intense and long-standing inter-community tensions."[13]

Towns like Ocean Shores, whose economic health is directly tied to the sense of welcome and well-being enjoyed by its visitors—including minorities from urban centers—can be badly harmed by a hate crime. Yet, perceptions notwithstanding, is Grays Harbor genuinely a racist place?

Probably not—at least, no more so than most other rural communities whose population historically have been homogenously white. Like nearly any small town in the Northwest—or any rural town in America, for that matter—the vast majority of the residents of Ocean Shores or Aberdeen are hard-working and well-meaning people who, beyond harboring the usual garden-variety racial stereotypes, are not racist or white supremacist in any serious way. They are usually disgusted by ideological racists and want nothing to do with them. And they are bewildered at suggestions they might be a haven for bigotry.

"Our police department received I don't know how many calls wanting to know if it was safe in Ocean Shores, is it a racist town?" says Carl Payne, who wound up taking the reins of the Ocean Shores Coalition, the group devoted to dealing with the town's unwanted new image. "They [police] didn't know it was a racist town."

"We aren't," insists Joan Payne, his wife, and executive director of the city's Chamber of Commerce. "We aren't a racist community. We have young people who were looking for trouble. And . . . it found them."[14]

But like most rural communities, the evidence of racist activity is not completely absent, at least in Grays Harbor County and the surrounding area. There is at least one proclaimed skinhead in Aberdeen who proselytizes among the local disaffected teens, though to little effect. A year before the July Fourth incident in Ocean Shores, at a retreat outside the town of Frances—about thirty miles south—a major Christian Identity gathering of about one hundred people was quietly held, with only local law enforcement aware of its presence. And in just the month before Minh Hong's trial, the nearby town of Elma was plastered with neo-Nazi fliers promising a parade down Main Street on New Year's Day. The fliers were bizarre, with rambling text that suggested a degree of mental instability: "Our fallen comrade Grand Admiral Donitz is our hero and George W. Bush is our leader," it proclaimed. "As the Nazi Party takes hold in the United States, we will respect the rights of the common citizen. We are a proud nation and a proud party. We proclaim Adolph Hitler as Satan and Devil and George W. Bush as supreme commander. Let us unite behind him and uplift his principles."

Idiosyncratic events like that are one thing. However, it is hard not to find a broader undertow of bigotry that usually lingers in the quiet places of rural communities like Grays Harbor. The few minorities who live there will tell you, privately, that racism in the town can be "bad," and even non-minorities see the signs. At times, the air in the local coffee shop wafts with smoke and complaints about "those damned Koreans" or "the stinking Mexicans" who have become the area's most visible minorities. Or a well-liked neighbor who's active in civic-minded organizations will, given the right turn in the conversation, suddenly spew a string of racist obscenities that surprise even his friends.

The response to these episodes is universal: simple silence. After all, there is a mantra common to all rural communities: "This is a nice town." People are nice to each other. If someone wants to be a racist, well, most people won't encourage them, but they won't speak out against it, either. They might even laugh at their nigger jokes just to go along.

Grays Harbor County is confronting a change that many other rural districts in America face: an influx of new, nonwhite faces. The bulk of these are Latino, who in the 1990 Census numbered only 1,173, or only 1.8 percent of the population, but by 2000 had grown to represent 4.8 percent of the population with 3,258 residents. (The county, which includes the Quinault Indian Reservation, has for years had a steady population of about 5 percent Native Americans.) More Asians, too, are moving in (they now constitute 1.2 percent of the population, up slightly from 2000), many of them taking over high-profile businesses like restaurants and convenience stores.[15]

This demographic change is happening broadly across rural America, particularly in the Midwest. As a report from the Department of Agriculture's Economic Research Service points out:

> Hispanics are the fastest-growing segment of the American population, and this growth is especially striking in rural America. The 2000 census shows that Hispanics accounted for only 5.5 percent of the Nation's nonmetro population, but 25 percent of nonmetro population growth during the 1990s. Many counties throughout the Midwest and Great Plains would have lost population without recent Hispanic population growth. Among nonmetro counties with high Hispanic population growth in the 1990s, the Hispanic growth rate exceeded 150 percent, compared with an average growth rate of 14 percent for non-Hispanics. Moreover, Hispanics are no longer concentrated in Texas, California, and other Southwestern States—today nearly half of all nonmetro Hispanics live outside the Southwest.[16]

These kinds of demographic shifts, as it happens, often become the primary breeding grounds for hate crimes—even in decidedly non-rural settings. A study published by Donald Green in 1998 focused on New York City, and it found that demographic change in 140 community districts of the city between 1980 and 1990 predicted the incidence of hate crimes. The balance of whites and whatever the target group happened to be in a given community district was an important factor, but the rate at which that balance changed was perhaps even more significant. The most common statistical recipe was an area that was almost purely white in the past that experiences the sudden and noticeable inmigration of some other group.

In the case of New York, what occurred was a rapid inmigration of three groups: Asians, Latinos and blacks, though in the latter case the migration was often a response to the other groups' arrival; blacks were in some ways moved around, or their neighborhood boundaries changed. A number of previously white areas—Bensonhurst being the classic case, or Howard Beach—experienced a rapid inmigration of various nonwhite groups. What was particularly revealing about the hate-crime pattern was that the crimes reflected the targets who were actually moving in—that is, they revealed that this was not a kind of generalized hatred. Where Asians moved in, the researchers found a surge in anti-Asian hate crimes, and likewise with Latinos or blacks. Bias crime has more of a kind of reality-based component, at least in the aggregate, than is implicated by those psychological theories that suggest that there only exists a generalized sense of intolerance on the part of those who practice extreme forms of bigotry.[17]

In a later study, Green found this trend replicated itself elsewhere—namely, in Germany after the fall of the Iron Curtain in the late 1980s. In that case, there was rapid inmigration of immigrants into formerly homogeneous eastern Germany, which replicated the conditions in New York as the perfect recipe for bias crime. And indeed, there was a huge surge in hate crimes, which only slowed when the flow of immigrants was halted in the summer of 1993.[18]

"Thinking about the kind of spatial and temporal dimensions of hate crime is a start in the right direction," says Green. "What it helps to think about is the difference between the static and the dynamic dimensions of this problem. People talk about the problem of hate crime being hate—of course, it is a problem, but hate isn't necessarily rising or falling in the society as a whole. What's changing is your proximity to people that you find onerous. And also your ability to organize or to take action against them.

"There are two hypotheses about why it is that hate crimes subside when demographic change runs its course. One hypothesis is that the haters either accept the fact changes occur to them or they move away. Another hypothesis is that nobody really changes their attitude, it's just that the capacity to organize against some outsider—meeting at the back fence and conspiring against somebody—no longer becomes possible when one of your back-fence neighbors is now no longer part of the old nostalgic group."

Green says that both suburbs and rural areas are the next frontiers for hate crimes, partly because the demographic change is beginning to hit there now, "and they will lack the political will to deal with it."[19]

✳

Though there are no guarantees for anything; at many points along the trajectory taken by Chris Kinison to his death, the intervention of authorities potentially could have altered that course and prevented the tragedy. Studies of the psychology of hate-crimes perpetrators make clear that most of the "thrill-seeking" types of bias offenders are often easily deterred by the strong intervention of authority and the open condemnation of society for such behavior.

Had Ocean Shores police, as well as the other law-enforcement officers with whom he came into contact while harassing minorities, effectively intervened when they had the chance, Kinison may have realized that taking on the persona of a white supremacist wasn't such a clever way to get into fights, and the spiral of violence may have been blunted before spinning out of control. And they had many chances with Kinison: his harassment of the black teenagers in 1997, when he escaped with not even a slap on the wrist; the confrontation with the Filipinos; the subsequent alleged threats against minorities on the beach at Long Beach and Ocean Shores through the weekend before the stabbing.

However, there were other indications that, unlike most "thrill seekers," Kinison had a higher level of ideological commitment to the hateful rhetoric he spewed. There was his possession of the Confederate flag, the nature of the taunts, and the suggestion by people who knew them that Kinison and his gang were unhappy about the "invasion" of Ocean Shores by minorities. For someone like that, bound up in the idea that being American means being white, the Fourth of July would have been the time to make a statement.

No one will ever know for sure. The presence of the "mystery man" attested to by numerous witnesses at the Texaco that night—an apparently older man with a "skinhead" appearance, who joined loudly in the verbal assaults—suggests that Kinison may have been led by someone with actual hate-group connections. Ocean Shores police say they scoured the witnesses and their recollections for more details, and were unable to trace the person, if he even actually existed. (Eyewitness accounts can be notoriously unreliable.) But at best this is only a dark hint that may possibly explain something that was plain at the time of the fight: Kinison was well steeped in hate rhetoric and its ideas, and seemingly well practiced at wielding them.

Moreover, if indeed ideology had no part in that night's events, if Kinison in fact was just "playing around" with race-baiting as an excuse for getting into fights, then it is likewise clear that he had little conception of the lethal nature of the forces he was tapping into—a fear that, as Lynne Varner suggests, is deeply visceral.

While I was attending Minh Hong's trial, I had lunch with James Arima, president of the Japanese American Citizens League's Seattle chapter, and asked him whether the experience in small rural towns was the same for Asian people. "I don't think Asians have nearly the same kind of stigma as black people," he said. "You know, certain episodes aside, I think Asians have generally had good experiences with white people over the years, even in these small towns. They're kind to us, friendly to us, polite, helpful.

"But I think there is an underlying belief—and I think this is cultural, going back to the days when it was bad around here—that if there's trouble, they won't help you," he said. "I think we believe that in those situations, you're going to have to look out for yourself."

This was what happened to Minh Hong that night in Ocean Shores, what went through his mind inside the mini mart. He looked around, and it was clear no one was going to help him. While Kinison banged on the windows, the clerk behind the counter studiously acted as though nothing was going on outside his store. The others inside the store, all apparently white, seemed oblivious. The only one who wasn't—a friend of the tormentor—seemed to think it was a joke, even as Kinison drew his finger across his throat, again and again.

So he started looking around for a way to defend himself, since it was clear no one else was going to.

CHAPTER 16

THE VERDICT

IF THERE WERE HOPES FOR A QUICK END TO THE TRIAL in Montesano shortly after closing arguments concluded on Tuesday, they slowly seeped out as the unseasonably warm afternoon ticked away and the jury remained behind its closed doors. The judge had turned the case over to them shortly before noon, but the doors to their ad-hoc jury room remained closed for the remaining hours of the afternoon.

Considering the complexity of the case, this was not surprising. The jurors faced a tangled web of conflicting evidence and varyingly reliable testimony, and sifting through it would not be easy. Indeed, if they had managed to review the evidence in that short of time, it may have suggested something amiss.

Outside, there was a dull sense of expectation. The remaining observers—a handful of reporters, friends of the participants and some of the trial regulars—were forced to hang outside the courtroom in the narrow hallway at the top of the stairs leading to it, or simply linger in the downstairs halls or outside the city hall. Most doubted that any word was going to come down that day, but some hoped—Minh Hong especially.

I chatted with Minh that afternoon as we hung about outside in the warm afternoon sunshine. It was our first chance to talk since the trial had started, and one of our first conversations in over a year, since I only infrequently visited the teriyaki shop then. Mostly it was small talk: how his parents were doing, what he was studying at school, how his degree was coming along.

He said he had been surprised to see me there, and I explained that I was just as surprised that first day in court—my interest in the case, I told him, arose from my previous work with white supremacists and hate groups, and I hadn't connected him to the case until I saw his mother. We talked a little about my first book, about the far-right Patriot movement in the Northwest, and I told him I was drawn to this case because I was interested in the effect of hate crimes on small towns.

I thought that Chris Kinison, I explained, represented one of the realities of hate crimes: Very few perpetrators of hate crimes are actually affiliated with organized hate groups. They range from skinhead wannabes to thrill-seeking young men out to start a fight to random haters who act out of a visceral animus to minorities. They may not be real skinheads, but they often present themselves as such, and the damage they cause—the physical and psychological trauma, the terrorization of the target community, the damage to the broader community—is every bit as present.

This is when he talked to me about what went through his own mind that early morning of July Fourth: "I just know what I saw, and they all had shaved heads and a Confederate flag, shouting stuff," he said. "I thought they were going to kill me. I just knew I didn't want to end up like that guy in Texas."

A little while later, around 4 P.M., the word came down from upstairs: The jury was retiring for the evening. Deliberations would resume in the morning.

✳

Things were much the same the next morning. After brief consultations among the lawyers, the judge restarted the deliberations, and everyone but the jurors left the courtroom. The remainder of the morning went quietly, like the day before.

The difference was that a media horde of sorts finally had descended on the trial. Two Seattle-based TV trucks had set up shop outside the city hall, and reporters and cameramen could be seen that morning out setting up their spots and testing their equipment. At least one radio reporter had arrived on the scene. The *Post Intelligencer*'s reporter, Bill Miller, had arrived the day before, and the *Olympian* had a staff writer there too. But inside, things were as quiet as before.

Occasionally, people in the hall could hear raised voices through the doors to the jury room—sometimes male, sometimes female. It was only intermittent, though at one point one of the women jurors emerged, crying, and fled to a back room, only to return a little while later with tissues, walking back silently through the door.

Finally, a little after two o'clock, word circulated that the jury had reached a decision. The crowd shuffled quietly back into the courtroom and took their seats. There was a low murmuring of anticipation in the air. The windows again were open to try to keep things circulating as the sun heated up the room, and trucks still occasionally rumbled by and filled the chamber with their noise.

Judge Foscue looked slightly disheveled, and definitely disconcerted, when he entered and took his seat. Jury foreman Gene Schermer delivered an envelope to the clerk that was taken to Foscue, who opened it, read its contents and delivered them to the audience: "The jury has announced that it is deadlocked," he said.

Foscue consulted briefly with the jurors. Was it possible, he asked, that further deliberations could relieve the logjam? "We reached this conclusion very reluctantly, your honor," Schermer said, noting that he had polled all twelve jurors on the question. "There is no probability of resolution."

Fuller was dismayed and argued strenuously for further deliberations. "They have been deliberating for over a day," Foscue retorted. He officially declared a mistrial.

No one was sure what it meant right away—except that the prosecution's case had failed, which meant Minh Hong was free to go home.

Molly Kinison fled the courtroom in tears. "I can't believe this, I just can't believe this," she said. "He's not going to walk free, is he?" she cried to a friend comforting her as she crouched in an elevator.

Minh Hong looked relieved but still stunned: "I am speechless right now," he said. His father and girlfriend were beaming as they and the lawyers chatted afterward.

But there was an edge to the elation: A hung jury meant that prosecutors could refile charges and try Minh Hong all over again. James Arima of the Japanese American Citizens League, who attended the trial as a show of support for the Hong family, was dismayed that there had not been an acquittal.

"The nightmare continues for Minh," he said. "He just continues to be victimized. He's got the cloud still over him."

"Whenever a person goes home at the end of a trial, it's a success," Brett Purtzer said outside the courtroom.

"We put on our best case," said Jerry Fuller. "The jury deliberated long and hard but they couldn't reach a verdict. In the next few days, we'll look at it long and hard and decide where to go from here."

The *Daily World*'s David Scheer managed to track down Gene Schermer at his home that night. "We worked very hard to come to a joint verdict," he said, but told Scheer that he couldn't talk any further because jurors had made a pact not to discuss their deliberations with the press or the public.

Doug Twibell, another juror who was co-owner of an Aberdeen funeral home, told Scheer that jury members were concerned that the media would report their feelings on the case, which in turn might taint any future jury pools if the case returned to court.

"There were some tears shed," Twibell added. "You put a week-and-a-half into something like that with feelings on both sides of the aisle and to come out empty-handed—you have some emotion.

"We saw Kinison's mom sitting there," he added, "and we saw the (emotions) going on in the other family, too."[1]

The vow of silence prevented anyone from getting a handle on the most important question: How had the jury voted? Those results, after all, were likely to affect prosecutors' decision whether or not to refile.

The next day, at Judge Foscue's insistence, that result was released to the attorneys: eleven-to-one for acquittal. One juror—a middle-aged white male—had refused to acquit on the grounds that Minh Hong "shouldn't have brought a knife to a fistfight."

The rest of the jury felt strongly enough about the verdict that it made certain Fuller was aware of the count. "I talked to the prosecutor," foreman Gene Schermer told me a week later, after the jurors had relented on their vow of silence. "I wanted the prosecutor to know it was eleven-one—I think it might make him think again before he tried the poor guy one more time.

"I don't think there was anyone on the jury that wasn't really upset about the hatred that the accused was subjected to."[2]

※

Though the jury had left little doubt about its findings (in many states, an eleven-one vote is an acquittal), Jerry Fuller and his boss, County Prosecutor Stew Menefee, still had the option of reopening the case by filing new charges. Indeed, a tentative new trial date of March 3 was announced a few days after the trial.

The cloud continued to hover over Minh Hong for another three weeks. Finally, on January 3, 2001, Menefee announced his office would not seek a retrial. Fuller filed a motion to dismiss the case that day, and Judge Foscue granted it.

Considering the difficulty prosecutors clearly faced in obtaining a conviction, "it didn't seem appropriate to put everyone through a trial again," Menefee told the *Daily World*. "We presented all the evidence and all the witnesses. Absent minor tuning here and there, there weren't any substantial changes we would make in the way the case was presented.

"It wasn't a case where the jurors didn't know what was going on or something like that. And we didn't find anything unusual or unique about the panel.

"Given those two things and the divisiveness of the case in the community, we made a determination that it wasn't in the interest of anybody to go forward with a second trial. . . . There is no purpose to be served in going forward if we didn't believe we would get a different result," Menefee said.

Brett Purtzer was elated. "We're happy for our client and we think it's the right decision for the prosecutor," he said. "We think enough is enough. The jury spoke and loudly."

Minh Hong, he added, was relieved: "This has been a nightmare for his family."

Doug Chin of the Organization of Chinese Americans in Seattle was also pleased with the announcement, noting that it likely was difficult for an all-white jury to reach, since it may have been hard for them to understand what had happened "if you are not a non-white and you haven't experienced racial threats."

The case was monitored closely by the Asian American community, Chin said: "I think they will feel a sense of relief. But I think most of them will say that Hong shouldn't have been charged in the first place."

Molly Kinison, on the other hand, was apparently dismayed by the decision. "We spoke with her, and my impression is that she feels that the defendant has gotten away with it," Menefee said. "She thinks that her son was killed out of anger and not out of fear or self-defense. She was not happy with the hung jury and she's not happy with the decision not to go forward."[3]

✳

It was inescapable that whatever he had done, Chris Kinison was the one who was dead, and no one deserves to die simply for being racist, or behaving like one. However, in the end it was only by a twist of fate and impulse—Minh Hong's theft of those knives—that the story ended differently than most hate crimes. So if Kinison indeed just used the Confederate flag and the racial slurs and the throat-slashing gestures as a way of looking for trouble, it found him with a vengeance.

A few days after the jury delivered its verdict, Molly Kinison granted an interview to the *Daily World's* David Scheer. "My son is not a racist," she told him. "He was not a skinhead—I wouldn't stand for it. I wouldn't stand for anybody to be treated badly."

She told Scheer she believed Minh Hong lied on the stand to get away with the killing. She had little doubt that no one had stopped the Hongs from leaving in their Honda, and contended that when they got out, the insults went "both ways." "If you were that scared for your life, why would you get out of the car?" she asked.

She disputed the defense's depiction of him as a "skinhead" because of his short hair, arguing that Kinison had planned to join the Navy, like his father. And she doubted the contention that he was a serious threat.

"I know my son wouldn't have hurt those boys the way they hurt my son," she said.[4]

Molly Kinison may have known that, but there is no reason Minh Hong would have—nor, for that matter, any reason why a juror would believe he wouldn't have, at bare minimum, inflicted serious harm on Minh Hong. Too many witnesses had testified that he had made that intention clear.

In the end, Molly Kinison's view was one small, and ultimately very narrow, slice of the Rashomon tragedy that played out that night in Ocean Shores. Like all such dramas, the truth only emerges as more voices are heard.

In most criminal trials, there are only two versions of reality that are officially presented, but many more are likely to emerge as the evidence mounts. The narrative version of those events that Jerry Fuller tried to concoct ultimately rang false, in no small part because of the weight of evidence produced by his own witnesses that demonstrated with stark clarity what kind of hell Chris Kinison made his victims endure that night. Moreover, asked to decide if a person was reasonable to arm himself with a knife when faced with such threats, most people would readily say yes: What would not be reasonable would be to proceed naively as though such assailants were harmless. Minh Hong's understated and ultimately convincing testimony only served to confirm that the version of reality presented by his defense team was closer to the truth, if not that exactly.

It may have been true, for example, that just as prosecutors contended, Chris Kinison's taunts had angered Minh Hong; it would have taken saintly forbearance not to have taken some umbrage. But the prosecutor's case depended on the notion that somehow fear and anger are mutually exclusive emotions. Hong probably did feel at least pangs of anger—but that doesn't mean his state of mind at the same time was not overwhelmingly gripped with sheer terror.

There were other aspects of the drama that emerged in court which were not part of the official narratives, but which also became clear as testimony proceeded. There were hints—mostly Minh Hong's cuts, and his testimony that he felt a sharp pain in his hand and arm before reaching for the knife—that Kinison may have had a knife of his own. And though the evidence was never presented in court, only three hours before the stabbing, a black man had been threatened by a man he identified as Kinison, wielding a large Bowie knife.

Several witnesses, including one with a clear view, had seen one of the three Asian men reach for a pants leg as they exited the convenience store, evidently trying to suggest he had a weapon, sparking the response: "No knives." Again, however, this presumes that such displays of anger excluded the men from feeling terrorized. In fact, they were in some ways at least understandable reactions to the threats they faced—bluffing with a counterthreat may reek of desperation, but it may have bought them the time to reach their car, too.

The key to the drama ultimately revolved around that moment when Minh Hong stole the knives. Because one more question, one more perspective, lingered: What if he hadn't stolen the knives?

What if Minh Hong and his brother and friend had ventured unarmed against Kinison and his friends? What if they had been severely injured, as was more than likely? (As it was, Minh Hong was hospitalized with injuries inflicted in the fight.) Would Christopher Kinison have been standing trial that December for committing a hate crime?

Given the behavior of Ocean Shores police in handling the incidents leading up to the stabbing, and their strenuous denials of wrongdoing or misfeasance in those cases, and especially given the insistence by prosecutors that the Hongs were not facing a serious threat of bodily harm on July Fourth, it is not hard to conclude that the answer may well have turned out: "No."

This was the most troubling reality that emerged from Minh Hong's trial: Much of the testimony, including the prosecution's, made abundantly clear that Chris Kinison was not alone in harassing and assaulting, verbally and physically the three Asian men. He had at least three, and possibly as many as seven, accomplices who joined him in shouting racial epithets, making threats to inflict various kinds of harm, and generally putting them in fear for their lives. It was clear, in fact, that Kinison couldn't have terrorized them alone.

And each of those people, to varying degrees, had also participated in a hate crime: specifically, Washington's malicious harassment law, which outlaws precisely this kind of activity, designating it a Class C felony with stiff penalties.

Did Minh Hong get away with killing Chris Kinison recklessly? Perhaps. Did other people at the Texaco that night get away with committing a hate crime? Almost certainly.

The Grays Harbor prosecutor, however, did not see it that way.

✳

One of the real weaknesses of the county prosecutor's case in the trial was that it consistently downplayed Kinison's behavior, describing it variously as "rude, obnoxious, and obscene" and "racist," despite the near certainty that it was also *criminal*. The recognition that Kinison committed a hate crime, and that he was not alone in doing it, was utterly absent in nearly every step the prosecutor took.

It was clear from testimony presented in the court from all sides that the Hongs were the victims of a hate crime—and more to the point, that Chris Kinison was not alone in committing it. He had accomplices. But the Grays Harbor prosecutor, H. Steward Menefee, made it plain he had no intention of pursuing hate-crimes charges against any of them: "Given what I know, I don't see that as happening at this point in time," Menefee said, citing the widely conflicting testimony and lack of evidence.[5]

I spent an hour or so talking about the case with Menefee, and not once did he indicate that hate crimes entered into his office's calculus. He repeatedly contrasted what the Hongs went through that night, particularly the fatal fight itself, with a bar fight—a kind of prosecution with which he is abundantly familiar—as though a hate crime were comparable.

"OK, you've got a fistfight and that happens every day," Menefee said. "You're not going to hear me saying that what Mr. Hong experienced was not atrocious. I am not going to condone what Mr. Kinison was doing out there. But that's not the issue for me. We don't kill people because they've behaved that way.

"I think the jury focused on Mr. Kinison's behavior, and did not address the harder issue of when was Mr. Hong lawfully using deadly force. And that's what happened here: Deadly force was used in a fistfight.

"And the question is: Is it reasonable to use deadly force in a fistfight when your grounds for that is your perception is that he's white and he's using racial [epithets], therefore that in and of itself, raises deadly force? The second he punches you, it goes from fistfight to deadly force."

To Menefee, it was unimportant that Washington law stipulates that you are allowed to bring deadly force if there is an imminent threat of substantial bodily injury or death. Menefee, who consistently overlooked Chris Kinison's use of the throat-slashing gesture that had been attested to by several prosecution witnesses, didn't believe Minh Hong faced such a threat. He evinced no awareness at any time that the context of a hate crime, particularly when physical violence comes into play, carries with it an innate death threat that is not present in a typical bar fight.

"I don't believe the fight that we are talking about here rises to that level," he said. "We had one or two punches thrown, the rest of the time they were wrestling.

"If that's the test, if you leave all the other stuff out, then every bar fight that I ever prosecuted, then someone can pull a knife, you know what I mean? Because any fistfight can produce substantial bodily injury.

"I think that issue was one that had to be explored by the jury, and they did. And I've abided by the jury's verdict. I think reasonable minds can disagree."

He defended his office's decision to file the charges, saying he thought the evidence was clear the Hongs were not fearful or scared. "I think the evidence in this case indicates quite clearly that that was not what was going on. If I thought they were in terror of their lives, we would not have filed this charge."

What made the difference for him, he said, was the number of times Minh Hong stabbed Kinison: "Twenty-three wounds in these circumstances, given the facts of this case, not just the wounds themselves but the facts of this case, that was excessive. There's a lot of people who think that. I'm not on my own out here." Menefee said there was considerable support for the charges from the Grays Harbor community.

Yet even though he thought what happened was comparable to a typical fist-fight, he thought Kinison had in fact committed a hate crime. He said that, had Minh Hong been able to phone police, or if he had been the victim of an assault by Kinison without the stabbing, there would have been malicious-harassment charges filed.

"Yes, I believe that—probably, if there had been an investigation, assuming the facts as I know them, that there could have been a charge filed against Mr. Kinison," he said. "If somebody had called the police, and the police had investigated it, if Mr. Hong had used the phone at the Texaco instead of stealing two knives, we might have had an entirely different result. Probably Mr. Kinison would have been facing charges." (Prosecution witnesses testified, incidentally, that the pay phone at the Texaco was being used by someone else during the entire incident.)

But Menefee said that he saw nothing in the testimony to support malicious-harassment charges against any of Kinison's friends. "I think that the majority of the testimony, particularly the testimony of people who were not in Mr. Kinison's group, indicated that was not the case—that Mr. Kinison's activities at the time of the fight were pretty much on his own, that there was nobody else with him at that point," said Menefee, who went on to note that he couldn't charge anyone for their mere presence or for failing to stop Kinison. All this was true, but it elides what had just occurred beforehand: Five of the prosecution's fifteen eyewitnesses had testified that both Kinison and his friends had participated in the verbal assaults before the Hongs got in their car; most of the remaining ten, except William Keys, were all part of Kinison's group or knew him in high school; and three of those who did say they heard threats from others knew Kinison as well.

Menefee complained that "a lot of people who are talking about this case are utilizing a perspective that involves the race of the party instead of the facts of the case." He contended that Kinison was "stereotyped" as a "skinhead," which wasn't grounds in itself to kill someone. He saw no reason why a minority encountering someone who acted like one, intentionally looked like one, and threatened his life like one, would fear that he might become another James Byrd.

He said there was no basis for anyone to believe that "because he might be the white man that will drag me by a chain, if he takes any kind of action toward me, I must respond with deadly force.

"I'm afraid that in this population of this country, if that equates to ground to stab someone twenty-three times, then we are in deep trouble. That's mass hysteria fear is what you're talking about."

As it happens, Menefee has never prosecuted a malicious-harassment case in Grays Harbor County.

※

The FBI had earlier investigated the case at the behest of Seattle-based Asian American groups and had concluded initially that it was out of their jurisdiction. The state attorney general's office usually leaves decisions on seeking charges in such cases up to local prosecutors like Menefee.

And Menefee's decision to let the whole matter drop made a certain sense in the short run, since the incident continued to divide the community, and in fact prosecuting such a case would be difficult on an evidentiary level. Ocean Shores police conducted a vigorous investigation of the potential that others had taken part in a hate crime that night, but it began nearly a week after the fact, and by then, the evidence had gone cold. None of Kinison's crowd was talking, and neither were any of their friends who had been at the Texaco that night.

But it was akin to letting a deeply infected wound just scab over, since it also left urban Asians and blacks wondering whether Ocean Shores was committed to protecting them if they visited.

Up close, it was clear why officials in Grays Harbor would not pursue the case. From a distance, it became increasingly hard to look at them as substantially different from Southern sheriffs from another era who jailed uppity Negroes for resisting being lynched.

The difference, in this case, had been the jury. In the end, it stood up for the underlying decency of its own community by making clear it understood what a nightmare like that of July Fourth in Ocean Shores might mean to someone who happened to be a minority. Its verdict in essence made the same kind of statement as the one at the root of hate-crime laws: that death threats and violence by bullies aimed at oppressing other citizens will not stand. By recognizing that Minh Hong indeed had good reason to fear for his life, it refuted the argument that such acts are no different than a typical bar fight.

The key point for the jury, as it turned out, was a factor in the case that neither prosecutors nor defense attorneys dealt with directly: Minh Hong's role in the final fight. Because *he was not driving*, several of the jurors found that there was more than "reasonable doubt" that he had any role in instigating the fight.

"We had some serious questions about why [Hong's brother] turned back that way rather than go out on the highway," jury foreman Gene Schermer told David Scheer. However, "I realize the accused wasn't driving the car and there was no evidence that it was his decision to [stop]."

Of even greater weight, though, for most of the jurors was the level of threat that was emanating from Kinison and his crowd. "Considering all of the taunts and everything that had come to that point, it seemed reasonable that [Hong and his brother] could have feared that they would be subjected to severe injury," Schermer said.

"I believe it was self defense, and I think the majority of the jury felt that way." Not everyone did, Schermer noted. "For some folks, reasonable doubt was the issue." And one juror never doubted that Hong was guilty.

Overall, Schermer said the discussion was civil. "It was an emotional trial, so it wasn't without emotion, but I thought people handled themselves with great decorum," he said. "There were no personal attacks on anyone's integrity."

And Schermer said the presence of both Kinison's and Hong's family members did not have "one iota" of impact on their verdict.

"I think that all the jurors felt that it was very sad that someone had died and they didn't want to excuse that," he said, but the requirements of the law left no room for a conviction.

Juror Doug Twibell, the funeral-home owner who also voted to acquit, had a similar reading of the case. Most of the jurors were struck by the dimensions of the tragedy, he said: "I feel for Mrs. Kinison. She lost her son."

But, he said, the case did not fit the court's definition of manslaughter. Moreover, the jury understood that Minh Hong's fear was perfectly reasonable.

"We really understood the fear that Minh might have been experiencing," Twibell said. "Some of the jurors had been through some similar situations . . . Can you blame the Asians for that kind of action? A lot of us didn't think so."[6]

※

Minh Hong has a nice job now, in downtown Seattle, away from the teriyaki shop. No one at work knows anything about his past. That's the way he likes it. He says he only goes back to his parents' restaurant about once a week now, though he says Hung still works there occasionally.

He is still shy, still quiet, and still shows glints of hidden strengths. He seems haunted now. There is a sadness to him that used to not be there. Perhaps it comes from the inescapable knowledge that he killed a man.

Monte Hester told me the first time he met Minh Hong, he was struck by his "gentle soul." I know what he means. And gentle souls do not bear the burden of blood very easily.

Three years later, Minh says he still hasn't left town since the trial. He said he and Hung and his girlfriend nearly drove down to Portland a few weeks ago. But his parents said no. So they stayed home. He doesn't think he'll be leaving anytime soon.

"Everything's changed," he says, with a quiet finality. "Everything."[7] There are no tears in his eyes. Only endless regret.

CHAPTER 17

THE AMERICAN LANDSCAPE

HATE CRIMES ARE A PROBLEM IN AMERICA ONLY because it is a democratic republic. They do not really arise as serious pathologies in authoritarian societies, because equality of opportunity and ethnic harmony are not values that by necessity arise from within the warp and weave of the culture; to the extent that these values exist in such societies, they are imposed from without. Consider, by way of recent historical example, how Marshall Tito's Communist regime kept a lid on the bloody and ancient ethnic rivalries that were inherent in Yugoslavia. Part of this, of course, is due to the repressive nature of authoritarianism; but in a larger sense, even if such crimes do occur, they are not the same kind of social problem, because they don't cut so directly against the grain of its foundation, any more than any other crime.

Democracies, in contrast, intrinsically depend on an egalitarian body politic that encourages and enables opportunity and access to all of its members. Thus, hate crimes are innately anti-democratic, because their entire purpose is to terrorize, oppress, intimidate, divide, disenfranchise. They strike hard in nearly any kind of democracy, including those of Europe, because they directly undercut basic principles of equal participation and fair play.

But they are acutely a problem in the United States, not only because it is the beating heart of democratic society in the world, but because we are in reality a genuinely multicultural society, more so than even modern European states. Hate crimes cause intense damage right at the most fragile point of such societies, because they erupt along the contiguous fault lines of race and culture, rupturing whatever fabric of racial harmony may exist and sowing distrust and fear. As long as there are crimes that are intended to terrorize and oppress others, then it is incumbent on democracies like America to pass and enforce laws against them. As Boston University legal expert Frederick Lawrence says, "It's a recognition of what a multicultural society *should* do in terms of reacting to these kinds of crimes."[1]

Bias-crimes laws are largely failing in America, mostly because of inadequate enforcement, which in turn is entrenched by misconceived opposition to them. And to the extent that they fail, whatever progress the nation has made in healing its racial and cultural divides is undermined. It is almost unquestionable that great strides have been made in relations between the majority white culture and various minorities in the past half century, with notable strides not only on the racial and religious fronts, but in recent years, tolerance of gays and lesbians and other sexual minorities has dramatically improved.

Hate crimes, in fact, represent a violent reaction against that healing, and to the extent that they spread, the gap is widened and the wounds reopened. This failure is occurring in both rural and urban settings, across the landscape. Cities are better equipped and generally better prepared, but even their capacity to deal with them adequately can be overwhelmed at times, and even the best-trained officers can miss key signposts. And as the jury in Grays Harbor County established, small towns are, in the end, every bit as capable of doing the right thing, even if the route there is long and difficult.

The significant difference in the rural and urban response to bias crimes is how it affects the cultural landscape. Rural hate crimes make minorities even more apprehensive about setting foot in such places, just as urban black-on-white hate crimes compound the already common misgivings of whites in the surrounding areas about visiting the city. Likewise, the failure to adequately deal with hate crimes compounds and widens that mistrust, on all sides.

In real-world terms, there is a profound effect arising from the geographical and demographic differences between urban and rural America. The urban world, because it represents the majority of the nation's population, tends to dominate its cultural life. But cities and suburbs represent only a tiny portion of the nation's total landscape. When you get out a map and look at America, its mass is dominated by its cultural rural half. There are many more rural places in the United States than urban or suburban.

When hate crimes erupt, the racial and cultural discord they sow manifests itself in a kind of balkanization of the country: their respective target communities feel unsafe or disinclined to travel there, even in passing. For minorities who are cut off from white rural America, though, this effect is multiplied exponentially by the extent of the landscape which has become off-limits to them. This is what African American journalist Lynne Varner meant when she wrote, "Suddenly, the country seems a lot smaller."

Hate-crime expert Donald Green puts it this way: "If you had to kind of step back and ask, does hate crime pay? You'd say yes."[2] If, as Green argues, this effect is to create "a massive deadweight loss of freedom," then it is incumbent on all Americans, right and left, urban and rural, regular citizens and law-enforcement officials, to take them seriously—to finally, after generations of grappling with the problem, grasp its enormity and bring it to heel. At some point, the debate over hate crimes must evolve beyond meaningless and distorted myths and mature into a serious discussion of how to wisely deal with them, through means that preserve our cherished rights to free speech while simultaneously standing up for the rights of equal opportunity essential for democratic society and against the bullies and thugs who would use violence to harm it.

Though we have, as a nation, been tracking hate crimes since 1991, we still do not have a firm handle on the scope of the problem some thirteen years later. As the Department of Justice's 2000 study of hate-crimes reporting concluded, there is a massive gap between the bias crimes that are reported annually and the numbers that actually occur—which, by the Southern Poverty Law Center's estimate, could run as a high as 42,000 more crimes than the annual 8,000 or so that show up in FBI statistics. Most significantly, the DOJ study found that the problems are not simply endemic to the system of laws themselves. The study demonstrates that hate crimes can be effectively countered through education and training, both of the public generally and law officers particularly. If the nation's law officers are better trained, they will be able to provide a more accurate picture of the phenomenon's reach before hate crimes can be effectively addressed through broader policy measures that attack its even deeper roots. In order to close the persistent gap between enforcement and the real levels of bias crime, there has to be a commitment on the part of both law enforcement and society to take the problem seriously.

This means especially emphasizing rural America, where the mass of smaller departments reside, and concurrently where the problem of underenforcement of bias-crime statutes persists most sharply. Although, clearly, urban police departments are not immune to this problem, it only takes a brief survey of the statistics to gain an appreciation for the breadth of the shortfall. In 2001 in Washington state, for example, the largest numbers of hate crimes reported by far came from three urban police departments: Seattle, Spokane, and Tacoma, all with extensive experience with and training in bias crimes (these three reported roughly 30 percent of all hate crimes in the state). Meanwhile, the vast majority of law-enforcement agencies in the state, 189 jurisdictions in all, reported zero hate crimes or did not report at all.[3] As we have seen, this does not necessarily mean there are in fact no hate crimes occurring in these districts—it only means that within at least some of them an inestimable number are going either unreported or uninvestigated.

Most of the time, as in Ocean Shores, hate crimes are underinvestigated because they are not commonplace events. "No matter where you are, hate crimes are rare events and they won't be encountered by an officer very often," says Jack McDevitt, co-author of the DOJ study and dean of Northeastern University's Center for Criminal Justice Policy Research. As a result, he says, their studies have found that very few places employ the model that the FBI recommends—namely, a two-tiered response in which departments designate a trained officer for whom part of their responsibilities is to investigate these kind of incidents. That officer in turn is a sort of institutional repository of expertise around these incidents, and serves as a resource to everybody in the department, helping other officers on the force become familiar with at least the basics of identifying bias crimes.

"In small agencies, they just don't do this," says McDevitt. "And the vast majority of agencies in the United States are small, so the vast majority of agencies don't do it."

Many of the reasons for this became clearer after McDevitt's team conducted a follow-up study to the 2000 DOJ report in the fall of 2003, also for the Department of Justice Statistics, titled, "Bridging the Information Disconnect in National Bias Crime Reporting." It sampled some of the respondents to the earlier study and tried to examine them more closely to determine why bias crimes were being underreported to the extent found in the first study.

What the study found, McDevitt says, is that "there was a real set of incentives to not identify bias-motivated incidents as such. Generally speaking, we went to focus groups with police officers in these communities, and they would say, 'Oh, we haven't had any bias crimes,' and then in the course of fifteen or twenty minutes of discussion, they would relate two or three incidents that could have been.

"What we found when we went into it deeper was that, for many of these communities, the definition of a hate crime is something like what happened in Jasper, Texas, or Laramie, Wyoming. That's what the officers see in their head when they think of a hate crime. Or someone with a shaved head. The extreme examples.

"Smaller examples are generally sort of identified as something that—you know, it's not that serious. And we found that the lack of training is one of the most significant barriers; most police officers get very little training on this in the academy and none after that. And then once they get through that, they forget about it quickly because they don't encounter it regularly. And then, when they do encounter them, they have these incredible ways to sort of minimize incidents that don't involve actual physical violence.

"One of the stories that was related to us that was put in the report was this one officer who told us: 'Yeah, we thought we had a hate crime one time. We went out to investigate, there had been a cross burning on a black family's lawn. And when we went out there, we saw it—there were three crosses, but they were really little crosses, so it wasn't a hate crime.'

"All the tendencies of small departments are that if, you just call it an assault or a vandalism, it can be handled regularly. If you label it as a hate crime it kicks in all these other things, as well as the publicity and the media and stuff. So if you're an officer, there really has to be leadership from the department that says they want you to do this, because otherwise, you're making your job more difficult, and the chances are they are not going to identify it."[4]

Another co-author of the earlier DOJ study, Joan Weiss of the Justice Research and Statistics Association, found a similar trend in police departments: when the leadership made hate crimes a priority and made it clear why, beyond mere "political correctness," then officers were far more likely to respond adequately. This is especially critical in smaller departments, where it is rare to find an officer designated as the hate-crimes specialist.

"If you have a small rural department, everybody in the department has to be involved," Weiss says. "You can't just have one person and say, 'That person is the hate crimes officer.' In a large department, there's obviously much more compartmentalization, but in rural areas, it doesn't work unless the department as a whole buys into the need for this so that everybody is on board with it."[5]

Large police agencies will contain segments that are never going to come into contact with a hate crime or victim. In a rural area, every officer potentially could come into contact with such a crime. However, the resistance to the very *idea* of a hate crime is most likely to arise in such areas as well.

"We see that resistance all the time," says McDevitt. "When we did the interviews in the second study with police officers, there was a lot of resistance along the lines of: 'This is a special law for special people; this is not a general law; why do we have to do this differently for these people?' There was a real lack of appreciation for any kind of differences that might exist.

"And there was also what we saw as a sort of natural conservatism of the police. This idea, politically, of protecting a group was something that is sort of antithetical to the way most police officers would sort of see the world, coming from the place they are, their social status, that sort of thing. We found consistently that there was a real non-support for hate-crime legislation."

This picture changed dramatically for police departments that, like the one in Ocean Shores, had a good look not just at the crimes themselves but at the damage they cause. "There's also a near-universal appreciation for the victims from among officers who've had to deal with these cases," says McDevitt. "When they see what the real pain and the real victimization is among these people, it overcomes their natural conservatism and becomes something that they believe in.

"Like any kind of prejudice, it doesn't necessarily transfer across groups quickly—if you find a young black victim who's been beaten and you become empathetic to that, you're not all of a sudden going to always say, well, I'm going to be empathetic to gay men next. But I do think that what we found was that police were naturally non-disposed to dealing with this, which is another element of why it's hard to identify them, and almost hostile to the idea of legislation, particularly if it involved additional paperwork for them. And that message didn't get out very much—it wasn't until it became personal that you could get them past that."

Weiss argues that, in the end, it comes down to education and training coupled with the commitment on the part of the department leadership. "I believe the majority of people in law enforcement are capable of understanding and implementing the bias crimes laws. But for them to be enforced as they were intended requires effective training by those of us responsible for communicating what it is we want them to know and how we want them to proceed. It has got to be talked about in a police department; the subject has to have credibility."

"It's not just that they have to buy into the fact that hate crimes are important and they have terrible impacts on people and the community, and they have the potential for escalating into greater violence if they are not dealt with. You have to know what it is you're looking for. Even if police departments are well-intentioned, some officers may miss hate crimes—they may not recognize the bias motivation because they don't know what to look for or the questions to ask."[6]

✯

Insofar as bias-crime laws are failing in America, the blame ultimately falls not so much on the laws but on the system itself. If thousands of police departments are failing to adequately enforce them, it is not because they are incapable of it, or of understanding the laws. It is that the system itself not only fails to enable these agencies, but in some regards acts to impede the proper handling of the crimes.

Hate-crimes laws are, in this sense, a classic unfunded mandate: Politicians at the top of the system have passed them in increasing number, but have done little to make sure that the people in charge of enforcing them have the proper tools to do so. Even though the laws are, as I have argued, a product of long American traditions both in terms of the law and in our undergirding democratic beliefs, they also are decidedly new kinds of laws, especially from a law-enforcement perspective. With their passage, officers are expected to almost automatically possess a sophisticated ability to differentiate a bias crime from an ordinary crime—and of course, relatively few do. The system itself, having passed these laws, does little or nothing to give them that ability.

Fixing the problem will require proper funding for the mandate. In this case, the costs, from the perspective of Congress and state legislatures, are not prohibitive—but their allocation is essential. And the solutions must focus on the three components that are grappling with bias crimes: the political arena, law enforcement, and the general community.

CHANGING THE LAWS

Legal reform at both the federal and state levels is required to make hate-crimes laws consistently effective. As matters currently stand, the federal statutes are toothless and effectually meaningless, and their intersection with state laws—which are themselves a hopeless and sometimes unconstitutional tangle, and often equally useless—is fraught with miscommunication and bu-reaucratic bungling.

• **Federal laws:** As Frederick Lawrence points out: "We actually do not have a real federal bias-crime statute at present."[7] The 1990 Hate Crimes Statistics Act only created the federal data-reporting system, while the 1994 Hate Crimes Sentencing Enhancement Act only allowed prosecutors to enhance sentences for certain federal crimes committed with a bias motivation, but it was written in a way that placed extraordinary limits on the kinds of cases that can be considered, rendering the laws of little use to most law-enforcement officials.

The legislation that has been pending in Congress since the spring of 2000, the Local Law Enforcement Enhancement Act, would represent the nation's first genuine federal hate-crimes law—were it ever to pass. It would finally enable FBI and other federal agents to deal with a broad range of bias crimes—including, for the first time, those against gays and lesbians.

"It would do several things," says Lawrence. "First of all, it would have provided a federal statute so that, in those states that didn't have the resources or didn't have the statute, they would be able to use the federal option. The other thing it would do is it probably would encourage states to put in appropriate resources, because otherwise the feds might show them up. If you don't want the feds coming into your territory and prosecuting one of these things, then what it would do is it would take a crime that has a national aspect to it—the impact on the racial divide in a multicultural society—and it would elevate it to the level that crimes, for example, narcotics laws have, namely, laws that have both federal and state elements. And what that would call for in any given case is a federal and state discussion—and whoever's got the better statute, use [that agency] to lead the case."[8]

Unfortunately, most of the debate over the LLEA has revolved around the mythology of hate crimes, particularly on the issue of including sexual orientation among the categories of bias. But, as we have seen, there simply is no sound legal or even logical argument for not including anti-gay violence in a bias-crime law;

such acts, after all, clearly constitute the kind of large-scale social pathology that the laws are meant to address (by most estimates, gays and lesbians represent the second-most-common target of hate crimes, and they likewise are victims of some of the most violent hate crimes). The arguments against their inclusion—which to date have been the chief reason for the failure of the LLEA—are almost purely of the emotional kind, highly moralistic and innately amoral in the way they equate crimes with free speech. What has been sadly lacking is a more serious debate that examines the real effects of a federal hate-crime statute and what its proper breadth and scope should be, especially concerning free-speech rights and the issue of extending federal control in law enforcement.

In this regard, however, the LLEA is extraordinarily circumspect. While giving federal authorities broad abilities to support, financially and logistically, local law enforcement in pursuing these crimes, it specifically delimits the points at which federal agents may become involved in them. As its name suggests, it places a heavy emphasis on empowering local police departments to go after hate crimes. And, since it is carefully drawn on the free-speech guidelines laid down by the Supreme Court in *Wisconsin v. Mitchell* (and, more recently, in *Virginia v. Black*), it avoids creating such "thought crimes" as the outlawing of hate speech. In all, the legislation as written treads carefully within both the free-speech and states-rights arenas.

"The critical point is that this is not about saying that the states don't have the desire to do it—though there's part of that too," says Lawrence. "But this is not a retread of the civil-rights enforcement in the '50s and '60s in the South. There really is special training that goes into these kinds of crimes. And those of us who live in places like Boston or New York or Chicago sort of blithely assume that a good police department will have a separate bias-crime unit and it will be trained, and for that matter, the average cop on the street will be sufficiently trained to know how to tag something as a case that ought to be sent to the bias-crime unit. But the fact is, small police departments don't have the resources.

"What this federal statute would have provided, and may yet provide, is the kind of federal stopgap that backs up local agencies. One would expect that U.S. Attorney's offices in places like New York and Boston, where departments already have hate-crime units, would not have to do quite so much, but you would expect that U.S. Attorney's offices in other parts of the country would be able to hack into the Department of Justice and put somebody on the case who's got expertise."[9]

Moreover, language written into the LLEA would authorize funding for providing grants to small departments that would enable them to get the training in bias crimes they need. As we have seen, this training is an essential component of making hate-crimes genuinely effective.

• **State laws:** The forty-six states that have passed bias-crime laws have done so remarkably haphazardly. (This is equally true of the variety of local jurisdictions that have passed some form of bias-crime law.) Some states, like Washington, have freestanding "malicious harassment" statutes whose usefulness is often very limited.

A "malicious harassment" statute typically makes anyone committing such a crime liable for a Class C felony. As such, it is useful for stiffening the sentences of lesser "parallel" crimes such as threatening, intimidation and vandalism when committed with a bias motivation. Conversely, it is utterly useless when it comes to more serious crimes, especially most forms of assault—only fourth-degree assault is less than a Class C felony (it is a gross misdemeanor), and first-degree assault is a Class A felony.

In other words, a prosecutor confronted with the choice of prosecuting someone for aggravated assault or malicious harassment would naturally, under such a state law, choose the traditional "parallel" crime to pursue, because it carries stiffer penalties and is a more serious crime. This problem manifested itself in the spring of 2001 in Seattle, when police investigators recommended hate-crimes charges against various participants in the city's February 2001 Mardi Gras riots, only for prosecutors to decide not to file such charges primarily because of just this weakness in the law.[10]

The constitutionality of such standalone laws in any event is suspect, since they do not follow the "sentence enhancement" model endorsed by the Supreme Court, though most of them do maintain the distinction between speech and conduct that is at the basis of the courts' core rulings. Others have adopted almost absurdly (and plainly unconstitutional) vague language as a sop to the forces aligned against the laws. Even those states that employ sentence-enhancement laws vary widely by the kinds of biases they specify. And of course, the lack of any kind of a hate-crime law in four states—Wyoming, Indiana, South Carolina and Arkansas—not only remains a serious problem in those places, but it creates a vacuum in their dealings with other jurisdictions.

The result is a thicket of confused communication and displaced priorities, especially if police officers move about from state to state or even to other departments within a state where priorities are aligned differently. When hate crimes do occur, many police officers have little idea just what acts constitute such a crime under their state's own laws, particularly if they involve a bias other than a racial one.

Of course, many of these laws were passed early in the 1980s, well before there was an established body of law and court rulings considering their respective worth and constitutionality, as well as any kind of a clear idea just which kinds of laws are actually effective in addressing bias crimes. Others remain clouded by the politics of anti-homosexual activism. Whatever the cause, many of the least worthy state laws remain entrenched through the same kind of political inertia that is at the root of so much of the nation's racial and cultural divides.

If states wish to seriously address hate crimes in their communities (and as a national problem as well) then a review of the status of their laws is in order. Legislators and rights activists should determine whether or not the laws on their books fit the models engendered by court rulings that have followed their passage. The most broadly used (and legally ideal) model is the one drafted in 1994 by the Anti-Defamation League, which some states have in fact adopted (Hawaii being the most recent example). This model emphasizes the sentence-enhancement approach, and recommends the following categories of bias motivation: race, religion, national origin, sexual orientation or gender. It also includes a section on institutional vandalism, such as the defacement of synagogues or arson of black churches.[11] If states were to uniformly adopt this model—with slight variations depending on regional needs to address specific pathologies—law-enforcement officials more readily could eliminate the miscommunication and misunderstanding currently plaguing the system.

Unfortunately, because of political inertia, most states and local jurisdictions are unlikely to act to review the laws. It usually takes a horrendous event, like Matthew Shepard's murder, to get bias-crime laws on legislators' radar, and even then, that is no guarantee that anything will happen. This is true not only of places like rural Wyoming, but also urban Seattle. Institutional problems keep hate crimes from being adequately prosecuted. And cultural dispositions keep them from being squarely confronted by the communities themselves. When that happens, they often fade into the region's memory hole within a few short weeks. Advocacy by grass-roots community, church and civil-rights groups may be the best answer for moving these legislative mountains. Unfortunately, because of political inertia, most states and local jurisdictions are unlikely to act to review the laws. It usually takes a horrendous event, like Matthew Shepard's murder, to get bias-crime laws on legislators' radar, and even then, that is no guarantee that anything will happen. This is true not only of places like rural Wyoming, but also urban Seattle. Institutional problems keep hate crimes from being adequately prosecuted, as both the Mardi Gras and Ocean Shores cases demonstrated. And cultural dispositions keep them from being squarely confronted by the communities themselves. When that happens, they often fade into the region's memory hole within a few short weeks. Advocacy by grass-roots community, church and civil-rights groups may be the best answer for moving these legislative mountains.

LAW ENFORCEMENT

The linchpin for making bias-crimes laws work is the people who enforce them. If law-enforcement officials misunderstand the laws or are improperly trained to deal with them, then no amount of lawmaking will do any good.

The best place to start, perhaps, is with the creation of an FBI-recommended two-tiered system, one in which a single officer is assigned primary duty to bias crimes and then acts as a resource in training and assisting the rest of the department. But the DOJ study of hate-crime reporting also offers further suggestions, including:

- Law enforcement officials should strive to enhance their relations with victims and the target communities of bias crimes to ensure their full assistance investigating the crimes.
- Since public awareness of hate crimes is an essential component of police outreach, officials should make a concerted effort to educate and inform their citizens about their efforts to combat the crimes. This can range from holding town meeting to discuss crimes to publicizing the department's bias-crimes officer. Police should also try to publicize bias-crime data within their communities.
- Local agencies should try to establish "formal, step by step procedures for the investigation, recording, and reporting of bias crimes," as well as verifying bias motivations and dealing with the victims and target communities.
- Federal grant-making to small communities where bias-crime training is not offered in-house should be encouraged, both within the community and the agencies.
- Federal officials should undertake an emphatic campaign to make local law-enforcement officials aware of the advantages of obtaining proper training in bias crimes, as well as the disadvantages of failing to do so.
- Any bias-crime training program should include: "the role of departmental policies about bias crimes; local, state, and federal hate crime and civil rights laws; and resource lists for additional information when officers have questions. . . . Bias crime training should help officers to identify their own pre-conceptions of minority groups. . . . Hate crime training must also include tools for building relationships with minority groups. Working on these relationships prior to an incident of hate crime is as important—if not more so—than the events immediately following a hate crime incident. Proactively working on these relationships requires tools from community policing strategies, such as developing multidirectional lines of communication, changing the role of officers into active members of community problem solvers, etc."

The more thoroughly police officers are trained, the more likely they are not only to properly identify and investigate hate crimes, but also to enhance police relations with the target communities. Doing so further enhances their abilities to prevent or investigate other hate crimes. Failing to do so has the unfortunate effect of widening the gulf between police and minority communities, and by extension furthering the racial and cultural divides that exist within communities.

Jack McDevitt says that this effort is critical to recognizing and curtailing the divisive effects of bigotry within communities. "What we've seen over and over again, starting with what we wrote about Boston and over and over, is that when the police say they'll take this seriously and they make a good-faith effort to a community, then that community comes forward and brings incidents forward," he says. "When the police ignore it, the message to the community is that it's not important to the police.

"So if you have small towns where you have small numbers of officers, where this isn't a regular occurrence, it's something that's rare, then everybody gets confused and troubled as to what they should be doing. And that sends the message to victims not to come forward, so it becomes a self-fulfilling prophecy."[12]

THE COMMUNITY RESPONSE

While the role of law enforcement and the laws themselves is indispensable in grappling with hate crimes in America, in the long run society cannot depend on this effort alone to deal with them. They are at worst only a band-aid for the problem, although when functioning properly they can serve as a catalyst for broader social change by educating the public and leading by example.

The historic example of the "lynching era" phenomenon is perhaps the most instructive in this regard. Even though laws against lynching were at best scattered and haphazardly enforced, the popularity of this mass violence was effectively diminished by the widespread approbation that grew around them, beginning with grassroots efforts in the South and elsewhere in the early 1920s and continuing through the next three decades. By 1950, lynching had become only a scattered phenomenon, and unlike a half-century before, there was no doubt about where the larger society stood in relation to it.

Likewise, hate crimes will only be effectively diminished when both individual communities and the larger society rise up to thunder their condemnation. This will only happen when communities stand up and confront the kind of terrorization and disenfranchisement that is part and parcel of the bigoted rhetoric and scapegoating endemic to hate groups and their ideologies. It is particularly important in areas where significant demographic change is occurring, because these are the places where bias crimes are most likely to arise.

"I've come to the realization that it is maybe a more complex phenomenon than I had originally thought," says McDevitt. "You don't have vast groups in most communities who share the feelings of the offenders. In general, people are of no mind about it—they just don't think about it much in their daily lives. The fact that most people abhor violence means that when we have one of these incidents, the community tends to come together to try to make the victim whole. I think that a whole second dynamic comes in, which is the sort of labeling of the community that happens around these crimes, and then you have people deciding whether they want to stay in that community, and different groups avoiding that community. That becomes the costs of these that are more than what you find with ordinary crimes."

The most effective response, McDevitt says, occurs when communities stand up to haters and their rhetoric in its nascent phase, before it ever spirals into violence. As he points out, typical bias criminals receive relatively little gain for their acts, and if social condemnation is attached to them, they are that much less likely to carry through. Numerous studies have found that a broad condemnation of hateful rhetoric and acts, particularly when backed up by law enforcement, effectively deters the crimes.

"In responding to incidents when they're beginning—even though they may be minor, and they may be things that even might be protected speech, like calling names—that still doesn't mean you don't respond as a community," says McDevitt. "The lack of response is always seen by the offenders as acquiescence—they see themselves as heroes, as people who are acting out the beliefs of the majority of people who live in the community. So there's no question in their minds when they do something and they don't hear anything negative that everybody's agreeing with them. That empowers and emboldens them more.

"I think that one thing that we as a community can do is that we have to take these kinds of individuals more seriously. We're all too often willing to sort of say, 'Yeah, but they are just crazy.' So I think that in the community point of view, we have to be more vigilant and challenging of individuals who demonstrate this kind of rhetoric.

"And the second thing, I think, is that the nonminority community has to take the lead in that. I really do believe that when African Americans or Jews or Asians are the ones saying that it's a problem, that it doesn't reverberate the way it does if it's a white male or female saying it. So I think we need to band with those groups, but we have to be in a leadership role in condemning that kind of behavior.

"I always talk to people about the fact that the laws constrain the police and the courts from acting in cases of free speech, but it doesn't constrain us from challenging the speech. And again, by challenging them, what you do is confront the ideology of these people in a way that reflects a broad public awareness, and you force that issue. With the Internet, these people get this false sense that there are millions of people sharing their ideology, and we need to send them a series of directed messages at the initial points when they start to do this that this is something we abhor and disagree with everything they're standing for. That kind of thing has the ability to cause them to pause before they escalate up the scale.

"And I think that's hard—it's very hard to do as individuals, because you sort of put yourself at risk that this person may react violently when you challenge him. It's unclear how one does that. How can we as community set boundaries and send messages back? I'm not sure. I only know we have to try."[13]

✻

In Ocean Shores, the police, at least, are trying. Chief Rich McEachin says that in the wake of the Fourth of July stabbing, he gathered his officers and began reviewing just what they knew about hate crimes.

"When we started discussing after the incident what officers knew about hate crimes and what charges could be pressed, I found that everybody wasn't on the same page," he recalls. "A lot of officers, or the majority of officers, thought that hate crimes were only specific to race and had to have some kind of assault with it."

McEachin, who reviewed as much literature on bias crimes as he could find, decided to solve the problem by holding a training session for all his officers on hate crimes, ostensibly provided by federal officials in Seattle—who kept backing out at the last moment. "They kept canceling on us. So I had a bunch of officers sitting here for this training and they didn't show up. So I finally just put it on myself."

The Ocean Shores chief knows intimately just how damaging hate crimes can be to a community, and—like many other law-enforcement officials who have firsthand dealings with the crimes—is now adamant that they are indeed "special" crimes that warrant the attention.

Were he to offer advice to his fellow small-town police chiefs, it would be this: "I would tell them to make sure that all the line officers that are actually doing the job know exactly what they can and can't do," McEachin says. "Because somebody says they'd rather not press charges really doesn't fit into the scheme of prosecuting a hate crime. The incident that we had prior to the homicide [in which Kinison's friends harassed the family of Filipinos]—even though they didn't want to do anything, they just wanted to leave, if the officers knew what they could do, maybe they would have handled it different."

In Washington state, malicious harassment is a Class C felony—at which level of crime, McEachin says, the officers should simply take over. And he has outlined steps for his own officers to take: "To fully investigate, first of all. And to separate witnesses, and find out the entire story before they make a judgment of one or two people saying, well, this is what happened, but we don't really want to do anything.

"Once you have what you consider to be the minority saying they don't want to do anything, the officers historically have been taught, OK, well, we don't have anything. You have no victim, you have no crime. But I think the policy we came out with after this incident, that it would be fully investigated, and everybody would be talked to, and if you're indecisive, then you call your manager at home and tell him this is what I have, what should I do?"

He says his department has grown a great deal through the ordeal, and is if anything highly sensitive to the issue of hate crimes now. He knows all too well how easily the crimes can hit a community from out of the blue, too—and if his department made mistakes, they were the kind common to small-town departments. Human mistakes.

"When you get a small town like this and you have 60,000 people in it, and officers are running from call to call to call to call, and not having the totality of a hate crime in the back of your mind, or the training, and you get a call like this, and nobody wants to press charges, you're ready to go to your next call. If it had been in the middle of winter and that had been the only call for service they'd had in the last four hours, it would have been handled a lot differently.

"I think that it's really hard to cover everything in the criminal-justice field for officers to know. And sometimes, unfortunately, things come up that you realize, not everybody's on the same page here, and it takes a tragedy to bring that forward. But I think this has pulled the community together, just to get the word out to outsiders that Ocean Shores doesn't have that kind of crime and doesn't tolerate it. And the training that I gave the officers, everybody understands now—and like I say, we emphasize now to the point that they really dive into these things now and investigate them."

He says that the Confederate flag has made a few reappearances since the stabbing. One resident flew the Dixie colors from his porch the following spring, and officers asked him to take it down, and he complied. It shows up from time to time on the beach, too.

"We had one this Fourth of July—someone from Oregon, we asked them to take it down and they did take it down—it was on the back of their truck, driving down the beach," McEachin says. "So we do have outside rednecks that come into Ocean Shores now and then and think it's cute. And you know, you talk to these guys, they don't understand what they're doing. They just think that flag is cool. They don't even know what it stands for."

If anything, the Ocean Shores force is extremely vigilant about bias crimes now, McEachin says, but has (perhaps unsurprisingly) not had much support from the county prosecutor's office.

"We have had an incident since then where we considered it a hate crime, and we made arrests, and sent the case to the prosecutor, who didn't think it was a hate crime and didn't press any charges," McEachin says. "Everybody being on the same page is important, all the way along the line.

"We're being very cautious now, I think. Anything that looks like a hate crime, we're making arrests. And if the prosecutor doesn't prosecute, then he doesn't, but we're not the bad guys. You have to be aggressive."

The larger Grays Harbor community got involved in raising awareness in the wake of the Fourth of July incident. An ad hoc committee of community leaders formed, which included several notable minority residents, some already locally prominent. Also on the panel was John Hughes, managing editor of the local Aberdeen *Daily World,* who is himself the adoptive father of two Asian American girls.

"The public rationale for the group," says Hughes, "was to put up posters that promoted diversity: 'Are your neighbors getting to know you?' With the idea that if you could bring people together, classically, that you could break down barriers.

"But the thrust beyond that was that the hate crime—and I don't think anyone didn't think it wasn't a hate crime that we had out there—was absolutely intolerable. And that by making people aware that these were not just garden-variety things that you could brush off as just little spot fires. Spot fires become conflagrations. A better analogy is a cancer metastasizing—it grows in the dark and pollutes the community."

Hughes says grappling with the issues of racial tolerance and its opposite have not been easy for Grays Harbor, but they have been essential, in no small part because of the significant demographic changes the county is undergoing. And, he says, there is real progress being made.

"We have seen and documented, on the part of the bigger police departments in the county, outreach efforts to do just what needs to be done in broadening our horizons," Hughes says. "People can really have their horizons broadened. I think we've made some headway in the wake of the tragedy. I think the burgeoning number of Hispanics here has really helped. We've done a pretty good job, but we can do a lot better job in writing about minority issues."[14]

In spite of the best efforts of officials, however, it is not so clear just how deep have been the changes in Ocean Shores since the tragedy. In most respects, the city has simply dusted itself off and moved on, choosing largely to ignore whatever clouds may linger over their nice town from the ugliness of Fourth of July, 2000.

Initially, there was little question that the events around Chris Kinison's death hurt Ocean Shores economically. On July Fourth the next summer, none of the largest hotels in the area were fully booked, in contrast to previous years, when they filled up weeks in advance. Many blamed the shortfall on the struggling national economy, but even they agreed the tragedy had an effect. "It didn't help," said Jim Kim, owner of the Ocean Shores Best Western. "Something there is missing now."[15]

However, the events of September 11 that year, when terrorists attacked New York City and Washington, D.C., swept most of those clouds from everyone's minds. The travel and airline industry plummeted to depths few in Ocean Shores could recall seeing, and for the next year everyone struggled—as did nearly every other place in the world that relies on tourism dollars.

The national tragedy, however, became something of a springboard for Ocean Shores's own recovery. City business leaders astutely began marketing their town in urban areas easily within driving distance—particularly Seattle, Tacoma, Portland, and Vancouver. By the summer of 2003, the town was bustling again, and, indeed, thoughts of the fight at the Texaco hardly seemed to cross anyone's mind any longer.

The Ocean Shores Coalition, which once promised to promote racial diversity in the community and combat the stench of hate crimes, had faded to a distant memory. Carl Payne, its former leader, said he got out when other members began pushing for recognizing gays and lesbians as well. The group, he says, stopped meeting sometime in the summer or fall of 2001.

Payne's wife, Joan, is executive director of the Chamber of Commerce, and she too said the events of three years before have largely dissipated from people's minds. "September 11 is what pushed this out of people's memories so quickly," she said. "Because that became overall the problem. And actually, we've probably since capitalized on that to a degree, because you don't have to fly to come here if you live in western Washington. That helps us in many ways."

The change, she said, did not happen all at once. "It took a while for people to quit talking about it. It was scary for awhile.

"You know, the good thing with Ocean Shores is that they no longer relate it to the holiday. I mean, we got all through the holiday and I never thought about it. Which is good, really good. But that first year afterwards, everybody just thought, 'Oh my gosh, what are we going to have this year?' It's good we've gotten through that."

Payne said that by 2003, the attack on the Hongs seemed not even to be a concern for their Asian visitors. "There's not been even a comment about it," she said. "We have so many Asians come in here. I've never had one—that I'm aware of, or my volunteers tell me of—even mentioning the fact that we could be a racial community, or [asking], 'Is this the place where it happened?'"

Indeed, if there is any lingering sentiment in Ocean Shores, it is a quiet dismay at the outcome of Minh Hong's trial. Even though the Grays Harbor jury found otherwise, many in town, especially those who knew Chris Kinison, believe an injustice was done.

"Everybody was so disappointed in the outcome of the trial—not that they sat in judgment, but some people were just disappointed that there wasn't better closure to this," said Joan Payne. "That there wasn't something done. It was just like a death that happened and it's over, forget about it.

"Because a lot of people knew the young man involved. He didn't have the best reputation, like many young kids, but not a bad person. It was really disappointing. I think that was the most disappointing thing, was that the trial didn't give any real closure. Somebody . . . got away with something."

And was there any sense anywhere in Ocean Shores, I wondered, that perhaps other people—such as Kinison's friends—might too have gotten away with something that night? Something like a hate crime?

"I haven't heard that," said Payne, stopping and thinking. "No, I haven't heard that."[16]

✳

Minh Hong does not sleep well anymore. He says that ever since the Fourth of July, 2000, he has to take sleep medication. He received counseling afterward, which he says helped "a lot": "I was extremely depressed for quite awhile," he says.

Chris Kinison's death weighs on him. At times he still almost can't believe that he actually killed a man. His life mostly seems normal now. He's working steadily, and no one at work knows about his past. So when the memory hits him, as it does nearly every night, it comes from out of the dark of the soul. No one, not a gentle person like Minh Hong especially, wants to think of themselves as a killer, a bad person. Inside, it has changed him.

"No, I'm not the same person who drove to Ocean Shores that night," he says now. "I'm not as trusting. I wouldn't say I'm paranoid or fearful. I'd just say I'm more *alert*."

He knows that there are people in the Asian American community who think of him as a hero, who are glad he fought back, because it was past time that someone did. "I don't know what to say to that," he says. "Because they don't know what it's like. I'm just like anyone else, just trying to survive. I still am."

Nonetheless, part of what changed for him after the Fourth of July was the meaning of being American. It has been permanently colored by what happened to him—not just that night, but for the next six months. A sense of the injustice of it is now part of his outlook.

"I got a much closer view not just of what racism is, but how it is part of the system," he says. "I wouldn't say I've changed my view of America . . . I've just grown up a lot. I see both sides now."[17]

NOTES

CHAPTER ONE: THE KNIVES

1. See Robert L. Jamieson and Hector Castro, "Another racial incident preceded Ocean Shores stabbing death," *Post-Intelligencer*, Wednesday, July 12, 2000; Joshua Robin, "Ocean Shores victim was in earlier fight," *Seattle Times*, Wednesday, July 12, 2000; David Scheer, "Racial epithets in earlier case now in spotlight," (Aberdeen) *Daily World*, July 12, 2000; and Alex Tizon, "Storm over July 4 killing still raging in Ocean Shores," *Seattle Times*, Monday, April 8, 2001. See also the Ocean Shores police reports from the incident (No. 00–003744), filed July 7, 2000, which includes the anecdotal warning from Brouillard.
2. See Tizon, "Storm over July 4 killing."
3. See David Scheer, "Racial epithets."
4. Ibid.

CHAPTER TWO: FIREWORKS IN RED

1. See David Scheer, "Defense witness thought Kinison was a 'skinhead'," (Aberdeen) *Daily World*, December 9, 2000, p. A1.
2. See David Scheer and Ryan Teague Beckwith, "Minh Hong trial under way," (Aberdeen) *Daily World*, December 7, 2000, p. A1.
3. See David Scheer, "Anatomy of a death: Witnesses offer varying accounts," (Aberdeen) *Daily World*, August 8, 2000, p. A1.
4. See especially *Responding to Hate Crimes: A Police Officer's Guide to Investigation and Prevention*, a 1999 publication of the International Association of Police Chiefs, distributed as an educational guide to law-enforcement officers. It lists eight "key indicators" of hate crimes, including: 1) perceptions of the victim(s) and witnesses about the crime; 2) the perpetrator's comments, gestures or written statements that reflect bias, including graffiti or other symbols; 3) any differences between perpetrator and victim, whether actual or perceived by the perpetrator; 4) similar incidents in the same location or neighborhood to determine whether a pattern exists; 5) whether the victim was engaged in activities promoting his/her group or community—for example, by clothing or conduct; 6) whether the incident coincided with a holiday or date of particular significance; 7) involvement of organized hate groups or their members; and 8) absence of any other motive such as economic gain.
   The only component of this list absent from the scene at Ocean Shores was "whether the victim was engaged in activities promoting his/her group or

community—for example, by clothing or conduct." There was no overt or apparent involvement of hate groups, but the use of the Confederate flag and hate-group rhetoric was an indication that there may have been.

CHAPTER THREE: OPEN SORES

1. See Robert L. Jamieson, Jr., "One brother is released, other held in stabbing," *Post-Intelligencer*, July 6, 2000.
2. See Hector Castro, "Charges expected in fatal stabbing," *Post-Intelligencer*, July 7, 2000.
3. See Joshua Robin, "Stabbing victim liked to fight, his friends say," *Seattle Times*, July 10, 2000.
4. See Hector Castro and Robert L. Jamieson, "Ocean Shores killing leaves citizens caught in between," *Post-Intelligencer*, July 15, 2000.
5. See Joshua Robin, "Stabbing victim."
6. See Joshua Robin, "Ocean Shores victim was in earlier fight," *Seattle Times*, July 12, 2000.
7. Castro, "Charges expected."
8. Robin, "Stabbing victim."
9. Castro and Jamieson, "Ocean Shores killing."
10. See Isaac Baker, "Families grieve as man pleads not guilty to manslaughter," *Post-Intelligencer*, July 8, 2000.
11. See Bernadette Logue, "Customary to greet people with racial slurs?," Letters to the Editor, *Seattle Times*, July 19, 2000.
12. See Constance Daruthayan, "Man, brother faced white supremacists," Letters to the Editor, *Seattle Times*, July 16, 2000.
13. See Chi-Dooh Li, "Racial taunts reflect on the source," *Post-Intelligencer*, July 27, 2000.
14. See Ryan Teague Beckwith, "Asian community stunned, but not fearful," (Aberdeen) *Daily World*, July 16, 2000.
15. See Jamieson, "One brother."
16. There have been many accounts of the Northwest timber wars, but among the best is Timothy Egan, *The Good Rain: Across Time and Terrain in the Pacific Northwest* (New York: Vintage Press, 1990), especially pp. 160–179. For an account of the timber bubble of the 1980s, see Joe P. Mattey, *The Timber Bubble That Burst: Government Policy and the Bailout of 1984* (Oxford: Oxford University Press, 1990).
17. See Vlad Ivanovich, "If you are white, then naturally you are the villain," Letters to the Editor, (Aberdeen) *Daily World*, July 19, 2000.
18. See T. Evenrout, "Ocean Shores used to be such a nice, quiet place to live," Letters to the Editor, (Aberdeen) *Daily World*, July 19, 2000.
19. See Sean Izzarone, "We are all guilty," Letters to the Editor, (Aberdeen) *Daily World*, July 23, 2000.
20. See Timothy Egan, "A Racist Attack, A Town Plagued," *New York Times*, October 15, 2000.
21. See Stuart Eskenazi, "Minority groups want FBI to probe stabbing," *Seattle Times*, October 3, 2000.
22. See David Scheer, "FBI rules out Ocean Shores investigation," (Aberdeen) *Daily World*, October 11, 2000.

23. See Jenny Lynn Zappala, "Ocean Shores council issues anti-racism proclamation," (Aberdeen) *Daily World*, October 25, 2000.
24. See David Scheer, "Chamber-led coalition mulls ways to head off hate," (Aberdeen) *Daily World*, October 26, 2000.
25. See John Hughes, "Our View," (Aberdeen) *Daily World*, October 8, 2000.
26. See Peter Jordan, "Mayor finds our coverage profoundly disappointing," (Aberdeen) *Daily World*, October 20, 2000.
27. See Jenny Lynn Zappala, "Diversity panel says O.S. making headway," (Aberdeen) *Daily World*, November 15, 2000.

CHAPTER FOUR: WHITE FACES

1. See David Chapman, "Grays Harbor County Courthouse: A Crown for 'The Maid of Wynooche'," *Columbia: The Magazine of Northwest History*, Vol. 15, No. 3, Fall 2001.

CHAPTER FIVE: GROWING UP AMERICAN

1. See David Scheer, "'My son is not a racist,' Kinison's mom says," (Aberdeen) *Daily World*, December 20, 2000.
2. See Alex Tizon, "Storm over July 4 killing still raging in Ocean Shores," *Seattle Times*, April 9, 2001.
3. See Joshua Robin, "Stabbing victim liked to fight, his friends say," *Seattle Times*, July 10, 2001.
4. See Barbara Perry, *In the Name of Hate: Understanding Hate Crimes* (New York: Routledge, 2001), p. 107.
5. P. Finn and T. McNeil, *The response of the criminal justice system to bias crime: An exploratory review* (Cambridge, Mass.: Abt Associates, 1987).
6. See Jack Levin and Jack McDevitt, *Hate Crimes: America's War on Those Who Are Different* (Boulder, Colo.: Westview Press, 2001), pp. 65–98.
7. See Jack Levin and Jack McDevitt, *Hate Crimes Revisited: America's War on Those Who Are Different* (Boulder, Colo.: Westview, 2002), pp. 1978–198.
8. See Perry, *In the Name of Hate*, p. 61.
9. See also *Diagnostic and Statistical Manual of Mental Disorders*, fourth ed. (2000), American Psychological Association, pp. 645–650.
10. Quotes are from author's interview with Dr. Gary E. Connor, September 12, 2003.
11. Quotes are from author's interview with Donald P. Green, August 21, 2003.
12. The study referenced is by Donald Green, Robert P. Abelson, and Margaret Garnett, "The Distinctive Political Views of Hate-Crime Perpetrators and White Supremacists," in Deborah A. Prentice and Dale T. Miller (eds.), *Cultural Divides: Understanding and Overcoming Group Conflict* (New York: Russell Sage Foundation, 1999), pp. 429–464.
13. Ibid., p. 446.
14. See Federal Bureau of Investigation Hate Crimes Statistics, 2001, Table 7, p. 16, and Perry, *In the Name of Hate*, p. 29.
15. Perry, *In the Name of Hate*, pp. 16, 29.
16. Connor's explanation is largely drawn from the work of Joan H. Johnston, James E. Driskell and Eduardo Salas, "Vigilant and Hypervigilant Decision Making," *Journal of Applied Psychology*, Vol. 82, No. 4 (1997), 614–622.

17. See Hector Castro and Robert L. Jamieson, "Ocean Shores killing leaves citizens caught in between," *Post-Intelligencer,* July 15, 2000.
18. See Melinda Henneberger, "For Bias Victims, a Double Trauma," *Newsday,* January 9, 1992.
19. All quotes are from author's interview with Joan Weiss, September 5, 2003.
20. See Joan Weiss, Howard Ehrlich, and Barbara E. K. Larcom, "Ethnoviolence at Work," *Journal of Intergroup Relations,* Vol. 18, Winter 1991–92, pp. 27–29. See also Joan Weiss, "Ethnoviolence: Impact Upon the Response of Victims and the Community," in Robert J. Kelly (ed.), *Bias Crime: American Law Enforcement and Legal Response* (Chicago: Office of International Criminal Justice, The University of Illinois at Chicago, 1991), pp. 174, 182.
21. Berrill, K. T., and Herek, G. M. "Primary and secondary victimization in antigay hate crimes: Official response and public policy," *Journal of Interpersonal Violence,* 5 (1990), pp. 401–413.

CHAPTER 6: THE TRIAL, DAY ONE: RASHOMON

1. The details of the trial are largely drawn from my notes in covering the trial. In some cases I cross-referenced those notes with the quotes published by my journalistic colleague David Scheer at the (Aberdeen) *Daily World.* Transcripts were largely unavailable (I did obtain one day's worth of trial transcripts, thanks to the efforts of court clerk Brenda Johnston), and reporters' notes will always slightly vary. In some cases I deferred to Scheer's quotes—and those quotes are duly footnoted here—while in others I adhered to those in my notebook. See "A Note On Sources."
2. See David Scheer, "Minh Hong trial under way," (Aberdeen) *Daily World,* December 7, 2000.
3. Ibid.

CHAPTER SEVEN: HATE, AMERICAN STYLE

1. The Byrd case was covered voluminously in the national media. Probably the best single account is Dina Temple-Ralston's *A Death in Texas: A Story of Race, Murder, and a Small Town's Struggle for Redemption* (New York: Henry Holt, 2002), which also addresses the issues confronting a rural town in the wake of a horrific hate crime.
2. Ibid., pp. 144–151, offers a vivid and darkly hilarious account of the KKK rally.
3. See Dick Gregory, "Ku Klux Klan Terrorists Active In Texas," Pan-African News Wire, July 11, 1998, available online at http://www.dickgregory.com/dick/2_kukluxklan.html.
4. "Black's man's slaying horrifies Texas town," Associated Press report, June 10, 1998; datelined Jasper, Texas.
5. A copy of the postcard, as well as an account of Daniels's lynching, is available at the historical Web site *Without Sanctuary* (http://www.musarium.com/withoutsanctuary/main.html). The Daniels photo is available at http://www.musarium.com/withoutsanctuary/pics_49.html. See also Gregory Kane, "Postcards of Lynchings Illustrate Madness," *Baltimore Sun,* July 1, 2000.
6. See Philip Dray, *At the Hands of Persons Unknown: The Lynching of Black America* (New York: Random House, 2002), pp. 215–219.

7. See "Lynching Statistics: By Race, State and Year, 1882–1968," Tuskegee Institute, available online at http://www.law.umkc.edu/faculty/projects/ftrials/shipp/lynchstats.html.

8. See Dray, *At the Hands*, p. 21.

9. For more on the Nat Turner revolt, as well as a discussion of the antebellum treatment of slaves, see especially *Nat Turner: A Slave Rebellion in History and Memory* (Oxford: Oxford University Press, 2003); for a general discussion of slave revolts, see Herbert Aptheker, *American Negro Slave Revolts* (New York: International Publishers, 1963), especially p. 11, which provides an estimate of the numbers of black killed before the Civil War.

10. See Dray, *At the Hands*, pp. 35–39.

11. See Dorothy Sterling, *The Trouble They Seen: The Story of Reconstruction in the Words of African-Americans* (New York: Doubleday, 1976).

12. A copy of the Stacy lynching photo can be found at *Without Sanctuary* at http://www.musarium.com/withoutsanctuary/pics_51.html.

13. See Dray, *At the Hands*, p. 72.

14. See especially James H. Madison, *A Lynching in the Heartland: Race and Memory in America* (New York: Palgrave Macmillan, 2002), pp. 14–15, and Dray, *At the Hands*, pp. 70–77.

15. See Ida Wells-Barnett's 1909 address to the NAACP, reproduced in Robert Torricelli and Andrew Carroll (eds.), *In Our Own Words: Extraordinary Speeches of the American Century* (New York: Washington Square Press Publication, 1999), p. 182.

16. See Edward L. Ayers, *Vengeance and Justice: Crime and Punishment in the 19th-Century American South* (New York: Oxford University Press, 1984), p. 241.

17. For more on the underlying dynamics of the lynching phenomenon, see especially Stewart E. Tolnay and E. M. Beck, *A Festival of Violence: An Analysis of Southern Lynchings, 1882–1930* (Urbana: University of Illinois Press, 1992), which describes how lynching "served four functions: (1) to eradicate specific persons accused of crimes against the white community; (2) as a mechanism of state-sanctioned terrorism designed to maintain a degree of leverage over the African American population; (3) to eliminate or neutralize African American competitors for social, economic, or political rewards; and (4) as a symbolic manifestation of the unity of white supremacy," p. 50.

18. See especially Ida B. Wells, *A Red Record* (1895). Reprinted in Jacqueline Jones Royster, ed., *Southern Horrors and Other Writings: The Anti-Lynching Campaign of Ida B. Wells, 1892–1900* (Boston: Bedford Books, 1997), pp. 73, 75–78, 80–81, 82–87, 131–32, 138–40, 146–147, 153–155, and Miriam DeCosta-Willis, ed., *The Memphis Diary of Ida B. Wells: An Intimate Portrait of the Artist as a Young Woman* (Boston: Beacon Press, 1995), pp. 179–182.

19. Dray, *At the Hands*, pp. 114–116, 138–142, 169–172.

20. See *Savannah Tribune*, May 25, 1918; Walter F. White, "The Work of a Mob," *Crisis*, Vol. 16 (Sept. 17, 1918), pp. 221–22; Leon F. Litwack, *Trouble In Mind: Black Southerners In The Age Of Jim Crow* (New York: Knopf, 1998), pp. 158–162. See also "The Anti-Lynching Crusaders: The Lynching of Women," [1922], NAACP Papers, Part 7: The Anti-Lynching Campaign, 1912–1955, Series B: Anti-Lynching Legislative and Publicity Files, 1916–1955, Library of Congress (Microfilm, Reel 3, Frames 570–73), available online at http://womhist.binghamton.edu/lynch/doc7.htm.; and Dray, *At the Hands*, pp. 245–246.

21. See Alfred L. Brophy and Randall Kennedy, *Reconstructing the Dreamland: The Tulsa Race Riot of 1921* (Oxford: Oxford University Press, 2002), as well as recent news accounts regarding reparations for the Tulsa riots (e.g., see Charles Zewe, "Archaeologists to search for mass graves from 1921 Tulsa riot," CNN.com, January 20, 2000, online at http://www.cnn.com/2000/US/01/20/tulsa.riot/, and "Reparations For Tulsa Riot?" CBS News, February 8, 2000, online at http://www.cbsnews.com/stories/2000/02/07/national/main157781.shtml).

22. See Dray, *At the Hands*, pp. 256–267.

23. See Barbara Holden-Smith, "Lynching, Federalism, and the Intersection of Race and Gender in the Progressive Era," *Yale Journal of Law and Feminism*, Vol. 8, No. 31 (1996); online at http://www.soc.umn.edu/~samaha/cases/holden%20smith,%20lynching%20and%20feminism.htm.

24. Congressional Record, 67th Congress, 2nd Session, January 18, 1922, p. 1366. Also cited by Edward Sebesta, "Parallels of the Opposition to Anti-Hate Crime Legislation to the Opposition to Anti-Lynching Legislation in the Early 20th Century," *Temple of Democracy*, online at http://www.templeofdemocracy.com/Parallels.htm.

25. See Barbara Holden-Smith, "Lynching," p. 16.

26. Congressional Record, 67th Congress, 2nd Session: January 18, 1922, p. 1362. See also Sebesta, "Parallels."

27. See Dray, *At the Hands*, pp. 268–272.

28. Ibid., pp. 314–317,

29. Author's interview with Philip Dray, April 8, 2003.

30. See Valerie Jenness and Kendal Broad, *Hate Crimes: New Social Movements and the Politics of Violence* (New York: Aldine de Gruyter, 1997), pp. 21–36.

31. See Valerie Jenness and Ryken Grattet, *Making Hate a Crime: From Social Movement to Law Enforcement* (New York: Russell Sage Foundation, 2001), pp. 42–54. This text also discusses the emergence of the anti - hate-crime movement (pp. 17–41).

32. See especially Jenness and Grattet, *Hate Crimes*, pp. 73–101.

33. Ibid., pp. 102–126, and Frederick M. Lawrence, *Punishing Hate: Bias Crimes Under American Law* (Cambridge: Harvard University Press, 1999), pp. 80–109.

CHAPTER NINE: THE HATE DEBATE

1. See "Jury selection set to begin for Wyoming man allegedly responsible for Matthew Shepard's fatal beating," Court TV, October 8, 1999.

2. See Chris Dettro, "Man gets 12 years in 'hate' beating," *Springfield State-Journal*, November 26, 1998.

3. See "A Chronology of Hate Crimes," Human Rights Campaign report, 2002, available online at http://www.hrc.org/Content/NavigationMenu/HRC/Get_Informed/Issues/Hate_Crimes1/Background_Information5/chronology_hc.pdf.

4. See Lewis Griswold, "Murder charges dropped," *Fresno Bee*, April 20, 1999.

5. Among the most notorious of these was the "Blue Boys," who had a lengthy rampage in the Los Angeles area in 1988, detailed by Michael Collins, "The Gay-Bashers," in *Hate Crimes: Confronting Violence Against Lesbians and Gay Men* (Newbury Park, Calif.: Sage Press, 1992), pp. 191–200.

6. Gary D. Comstock, *Violence against Lesbians and Gay Men* (New York: Columbia University Press, 1991), p. 36.

7. National Institute of Justice, *The Response of the Criminal Justice System to Bias Crime: An Explanatory Review* (Washington: United States Department of Justice, 1987), p. 32.

8. National Gay and Lesbian Task Force, Anti-Gay/Lesbian Violence, Victimization and Defamation in 1994 (Washington, D.C.: National Gay and Lesbian Task Force Policy Institute, 1995), p. 18. For an illuminating discussion of the motivations of gay-bashers, particularly as a vehicle for establishing masculinity, see Barbara Perry, *In the Name of Hate: Understanding Hate Crimes* (New York: Routledge, 1999), pp. 106–110.

9. See, e.g., "Homosexuals on the March," a "Special Report" of Falwell's "Old Time Gospel Hour," March 1981, which featured various black-and-white photos of gay men parading and drag queens in full regalia, all with their eyes blacked over with small rectangles (including all the participants in a crowd shot of a gay-rights parade). The report was proffered as part of a fundraising drive for Falwell's organization; the author possesses a copy, but public copies may be difficult to obtain.

10. Congressional Record, 1989, 1076.

11. See Valerie Jenness and Ryken Grattet, *Making Hate a Crime: From Social Movement to Law Enforcement* (New York: Russell Sage Foundation, 2001), pp. 58–60.

12. See Elizabeth Tedesco, "Humanity on the Ballot: The Citizen Initiative and Oregon's War Over Gay Civil Rights," *Boston College Third World Law Journal*, Vol. 22, No. 1 (2002), pp. 163–200.

13. See Sara Diamond, "The Christian Right's Anti-Gay Agenda," in *Facing the Wrath: Confronting the Right in Dangerous Times* (Monroe, ME: Common Courage Press, 1996), pp. 82–84. See also Ian Young, *The Stonewall Experiment: A Gay Psychohistory* (New York: Cassell Academic, 1999), especially pp. 260–292, for more on the "AIDS concentration camp" meme.

14. See Fern Shen, "Hate Crime Bill Rejected in Md. House," *Washington Post*, March 22, 1991, p. C1.

15. See Terri Ann Schroeder, "Different Version," *Indianapolis Star*, March 7, 1994, p. A9.

16. See Stuart Eskenazi, "Chisum Casts Blame at Gay Victims," *Austin American-Statesman*, February 17, 1995, p. B1.

17. See James B. Jacobs and Kimberly Potter, *Hate Crimes: Criminal Law and Identity Politics* (Oxford: Oxford University Press, 1998), pp. 76–77, and Jenness and Grattet, *Making Hate a Crime*, pp. 44–45.

18. See Department of Justice, Attorney General Transcript, News Conference with USA John Brownlee, Indictment of Darrell David Rice, April 10, 2001, available online at http://www.usdoj.gov/ag/speeches/2002/041002newsconferenceindictment.htm.

19. See "Prosecutors drop hate-crime charges in lesbian hiker murders," *The Advocate*, May 7, 2003 (available online at http://www.advocate.com/new_news.asp?id=8560&sd=05/07/03). It's worth noting that this somewhat contradicts Ashcroft's assertion of a year before, during the press conference, that "[t]he utilization of the sentencing enhancement procedures that relate to both gender and homosexuality in this instance are key to our ability to request the death penalty in cases like this" (see Department of Justice, Attorney General Transcript, News Conference with USA John Brownlee, Indictment of Darrell David Rice, April 10, 2001, available online at http://www.usdoj.gov/ag/speeches/2002/041002newsconferenceindictment.htm).

20. See Erik Stetson, "Feds see to withdraw charges against hikers' accused slayer," Associate Press, February 6, 2004.

21. See Laurie Goodstein, "The Architect of the 'Gay Conversion' Campaign," *New York Times*, August 13, 1998, p. A10.

22. See Associated Press, "Friends say clearly a hate crime," Friday, October 9, 1998.

23. See "Local and National Groups Call for Hate Crime Legislation Following Brutal Wyoming Murder," Gay and Lesbian Alliance Against Defamation press release, Oct. 12, 1998, available online at http://www.glaad.org/media/archive_detail.php?id=128.

24. See Beth Loffreda, *Losing Matt Shepard: Life and Politics in the Aftermath of Anti-Gay Murder* (New York: Columbia University Press, 2000), pp. 9–11.

25. See "Remarks of Matthew's friend at D.C. vigil," October 14, 1998, Matthew Shepard Online Resources, at http://www.wiredstrategies.com/shepard3.html.

26. See Rea Carey, "Press Statement on Wyoming Attack," National Youth Advocacy Coalition, October 12, 1998.

27. See Loffreda, *Losing Matt Shepard*, p. 14.

28. See "Comments by Governor Jim Geringer on the Matthew Shepard Incident," Press Release, October 12, 1998, available online at http://www.state.wy.us/governor/press_releases/1998/october_1998/text_matthew_shepard.html.

29. See "Wyoming officials now downplay hate-bias motive," Wired Strategies, October 24, 1998, available online at http://www.wiredstrategies.com/shepard3.html.

30. See Loffreda, *Losing Matt Shepard*, pp. 49–52.

31. See ABC News staff report, "Do Anti-Homosexual Ads Contribute to Violence?," ABCNews.com, October 16, 1998, available online at http://more.abc-news.go.com/sections/us/dailynews/gayattack981011.html.

32. See Joan M. Garry, "GLAAD and National Coalition of Anti-Violence Programs Express Sorrow and Horror at Attack on Gay Man in Wyoming," Gay and Lesbian Alliance Against Defamation Media Release, October 10, 1998.

33. See Kim I. Mills, "Statement at Press Conference," Human Rights Campaign, October 10, 1998.

34. Phelps's hatred of homosexuals, and of American society's tolerance for them, apparently knows no bounds. Phelps at least once during the late 1990s visited Baghdad, Iraq, and made colorful public appearances, denouncing President Clinton and the "immoral" American actions against the Iraqi regime. Shortly after September 11, 2001, Phelps celebrated the terrorist attacks on New York City and Washington by referring to the event as "The Day of God's Wrath": "The message to get from this tragedy is not the message that these lying churches all across the nation are telling you. The message to get is that God is punishing this wicked, sinful, perverse, adulterous, murderous, sodomite nation. You need to repent!" See text of September 12, 2001, "Day of God's Wrath," from Phelps's Web site, http://www.godhatesfags.com.

35. See Family Research Council Press Release, October 16, 1998, "FRC calls on Phelps' group to abandon plans to picket Matthew Shepard's funeral," available online at http://www.brentpayton.com/phelps/FRC%20Calls%20on%20Phelps'%20Group%20to%20Abandon%20Plans%20to%20Picket%20Matthew%20Shepard's%20Funeral.txt.

36. See Justin Gillis and Patrice Gaines, "Pattern of Hate Emerges on a Fence in Laramie: Gay Victims' Killers Say They Saw an Easy Crime Target," *Washington Post*, October 18, 1998.

36. Family Research Council, "Action Alert: President Makes Hate Crime Agenda Clear: Use Schools, AT&T, Government and Television to Bully Students into

Acceptance of Homosexuality," July 15, 1999, formerly available online at http://www.frc.org/press/040699.html.

38. See *Hill Source*, Talking Points memo, October 20, 1998. The memo described "'Hate crime' proposals that criminalize motive rather than punish violent crime." *Hill Source* was the in-house publication of the House GOP Conference Chair, but it is no longer published.

39. See "Gays' critics accused of 'hate speech'," Washington Times, October 27, 1998, p. A2.

40. "Hate crimes legislation introduced in Congress," CNN.com, March 12, 1999, available online at http://www.cnn.com/ALLPOLITICS/stories/1999/03/12/hate.crimes/.

41. Among the groups and individuals supporting the Hate Crimes Prevention Act were 22 state attorneys general, the National Sheriffs Association, the Police Foundation, former Attorney General Dick Thornburgh and the U.S. Conference of Mayors.

42. See Judy Shepard, "Mrs. Shepard Statement in Support of HCPA," Human Rights Campaign, March 23, 1999.

43. See "Senate must reject unjust 'Hate Crime' legislation," Press Release, Traditional Values Coalition, July 26, 2001.

44. See Lawrence Morahan, "Hate Crimes Prevention Proposal Receives Mixed Reception," Conservative News Service, March 12, 1999.

45. See "Testimony of Timothy Lynch, Associate Director, Center for Constitutional Studies, The Cato Institute, On The Hate Crimes Prevention Act of 1999," May 11, 1999, available online at http://www.cato.org/testimony/ct-tl051199.html.

46. See Eric Pianin and Juliet Eilperin, "GOP Raises the Ante On Social Programs," *Washington Post*, October 21, 1999, p. A1; Charles Babington, "Wielding Veto, President Presses Hate Crimes Issue: Clinton Wants Congress to Add Homosexuals to Law as Protected Group," *Washington Post*, October 27, 1999, p. A2; and Charles Babington, "Clinton Signs Spending Bill, But Notes What It Left Out," *Washington Post*, November 30, 1999, p. A2.

47. See Susan Estrich, "George Jr. Courts the Right," Los Angeles Times, April 2, 1999.

48. See Molly Ivins, "A little background on that hate crimes bill," *Fort Worth Star-Telegram*, Monday, October 31, 2000.

49. See Jake Tapper, "Bush angers slain man's family," *Salon.com*, October 16, 2000.

50. See *The Second 2000 Gore-Bush Presidential Debate: October 11, 2000*, transcript, the Commission on Presidential Debates, available online at http://www.debates.org/pages/trans2000b.html.

51. See Michael Graczyk, "Attorneys say Bush comments won't hurt Texas dragging case," Associated Press report, October 12, 2000.

52. See Tapper, "Bush angers."

53. See Ann Coulter, *Slander: Liberal Lies About the American Right* (New York: Crown Books, 2001).

54. See "FBI Director Denounces Attacks Against Arab-Americans," U.S. Department of State International Information Programs, September 17, 2001, available online at http://usinfo.state.gov/usa/race/hate/s091701.htm.

55. See "Bush Remarks at Islamic Center of Washington, D.C.," U.S. Department of State International Information Programs, September 17, 2001, available online at http://usinfo.state.gov/topical/pol/terror/01091722.htm.

56. See "How Hate-Crime Laws Harm Religious Freedom and Lead to Same-Sex Marriage," Family Forum CitizenLink, June 1, 2001, available online at http://www.family.org/cforum/research/papers/a0016304.html.

57. See Helen Dewar, "Senate GOP Stalls Hate Crime Measure: Bill Would Federalize Crimes Motivated by Sexual Orientation, Gender or Disability," *Washington Post*, June 12, 2002, p. A4.

CHAPTER 11: THE MYTHOLOGY OF HATE

1. See Joseph Farah, "Not a hate crime," *WorldNetDaily*, October 22, 1999, available online at http://www.worldnetdaily.com/news/article.asp?ARTICLE_ID=14837.

2. See Louis P. Sheldon, "Jesse Dirkhising's Death Is Example of Media Double Standard," CNSNews.com, March 15, 2001. Available online at http://www.cnsnews.com/ViewCommentary.asp?Page=\Commentary\archive\200103\COM20010315e.html.

3. See "Media and the Murder Case: Is Media Ignoring Boy's Murder Case Because Suspects Are Gay?," ABCNews.com, April 10, 2000, available online at http://abcnews.go.com/sections/wnt/WorldNewsTonight/wnt010410_dirkhising_feature.html.

4. See Scott Hogenson, "Dirkhising Murder-Rape Trial Opens in Arkansas," CNSNews.com, March 15, 2001.

5. Author's interview with Frederick Lawrence, July 27, 2003.

6. See Andrew Sullivan, "What's So Bad About Hate," *New York Times Magazine*, September 26, 1999.

7. See Frederick Lawrence, *Punishing Hate: Bias Crimes Under American Law* (Cambridge: Harvard University Press, 1999), pp. 45–53.

8. See Oliver Wendell Holmes, "The Common Law: Lecture I—Early Forms of Liability," 1881, available online at http://www.llpoh.org/Law_and_Medicine/Holmes_LECTURE_I_EARLY_FORMS_OF_LIABILITY.html.

9. See Jack Levin and Jack McDevitt, *Hate Crimes: The Rising Tide of Bigotry and Bloodshed* (Boulder, Colo.: Westview Press, 1993), pp. 11–12. The schema of this argument is based on Lawrence, *Punishing Hate*, p. 39.

10. See Lawrence, *Punishing Hate*, pp. 40–41.

11. Ibid., pp. 41–43.

12. Federal Bureau of Investigation, Hate Crimes Statistics, compiled from annual reports.

13. See James Jacobs and Kimberley Potter, *Hate Crimes: Criminal Law and Identity Politics* (Oxford: Oxford University Press, 1998), p. 37.

14. See Edward Dunbar, "Hate crime patterns in Los Angeles County: Demographic and behavioral factors of victim impact and reporting of crime," paper presented at a congressional briefing co-sponsored by the American Psychological Association and the Society for the Psychological Study of Social Issues, November 1997, Washington, D.C.

15. See Donald P. Green, Jack Glaser and Andrew Rich, "From lynching to gay-bashing: The elusive connection between economic conditions and hate crime," *Journal of Personality and Social Psychology*, 75, July 1998, pp. 1–11, available online at http://www.yale.edu/isps/publications/green1.pdf.

16. See Jack Levin and Jack McDevitt, *Hate Crimes Revisited: America's War on Those Who Are Different* (Boulder, Colo.: Westview, 2002).
17. See Jacobs and Potter, *Hate Crimes*, pp. 56–64.
18. Valerie Jenness and Ryken Grattet, *Making Hate a Crime: From Social Movement to Law Enforcement* (New York: Russell Sage Foundation, 2001), pp. 18–21, and author's interview with Valerie Jenness, June 10, 2003.
19. See *Wisconsin v. Mitchell* (92–515), 508 U.S. 47 (1993).
20. See Lawrence, *Punishing Hate*, pp. 89–99.
21. See *Virginia v. Black* (01–1107), 262 Va. 764, 553 S. E. 2d 738, affirmed in part, vacated in part, and remanded.
22. Ibid., p. 159.
23. Ibid., pp. 161–167.
24. Royal Commission on Capital Punishment, Minutes of Evidence, Ninth Day, December 1, 1949. Cited in ibid., p. 164.
25. See Jenness, *Making Hate a Crime*, p. 18.
26. See Jacobs and Potter, *Hate Crimes*, pp. 5
27. Ibid., p. 131.
28. Lawrence, *Punishing Hate*, p. 169.

CHAPTER 12: THE TRIAL, DAY FOUR: IN FEAR

1. See, e.g., Joe Gyan Jr., "Duke admits lying, bilking supporters," *The Advocate* (Baton Rouge, LA.), December 19, 2002; and Cain Burdeau, "Facing prison sentence, Duke denies he bilked anyone," Associated Press, March 13, 2003.
2. See David Scheer, "Defense rests its case after Minh Hong takes the stand," (Aberdeen) *Daily World*, December 12, 2000.

CHAPTER 13: WALL OF SILENCE

1. See Sue Anne Pressley, "Alabama Killing Draws Comparisons," *Washington Post*, March 6, 1999, p. A3.
2. See Tad Dickens, "Gay describes himself as 'Christian soldier,'" *Roanoke Times*, March 3, 2001.
3. See, e.g., Monica Whitaker, "Soldier's death may be hate crime," *Tennesseean*, July 13, 1999.
4. See "Dover man, teen, held in Nazi graffiti incident," *Poughkeepsie Journal*, August 22, 1999. See also Mark Potok and Heidi Beirich, "Discounting Hate: Ten years after federal officials began compiling national hate crime statistics the numbers don't add up," *Southern Poverty Law Center Intelligence Report*, Winter 2001, Issue No. 104.
5. See Human Rights Campaign, "A Chronology of Hate Crimes, 1998–2002," available online at http://www.hrc.org/issues/hate_crimes/background/index.asp.
6. See "UNLV police investigating racial vandalism," *Las Vegas Review-Journal*, April 8, 1999. See also Potok and Beirich, "Discounting Hate."
7. See Stephen Hunt, "Two Suspects Enter Guilty Pleas To Assault in Gay-Bashing Case," *Salt Lake Tribune*, March 1, 2000.
8. See Steven Gray, "Man Faces Charges in Row with Lesbian: Incident Not Hate Crime in Md.," *Washington Post*, May 10, 2000, p. B1.

9. See Steven Gray, "Attack Case to Be Dropped: Witnesses Dispute Man Was at Fault," *Washington Post,* June 10, 2000.

10. See "'Oil Can' Boyd finds racial graffiti on fence," *Meridian* (Miss.) *Star,* November 6, 1999.

11. See Dennis Wilken, "Attempted murder alleged in attack on gay campers," *The Garden Island,* May 30, 2001; and Wilken, "Attack cases headed for trial," *The Garden Island,* June 2, 2001; and Wilken, "Teens sent to prison for attacking gays," *The Garden Island,* January 18, 2002.

12. See Jack McDevitt and Joan Weiss, *Improving the Quality and Accuracy of Bias Crime Statistics Nationally,* Justice Research and Statistics Association/Northeastern University Center for Criminal Justice Policy Research, September 2000, pp. 53–57.

13. See Potok and Beirich, "Discounting Hate."

14. See Donald P. Green, Jack Glaser and Andrew Rich, "From lynching to gay-bashing: The elusive connection between economic conditions and hate crime," *Journal of Personality and Social Psychology,* 75, July 1998, pp. 1–11.

15. See McDevitt and Weiss, *Improving the Quality,* pp. 85–91; p. 73.

16. See Potok and Beirich, "Discounting Hate."

17. See Valerie Jenness and Ryken Grattet, *Making Hate a Crime: From Social Movement to Law Enforcement* (New York: Russell Sage Foundation, 2001), pp. 80–83.

18. See, e.g., Barbara Perry, *In the Name of Hate: Understanding Hate Crimes* (New York: Routledge, 1999), p. 216.

19. See Joan Weiss, "Ethnoviolence's Impact Upon and Response of Victims and the Community," in Robert Kelly (ed.), *Bias Crimes* (Chicago: Office of International Criminal Justice, 1993), pp. 174–185.

20. McDevitt and Weiss, *Improving the Quality,* p. 114.

21. Ibid., p. 29.

22. See Kevin T. Berrill, "Anti-Gay Violence and Victimization in the United States: An Overview," in *Hate Crimes: Confronting Violence Against Lesbians and Gay Men* (Newbury Park, Calif.: Sage Publications, 1992), pp. 19–40.

23. Weiss and McDevitt, *Improving the Quality,* p. 114.

24. Ibid., pp. 115–117.

25. Ibid., pp. 72–73.

CHAPTER 15: THE GREAT DIVIDE

1. See Rob McDonald, "Slain man's son tells of 'superhero,'" *Spokesman-Review,* July 18, 1999, p. B1.

2. See Mick Holien, "Shooting suspect arraigned," *Missoulian,* July 1, 1999.

3. See Mick Holien, "Affidavit: Race a factor in shooting," *Missoulian,* July 9, 1999.

4. See Diane Cochran, "Zander given 60-year sentence to Warm Springs for murder," *Missoulian,* August 25, 2000.

5. See especially the author's *In God's Country: The Patriot Movement and the Pacific Northwest* (Pullman, Wash.: Washington State University Press, 1999).

6. See Lynne Varner, "I am infected with the same fear of white people that many whites have of black people," *Seattle Times,* October 29, 2000.

7. All quotes from author's interview with Ken Toole, August 18, 2003.

8. All quotes from author's interview with Donald P. Green, August 21, 2003.

9. Author's interview with Toole.

10. See Gary Jahrig, "Police still pursuing leads in burning of couple's home," *Missoulian*, February 12, 2002; Jahrig, "No anthrax in letter to couple," *Missoulian*, February 13, 2002; Michael Moore and Gary Jahrig, "Police narrow focus in arson investigation," *Missoulian*, February 16, 2002; Ginny Merriam," Angry reaction to media, police is result of years of discrimination, groups say," *Missoulian*, March 3, 2002; and Michael Moore, " Arson victim tells own side of story," *Missoulian*, August 22, 2002.

11. See Ericka Schenk Smith, "Police say arson case now cold," *Missoulian*, December 8, 2002.

12. Author's interview with Toole.

13. See Frederick Lawrence, *Punishing Hate: Bias Crimes Under American Law* (Cambridge: Harvard University Press, 1999), p. 42.

14. Author's interview with Carl and Joan Payne, July 11, 2003.

15. U.S. Census Bureau, Quick Facts, Grays Harbor County, 1990 and 2000.

16. William Kandel and John Cromartie, "Hispanics Find a Home in Rural America," Amber Waves, U.S. Department of Agriculture Economic Research Service, February 2003, available online at http://www.ers.usda.gov/AmberWaves/Feb03/Findings/HispanicsFind.htm.

17. See Donald Green, with D. Strolovitch and J. Wong, "Defended Neighborhoods, Integration, and Racially-Motivated Crime," American Journal of Sociology, 1998.

18. See Donald P. Green, Laurence H. McFalls, and Jennifer K. Smith, "Hate Crime: An Emergent Research Agenda," *Annual Review of Sociology*, August 2001, Vol. 27, pp. 479–504.

19. Author's interview with Green.

CHAPTER 16: THE VERDICT

1. See David Scheer, "After two days of deliberations, jury can't decide," (Aberdeen) *Daily World*, December 14, 2000.

2. Author's interview with Gene Schermer, December 15, 2000.

3. See David Scheer, "Hong won't face new trial in stabbing case," (Aberdeen) *Daily World*, January 5, 2001.

4. See David Scheer, "'My son is not a racist,' Kinison's mom says," (Aberdeen) *Daily World*, December 20, 2000.

5. All quotes from author's interview with H. Steward Menefee, January 10, 2001.

6. See David Scheer, "Foreman in Hong trial speaks out on 11–1 vote to acquit," (Aberdeen) *Daily World*, January 6, 2001.

7. Author's interview with Minh Duc Hong, July 18, 2003.

CHAPTER 17: THE AMERICAN LANDSCAPE

1. Author's interview with Frederick Lawrence, July 27, 2003.

2. Author's interview with Donald P. Green, August 21, 2003.

3. See Federal Bureau of Investigation, *Hate Crimes Statistics 2001*, available online at http://www.fbi.gov/ucr/01hate.pdf.

4. All quotes from author's interview with Jack McDevitt, September 16, 2003.

5. Author's interview with Joan Weiss, September 5, 2003.

6. Again, all quotes from author's interview with Jack McDevitt, September 16, 2003.

7. Author's interview with Lawrence.
8. Ibid.
9. Ibid.
10. See Alex Tizon, "Hate crimes: Is enforcement colorblind?," *Seattle Times*, March 30, 2001.
11. See Anti-Defamation League, *Hate Crime Laws: An Overview*, Part II: "Penalty Enhancement and the Inclusion of Gender," available online at http://www. adl.org/99hatecrime/penalty.asp.
12. Author's interview with McDevitt.
13. Ibid.
14. Author's interview with John Hughes, July 11, 2003.
15. See Chris McGann, "Ocean Shores still dealing with an image problem," *Post-Intelligencer*, July 5, 2001.
16. Author's interview with Joan Payne, July 11, 2003.
17. Author's interview with Minh Duc Hong, September 25, 2003.

BIBLIOGRAPHY

BOOKS

Gary D. Comstock, *Violence against Lesbians and Gay Men* (New York: Columbia University Press, 1991)

Philip Dray, *At the Hands of Persons Unknown: The Lynching of Black America* (New York: Random House, 2002)

Gregory M. Herek and Kevin T. Berrill (eds.), *Hate Crimes: Confronting Violence Against Lesbians and Gay Men* (Newbury Park, CA: Sage Press, 1992)

John C. Hughes and Ryan Teague Beckwith, *On the Harbor: From Black Friday to Nirvana* (Aberdeen: The Daily World Inc., 2001)

James B. Jacobs and Kimberly Potter, *Hate Crimes: Criminal Law and Identity Politics* (Oxford: Oxford University Press, 1998)

Valerie Jenness and Kendal Broad, *Hate Crimes: New Social Movements and the Politics of Violence* (New York: Aldine de Gruyter, 1997)

Valerie Jenness and Ryken Grattet, *Making Hate a Crime: From Social Movement to Law Enforcement* (New York: Russell Sage Foundation, 2001)

Robert J. Kelly, ed., *Bias Crime: American Law Enforcement and Legal Response* (Chicago: Office of International Criminal Justice, the University of Illinois at Chicago, 1991)

Frederick M. Lawrence, *Punishing Hate: Bias Crimes Under American Law* (Cambridge: Harvard University Press, 1999)

Jack Levin and Jack McDevitt, *Hate Crimes: America's War on Those Who Are Different* (Boulder, CO: Westview Press, 2001)

Beth Loffreda, *Losing Matt Shepard: Life and Politics in the Aftermath of Anti-Gay Murder* (New York: Columbia University Press, 2000)

James H. Madison, *A Lynching in the Heartland: Race and Memory in America* (New York: Palgrave Macmillan, 2002)

Jack McDevitt and Joan Weiss, *Improving the Quality and Accuracy of Bias Crime Statistics Nationally*, Justice Research and Statistics Association/Northeastern University Center for Criminal Justice Policy Research, September 2000

Barbara Perry, *In the Name of Hate: Understanding Hate Crimes* (New York: Routledge, 2001)

Deborah A. Prentice and Dale T. Miller (eds.), *Cultural Divides: Understanding and Overcoming Group Conflict* (New York: Russell Sage Foundation, 1999),

Dina Temple-Ralston, *A Death in Texas: A Story of Race, Murder, and a Small Town's Struggle for Redemption* (New York: Henry Holt, 2002)

Stewart E. Tolnay and E. M. Beck, *A Festival of Violence: An Analysis of Southern Lynchings, 1882–1930* (Urbana: University of Illinois Press, 1992)

ARTICLES

Charles Babington, "Wielding Veto, President Presses Hate Crimes Issue: Clinton Wants Congress to Add Homosexuals to Law as Protected Group," *Washington Post*, October 27, 1999, p. A2; and "Clinton Signs Spending Bill, But Notes What It Left Out," *Washington Post*, November 30, 1999, p. A2

Ryan Teague Beckwith, "Asian community stunned, but not fearful," (Aberdeen) *Daily World*, July 16, 2000

Kevin T. Berrill, "Anti-Gay Violence and Victimization in the United States: An Overview," in *Hate Crimes: Confronting Violence Against Lesbians and Gay Men* (Newbury Park, Calif.: Sage Publications, 1992)

Kevin T. Berrill and G. M. Herek, "Primary and secondary victimization in anti-gay hate crimes: Official response and public policy," *Journal of Interpersonal Violence*, 5 (1990)

Hector Castro, "Charges expected in fatal stabbing," *Post-Intelligencer*, Friday, July 7, 2000

Hector Castro and Robert L. Jamieson Jr., "Ocean Shores killing leaves citizens caught in between," *Post-Intelligencer*, July 15, 2000

Hector Castro and Lewis Kamb, "Police honor youth slain during Mardi Gras," *Post-Intelligencer*, Thursday, March 8, 2001

David Chapman, "Grays Harbor County Courthouse: A Crown for 'The Maid of Wynooche'," *Columbia: The Magazine of Northwest History*, Vol. 15, No. 3, Fall 2001

Michael Collins, "The Gay-Bashers," in *Hate Crimes: Confronting Violence Against Lesbians and Gay Men* (Newbury Park, Calif.: Sage Press, 1992), pp. 191–200

Diane Cochran, "Zander given 60-year sentence to Warm Springs for murder," *Missoulian*, August 25, 2000

Chris Dettro, "Man gets 12 years in 'hate' beating," *Springfield State-Journal*, November 26, 1998

Helen Dewar, "Senate GOP Stalls Hate Crime Measure: Bill Would Federalize Crimes Motivated by Sexual Orientation, Gender or Disability," *Washington Post*, June 12, 2002

Edward Dunbar, "Hate crime patterns in Los Angeles County: Demographic and behavioral factors of victim impact and reporting of crime," paper presented at a congressional briefing co-sponsored by the American Psychological Association and the Society for the Psychological Study of Social Issues, November 1997, Washington, D.C.

Timothy Egan, "A Racist Attack, A Town Plagued," *New York Times*, October 15, 2000

Stuart Eskenazi, "Chisum Casts Blame at Gay Victims," Austin *American-Statesman*, February 17, 1995

Susan Estrich, "George Jr. Courts the Right," *Los Angeles Times*, April 2, 1999

P. Finn and T. McNeil, *The response of the criminal justice system to bias crime: An exploratory review* (Cambridge, Mass.: Abt Associates, 1987)

Justin Gillis and Patrice Gaines, "Pattern of Hate Emerges on a Fence in Laramie: Gay Victims' Killers Say They Saw an Easy Crime Target," *Washington Post*, October 18, 1998

Laurie Goodstein, "The Architect of the 'Gay Conversion' Campaign," *New York Times*, August 13, 1998

Steven Gray, "Man Faces Charges in Row With Lesbian: Incident Not Hate Crime in Md.," *Washington Post*, May 10, 2000

Donald P. Green, with D. Strolovitch and J. Wong, "Defended Neighborhoods, Integration, and Racially-Motivated Crime," *American Journal of Sociology*, 1998

Donald P. Green, Jack Glaser and Andrew Rich, "From lynching to gay-bashing: The elusive connection between economic conditions and hate crime," *Journal of Personality and Social Psychology*, 75, July 1998

Donald P. Green, Robert P. Abelson, and Margaret Garnett, "The Distinctive Political Views of Hate-Crime Perpetrators and White Supremacists," 1999, in Deborah A. Prentice and Dale T. Miller (eds.), *Cultural Divides: Understanding and Overcoming Group Conflict* (New York: Russell Sage Foundation, 1999)

Donald P. Green, Laurence H. McFalls, and Jennifer K. Smith, "Hate Crime: An Emergent Research Agenda," *Annual Review of Sociology*, August 2001, Vol. 27

Melinda Henneberger, "For Bias Victims, a Double Trauma," *Newsday*, Jan 9, 1992

Ian Ith, "Mardi Gras: Police see hate crime in rampage," *Seattle Times*, Thursday, March 29, 2001

Barbara Holden-Smith, "Lynching, Federalism, and the Intersection of Race and Gender in the Progressive Era," *Yale Journal of Law and Feminism*, Vol. 8, No. 31, 1996

Mick Holien, "Shooting suspect arraigned," *Missoulian*, July 1, 1999; "Affidavit: Race a factor in shooting," *Missoulian*, July 9, 1999

Stephen Hunt, "Two Suspects Enter Guilty Pleas To Assault in Gay-Bashing Case," *Salt Lake Tribune*, March 1, 2000

Molly Ivins, "A little background on that hate crimes bill," (Fort Worth) *Star-Telegram*, Monday, October 31, 2000

Robert L. Jamieson Jr., "One brother is released, other held in stabbing," *Post-Intelligencer*, July 6, 2000

Robert L. Jamieson Jr. and Hector Castro, "Another racial incident preceded Ocean Shores stabbing death" *Post-Intelligencer*, Wednesday, July 12, 2000

Gary Jahrig, "Police still pursuing leads in burning of couple's home," *Missoulian*, February 12, 2002; "No anthrax in letter to couple," *Missoulian*, February 13, 2002

Joan H. Johnston, James E. Driskell and Eduardo Salas, "Vigilant and Hypervigilant Decision Making," *Journal of Applied Psychology*, 1997, Vol. 82, No. 4

William Kandel and John Cromartie, "Hispanics Find a Home in Rural America," *Amber Waves*, USDA Economic Research Service, February 2003

Chi-Dooh Li, "Racial taunts reflect on the source," *Post-Intelligencer*, July 27, 2000

Jack McDevitt and Joan Weiss, *Improving the Quality and Accuracy of Bias Crime Statistics Nationally*, Justice Research and Statistics Association/Northeastern University Center for Criminal Justice Policy Research, September 2000

Rob McDonald, "Slain man's son tells of 'superhero'," *Spokesman-Review*, July 18, 1999

Chris McGann, "Ocean Shores still dealing with an image problem," *Post-Intelligencer*, Thursday, July 5, 2001

Ginny Merriam, "Angry reaction to media, police is result of years of discrimination, groups say," *Missoulian*, March 3, 2002

Michael Moore, "Arson victim tells own side of story," *Missoulian*, August 22, 2002

Michael Moore and Gary Jahrig, "Police narrow focus in arson investigation," *Missoulian*, February 16, 2002

Eric Pianin and Juliet Eilperin, "GOP Raises the Ante On Social Programs," *Washington Post*, October 21, 1999, p. A1.

Mark Potok and Heidi Beirich, "Discounting Hate: Ten years after federal officials began compiling national hate crime statistics the numbers don't add up," *Southern Poverty Law Center Intelligence Report*, Winter 2001, No. 104

Joshua Robin, "Ocean Shores victim was in earlier fight," *Seattle Times*, Wednesday, July 12, 2000

Joshua Robin, "Stabbing victim liked to fight, his friends say," *Seattle Times*, July 10, 2000

David Scheer, " 'Gooks go home!' taunt led to stabbing," (Aberdeen) *Daily World*, July 5, 2000; "Racial epithets in earlier case now in spotlight," *Daily World*, July 12, 2000; "Anatomy of a death: Witnesses offer varying accounts," *Daily World*, August 8, 2000; "FBI rules out Ocean Shores investigation," *Daily World*, October 11, 2000; "Jury selection begins in racially charged stabbing case," *Daily World*, December 4, 2000; "Large jury pool in Ocean Shores stabbing case," *Daily World*, December 5, 2000; "Jury chosen in Hong case, trial begins," *Daily World*, December 6, 2000; "Witness says she heard Hong say, 'He's going down'," *Daily World*, December 8, 2000; "Defense witness thought Kinison was a 'skinhead'," *Daily World*, December 9, 2000; "Defense rests its case after Minh Hong takes the stand," *Daily World*, December 12, 2000; "Hong jury still out," *Daily World*, December 13, 2000; "After two days of deliberations, jury can't decide," *Daily World*, December 14, 2000; "'My son is not a racist,' Kinison's mom says," Aberdeen Daily World, December 20, 2000; "Hong won't face new trial in stabbing case," *Daily World*, January 5, 2001; "Foreman in Hong trial speak out on 11–1 vote to acquit," *Daily World*, January 6, 2001

See David Scheer and Ryan Teague Beckwith, "Minh Hong trial under way," (Aberdeen) *Daily World*, December 7, 2000

Ericka Schenk Smith, "Police say arson case now cold," *Missoulian*, December 8, 2002

Terri Ann Schroeder, "Different Version," *Indianapolis Star*, March 7, 1994

Fern Shen, "Hate Crime Bill Rejected in Md. House," *Washington Post*, March 22, 1991

Andrew Sullivan, "What's So Bad About Hate," *New York Times Magazine*, September 26, 1999

Jake Tapper, "Bush angers slain man's family," *Salon.com*, October 16, 2000

Elizabeth Tedesco, "Humanity on the Ballot: The Citizen Initiative and Oregon's War Over Gay Civil Rights," *Boston College Third World Law Journal*, Vol. 22, No. 1, 2002

Alex Tizon, "Storm over July 4 killing still raging in Ocean Shores," *Seattle Times*, Monday, April 8, 2001; and "Hate crimes: Is enforcement colorblind?," *Seattle Times*, March 30, 2001

Lynne Varner, "I am infected with the same fear of white people that many whites have of black people," *Seattle Times*, October 29, 2000

Joan Weiss, "Ethnoviolence: Impact Upon the Response of Victims and the Community," in Robert J. Kelly (ed.), *Bias Crime: American Law Enforcement and Legal Response* (Chicago: Office of International Criminal Justice, the University of Illinois at Chicago, 1991)

Joan Weiss, Howard Ehrlich, Barbara E. K. Larcom, "Ethnoviolence at Work," *Journal of Intergroup Relations*, Vol. 18, Winter 1991–92

Walter F. White, "The Work of a Mob," *Crisis*, 16 (Sept. 17, 1918)

Dennis Wilken, "Attempted murder alleged in attack on gay campers," *The Garden Island*, May 30, 2001; "Attack cases headed for trial," *The Garden Island*, June 2,

2001; and "Teens sent to prison for attacking gays," *The Garden Island*, January 18, 2002

OTHER PUBLICATIONS

Responding to Hate Crimes: A Police Officer's Guide to Investigation and Prevention, International Association of Police Chiefs, 1999

A NOTE ON SOURCES

In addition to those sources listed, I also relied heavily on interviews with numerous people involved with the case as well as a number of hate-crime experts. The former includes Minh Duc Hong; Grays Harbor County Prosecutor H. Steward Menefee; Hong's attorneys, Monte Hester and Brett Purtzer; Dr. Gary E. Connor; Ocean Shores Police Chief Rich McEachin, and department spokesman David McManus; Aberdeen *Daily World* editor John Hughes; Chamber of Commerce president Joan Payne; Ocean Shores Coalition president Carl Payne; Doug Chin of the Organization of Chinese Americans; and James Arima of the Japanese American Citizens League. The latter includes Frederick M. Lawrence of Boston University School of Law; Jack McDevitt of Northeastern University's Center for Criminal Justice Policy Research; Joan Weiss of the Justice Research and Statistics Association; Donald P. Green of Yale University; sociologist Valerie Jenness of the University of California-Irvine; and Ken Toole of the Montana Human Rights Network.

The chapters detailing the trial (Chapters 4, 6, 8, 10, 12, 14, and 16) are largely drawn from my notes covering the trial. In some cases I cross-referenced those notes with the quotes published by my journalistic colleague David Scheer at the Aberdeen *Daily World*, who was the only reporter to have covered both the case and the trial from start to finish, and the only person to obtain an interview with Molly Kinison. Transcripts were largely unavailable (I did obtain one day's worth of trial transcripts, thanks to the efforts of court clerk Brenda Johnston), and reporters' notes will always slightly vary. In some cases I deferred to Scheer's quotes, in others I adhered to those in my notebook. In any event, Scheer's body of work (duly noted above) was an invaluable reference and resource for my own work.

Index